Lincoln in New England

ALSO BY DAVID J. KENT

*Lincoln: The Fire of Genius: How Abraham Lincoln's Commitment to
    Science and Technology Helped Modernize America*
Lincoln: The Man Who Saved America
Edison: The Inventor of the Modern World
Tesla: The Wizard of Electricity
Abraham Lincoln and Nikola Tesla: Connected by Fate (e-book)
Nikola Tesla: Renewable Energy Ahead of Its Time (e-book)

LINCOLN IN NEW ENGLAND
In Search of His Forgotten Tours

DAVID J. KENT

Essex, Connecticut

Globe Pequot

An imprint of The Globe Pequot Publishing Group, Inc.
64 South Main Street
Essex, CT 06426
www.globepequot.com

Copyright © 2026 by David J. Kent

All rights reserved. No part of this book may be reproduced in any form or by any electronic or mechanical means, including information storage and retrieval systems, without written permission from the publisher, except by a reviewer who may quote passages in a review.

British Library Cataloguing in Publication Information available

Library of Congress Cataloging-in-Publication Data available
ISBN 978-1-4930-9222-2 (paper)
ISBN 978-1-4930-9223-9 (electronic)

*To my New England family
for keeping me grounded in reality*

Contents

Introduction ix

PART I. 1848—STUMPING FOR TAYLOR
Chapter 1: Zachary Taylor, the Whig?—New England Beckons . . . 3
Chapter 2: The Party Divided—Worcester Free Soilers Rebel 19
Chapter 3: The Abolitionists—New Bedford Whaling
and Wailing 33
Chapter 4: The Textile Mills—Lowell and the Power of Cotton . . . 48
Chapter 5: The Ancestors—Boston Burbs and the
New England Lincolns 63
Chapter 6: The Writers—Concord in the Shadow
of the Revolution 77
Chapter 7: The Hub of the Universe—Boston and Cambridge 91

Interregnum: 1848–1860 106

PART II. 1860—STUMPING FOR HIMSELF
Chapter 8: The Speech of a Lifetime—Cooper Union 119
Chapter 9: The Seward Rivalry Begins—Providence 133
Chapter 10: The Robert Visit—New Hampshire 146
Chapter 11: The Bedful of Snakes—Central Connecticut 160
Chapter 12: The Vice Presidential Abyss—Eastern Connecticut
and Rhode Island 175
Chapter 13: The Sculptors and the Showman—
Southwestern Connecticut 189
Chapter 14: The Missing New England—Maine and Vermont . . 204
Chapter 15: The End and the Beginning—Heading Home 220

Epilogue 233
Notes 245
Acknowledgments 257
Index 259
About the Author 263

Introduction

Abraham Lincoln poses presidentially despite the occasional paint flaking from the brick of the former textile mill. I am at the edge of the Riverwalk in Ipswich, Massachusetts, looking at a majestic mural depicting the history of my hometown, incorporated in 1634 and known as "The Birthplace of American Independence." Ipswich residents in 1687, led by the Reverend John Wise, protested taxation without representation to the English colonial governor, Edmund Andros. Wise and others were jailed and fined, but Britain backed down and they were released. Despite this impertinence, the Ipswich rebellion led to a new charter for the Massachusetts Bay Colony nearly a century before the Declaration of Independence. The town's history is filled with colonial lore and Revolutionary War heroes. George Washington, for example, rides his magnificent white charger Prescott across the mural to represent his presidential tour of New England, during which he made a stop in Ipswich. Having grown up here, I knew much about that era of the town's history, but nothing about any visit to Ipswich by our sixteenth president. The presence of Lincoln in the mural made me wonder if I had missed something.

Joining me along the Riverwalk is Ipswich historian Gordon Harris. Although he attended college in the Deep South not far from Vicksburg, Mississippi, the scene of one of the most consequential battles of the Civil War, Harris seems a quintessential New Englander with his trim gray goatee and a curved brim cap that reminds me of the kepi worn by Union soldiers. A retired carpenter who researches historic houses, he could easily be mistaken for a cast member of *This Old House*, the home fix-up television program that continues into its fifth decade on the local PBS station. Formerly the chair of the Ipswich Historical Commission, Harris has been the official town historian for the last dozen years.

Introduction

I had to ask him the one question stuck in my mind: "Why is Lincoln so prominently featured in the mural?"

Harris chuckles but admits that Lincoln never set foot in the town. "He represents the Civil War, in which many Ipswich natives fought to save the Union," Harris tells me. "In the painting, you can see the newspaper headline 'Lincoln Calls for Volunteers' after the attack on Fort Sumter." Ipswich immediately responded to the call for militia by forming the Ipswich Volunteer Company. Harris points me to a book called *American Town*—written by the mural's creator, local artist Alan Pearsall—that documents the history of the area through the mural. "Ipswich sent 348 men to the front, of which 54 are killed by Civil War's end," the book notes.[1] All told, something like 750,000 men died in the war, North and South combined.

I moved to the Washington, DC, area years ago after growing up in this quaint seacoast town northeast of Boston, famous for its miles of sandy beaches, its blustery nor'easters, and its fried clams and steamers. In the years since, I have grown used to the fact that every politician in Washington seems obligated to name-drop Abraham Lincoln whenever a microphone is handy. Still, the idea of celebrating Lincoln in Massachusetts seemed odd. After chatting with Harris, it made more sense. Here in the town's most prominent gathering place—free weekly concerts take place on the Riverwalk during the summer—is a full-size Abraham Lincoln, all six feet, four inches of him, stretched even taller by the four-foot pedestal he stands on. Lincoln made two trips to New England, and although he never made it to Ipswich, his 1848 visit to Boston and a few outlying cities did prove a turning point in his career. A return in 1860 came at a critical turning point for the nation. But why exactly was he in New England? Did anyone remember his visit? Did he make an impact on the local communities? These questions and others ran through my mind as Harris and I fell into a lengthy discussion at Zumi's, the local gourmet coffee shop.

The 2,700-square-foot painting was created by Pearsall over an eighteen-month period from spring 2005 to fall 2006. Ipswich has a long history of artistic talent, from the paintings of Arthur Wesley Dow to the poems of Anne Bradstreet (known as the "First Poet of America" in 1650)

Abraham Lincoln and Ipswich soldiers preparing to join the Civil War, on the EBSCO mural

to the modern novels of double Pulitzer Prize winner John Updike. Pearsall captured much of the long history of the town, including President George Washington's visit to thank the populace for supporting the fight for independence. While here George enjoyed a "cold collation" [light meal] and bought some of the town's famous black silk pillow lace to bring home to Martha. But Washington was not the only president to visit the town or be depicted on the mural. President James Monroe stopped by in 1817, and Theodore Roosevelt made a whistle stop here in 1912, giving a speech from Depot Square as he campaigned for president. Another future president, Massachusetts native John F. Kennedy, campaigned in Ipswich for his successful 1958 Senate run.

The mural highlights the town's share of infamy as well. Colonel Benedict Arnold, then only twenty years old, rested his troops on the town green on his way to Montreal during the Revolutionary War. He was still in Washington's good graces at the time and fought valiantly despite a disastrous defeat at the hands of the British in Quebec City. Four years later, however, the name Benedict Arnold would become synonymous with treason. During the summer of 1780, a disgruntled now-General Arnold plotted with the British to hand over West Point, then under his command. When it was discovered and he absconded over enemy lines, Washington sent an urgent message to Colonel Nathaniel Wade of Ipswich, ordering him to take command of West Point.

I will return to Benedict Arnold and West Point later, but Ipswich's history does not stop there. During the War of 1812, the British fired on the town's Castle Hill from ships in the bay. Townspeople fought back and held several captured British POWs in the Ipswich Prison. A century later, town residents marveled at the *Hindenburg* dirigible floating over Ipswich on its way to a horrific explosion in New Jersey. During World War II, German submarines were observed off the coast of nearby Plum Island; this time it was German POWs held in the town's prison.

More relevant to Lincoln, Ipswich has a long history of antislavery activity. Back in 1765, a full century before the Thirteenth Amendment ended slavery in all the United States, a wrongly enslaved African-American woman named Jenny Slew sued for her freedom from Ipswich resident John Whipple. Slew won her case in a time when African

Introduction

Americans had no rights, including in Massachusetts. It was not until 1780 that the Massachusetts Constitution came into force, written by none other than future president John Adams, declaring that "all men are born free and equal." Adams's records suggest that he sat in on the Slew trial, which no doubt encouraged his antislavery thinking. The Methodist Church in Ipswich, later an Underground Railroad stop, split over abolition, following a pattern that would split religious denominations into pro- and antislavery factions. Slavery was a catalyst of conflict connected to every aspect of American history. It would help Lincoln become prominent as well.

The mural takes up a large outer wall of an old brick textile mill building, so I ask Harris about the mills in town. I recall my mother telling me she worked at the Hayward Hosiery Mill farther up the river before getting married and starting a family soon after the mill phased out.

"That's on the mural too," he tells me. One of the more intricate details shows Benjamin Fewkes smuggling a disassembled stocking frame machine from England in crates of sugar. Wary of New England

Benjamin Fewkes smuggling a stocking frame machine into Ipswich, on the EBSCO mural BY PERMISSION OF GORDON HARRIS

competition and eager to relegate the colonies to mere provision of raw materials to feed the great mills of England, Britain banned the import of manufacturing equipment to the colonies. Skirting these limitations, Ipswich joined the Industrial Revolution, and it revitalized the town. Amos A. Lawrence bought the first rudimentary mill and created the Ipswich Mills Company, which would go on to employ 1,500 people. The original mill here on the downtown riverfront had closed back in the 1930s and was replaced by the Sylvania fluorescent lamp factory during World War II. More recently, the mill building was taken over by EBSCO, the publishing company that commissioned Pearsall to paint the mural alongside the newly built Riverwalk.

As Harris and I chatted, I came to realize that Ipswich was a microcosm of the conflicts that helped define our nation's history—our independence from Britain, internal economic splits over slavery and industrialization, the ever-increasing tensions between North and South, and struggles between the moral wrong of slavery and the industrial benefits of slavery-sourced cotton. All of this brought me back to Lincoln's two visits to New England.

Lincoln only spent time in Massachusetts once, although he would pass through the Bay State briefly on his second foray into New England. His depiction on the Riverwalk mural may primarily be to highlight the Civil War and Ipswich's contribution to it, but he also represents how a nation can so easily rend itself into two because of political, economic, and moral differences. Lincoln managed to reconstruct the country, and in fact, used that temporary fissure to end one of the moral deficiencies that taints our history. But it came at a terrible cost.

In the interregnum between the two visits, both Lincoln and the nation had changed dramatically. The 1848 visit came while he was serving his only term as a US congressman, after which he withdrew from political office for a dozen years. On that visit, New Englanders thought of him more as a sideshow, the kind of "uneducated western frontier man" who told off-color jokes and sported ungainly looks and ill-fitting clothes. He stood in sharp contrast to the self-avowedly more stoic and sophisticated men of the eastern United States. Since any eastern knowledge of him at that time arose from newspaper reports of his often biting

INTRODUCTION

and sarcastic humor, it should come as no surprise that Easterners in Massachusetts looked to Lincoln for his entertainment value more than his political policy strategies. While Lincoln may have played up this perception, he was already seeing himself in much different terms. By the end of this Massachusetts trip, he began the political and moral transition that would change the nation.

When he returned to New England in 1860, he was a vastly different man. He was much more serious a political strategist, much less sarcastic (although irreverent humor was still part of his repertoire), and much better known to the nation as a whole and to New England in particular. Moreover, the nation itself was immensely different. He made the first trip as the Mexican-American War was ending, and the United States had gained vast new lands. Soon the battle would begin over whether that new land was to be open to slavery. The Compromise of 1850 allowed California into the Union as a free state but left open the possibility of slavery in other states. The Compromise also created an iron-fisted Fugitive Slave Law to force Northern citizens and federal authorities to actively hunt down escapees from slavery and return them to their "owners." The Kansas-Nebraska Act of 1854 was widely regarded as a mechanism to nationalize slavery, which the 1857 Dred Scott decision by the US Supreme Court seemed to codify. Reawakened to the dangers of slavery and seeing the need to get back into politics, lawyer Abraham Lincoln campaigned for the US Senate twice, losing both times, although the 1858 Lincoln-Douglas debates made him a national figure. The caning of Charles Sumner in the Senate and other violence in Congress emphasized the North versus South, pro- versus antislavery split of the nation. When Lincoln had the opportunity to do a second speaking tour of New England after giving his memorable Cooper Union speech, he jumped at the chance. Unlike 1848 when he was campaigning for the Whig nominee Zachary Taylor for president, in 1860 he was effectively undertaking a campaign for himself and the new Republican Party.

As I toured New England in another contentious election year and its aftermath, it struck me how momentous Lincoln's two visits were. Both occurred during pivotal presidential election years, and both represented crucial inflection points in our nation's history. I wanted to see

Introduction

for myself where Lincoln traveled and dig into the historical questions that defined the national psyche. Along the way I discovered many New Englanders who played major roles influencing Lincoln's political and moral philosophies. Most people have heard about Frederick Douglass, who first made his way to New Bedford and Lynn, Massachusetts, after escaping slavery. But we hear less about Massachusetts natives William Lloyd Garrison and Theodore Parker, even though Parker later corresponded with Lincoln's law partner. We also often ignore the role of the great literary icons of the nineteenth century—writers like Nathaniel Hawthorne, Ralph Waldo Emerson, Henry David Thoreau, Louisa May Alcott, and Harriet Beecher Stowe—all New Englanders who used their influence to stimulate abolitionist fervor in the North.

Lincoln's two trips highlight the political divisions that significantly affected the elections. Intraparty fractures could be as striking as differences between the parties. Lincoln's Whig Party had started in opposition to Andrew Jackson's Democrats, but the Whigs in 1848 were experiencing devastating intraparty turmoil, with offshoots like the Liberty Party and Free Soil Party gaining steam in more radical areas such as New England. When the Whigs evolved into the Republican Party in opposition to the spread of slavery into the western territories, it was the New England leaders of those wayward splinters that led the new party's rapid growth.

All this breakup and reformation reminded me how the two major political parties we know today are the opposite of what they were in Lincoln's time. The Democratic Party back then was the more conservative party. Before the war they were national, but even then, the Northern Democrats were much closer in temperament to Northern Whigs. The Whig Party was the more liberal party, with a diversity of views on issues like tariffs and immigration, but most importantly on the main issue of the day, slavery. A small sliver of Northern Whigs considered themselves abolitionists, the far left of the political spectrum that their party sometimes only barely accepted. That sliver expanded significantly following the enactment of the Fugitive Slave Law of 1850. Another chunk were the more moderate liberals with conservative views on slavery but still in favor of the Whig push for progressive programs. Most were like

INTRODUCTION

Lincoln, who repeatedly disclaimed being an abolitionist while simultaneously speaking out against the immorality of slavery. When the Whig Party faded away, remnants of it joined with the antislavery factions from all parties despite their disparate views on other issues. The result was a new party, the Republican Party, based on progressive economic agendas and opposition to the expansion of slavery into the western territories. As we will see, New England epitomizes the complications of the intraparty political spectrum on the issue of slavery.

Meanwhile, the onset of the Civil War led to cataclysmic division of the Democratic Party. Northern Democrats were slavery apologists, vouching for the rights of slaveholding states to retain the slave-based economy relying on the forced labor of nearly four million Black men, women, and children, virtually all of whom had been born on American soil. What separated the Northern Democrats from the Southern Democrats was less the legitimacy of slavery as it was the belief in Union versus Disunion. Most Northern Democrats saw the Union as inviolate while Southern Democrats, at least those who controlled the political and economic strings, embraced the idea of separation. The reasons were both simple and complicated, which I tried to come to grips with on my travels.

The differences of the parties were also evident in ways apart from the primary issue of slavery. The more liberal party (i.e., Lincoln's Whigs and Republicans) believed in a strong and active federal government, Hamiltonian economic policies that empowered all individuals to better their condition, greater industrialization, and government facilitation of education. The more conservative party (nineteenth- and early-twentieth-century Democrats, especially in the South) eschewed widespread education and industrialization, favoring Jeffersonian policies that focused on agriculture, and preferring a weak federal government powerless to eradicate slavery. Southern Democrats focused entirely on maintaining a slave-labor system that funneled wealth to small numbers of landholding plantation owners, using the aura of aristocracy and power to maintain a strict social hierarchy. You can see how these characteristics fall into opposite camps today, with the current-day Democrats the more liberal party and the current-day Republicans the more conservative party. This switch in party roles has been extensively documented elsewhere so I will not belabor it here, but it is important to keep in mind whenever I use the terms *Democratic* and *Republican* for the parties of Lincoln's day. During my travels, this distinction became abundantly clear, but it also proved demonstrably more complicated.

I realized there were themes arising. In 1848, Lincoln's primary assignment was to stump for the Whig nominee, Zachary Taylor. But why Taylor? He did not exactly fit the Whig mold, and many in New England rebelled against the idea. Lincoln's first speech in Massachusetts was in Worcester, hotbed of the Free Soil spinoff that did not like the direction the Whigs had veered in their attempt to play a winning electoral hand. Then Lincoln spoke in New Bedford, the southeastern Massachusetts whaling town that had sheltered Frederick Douglass and other abolitionist sentiments. I put both cities on my itinerary to get a sense of the two big issues complicating the Whig path to the White House.

Textile mills were another obstacle. While Massachusetts had outlawed slavery in the 1780s and developed a vibrant abolitionist network, the mills continued to rely on slave-grown cotton for industrial expansion and huge individual profits. That one fact alone split the Whigs into factions, so I was off to the center of the textile mill industry at the time in Lowell, a city where Lincoln experienced firsthand the intraparty conflict. Meanwhile, Lincoln's tour took him close to his ancestral home. The suburbs south of Boston where Lincoln gave speeches—Dorchester, Dedham, and a bit farther south, Taunton—surround Hingham, the home of the first Lincolns to arrive in the United States. Lincoln had become interested in his fuzzy family lineage, so I decided to check them out.

North of Boston took me into Concord, one half of the "shot heard round the world" that started the Revolutionary War. The Concord Museum was hosting a special exhibit on the anniversary of the Lincoln Memorial Centennial, an event I was deeply involved in celebrating back in Washington, DC. While in Concord I discovered a fervent abolitionist community of writers, some of whom later met Lincoln in the White House. Lincoln ended his 1848 political tour in Boston. The Revolutionary War started here, the antislavery movement matured here, and Abraham Lincoln first met William Seward here. Already an established

INTRODUCTION

statesman, Seward would be a mentor, then a rival, of Lincoln as their political fortunes intersected. When the time came, together they would tackle the greatest existential crisis of the nation.

When Lincoln returned to New England in 1860, he was in effect stumping for himself, although so completely under the radar that newspapers barely mentioned him as a potential candidate. That would change quickly.

In the fall of 1859, Lincoln was invited to give a lecture at celebrated Reverend Henry Ward Beecher's Plymouth Church in Brooklyn, setting the date as February 27, 1860. Finding out on arrival that the venue had moved to Cooper Union in Lower Manhattan, Lincoln turned the opportunity into the speech of a lifetime. His clear, logical prose defined the slavery positions of North and South, galvanizing the public for the upcoming presidential election. With the Whigs now morphed into the Republican Party, Lincoln helped the new party coalesce around a central theme while driving a wedge between factions of conservative Democrats. So impressed were the party leaders that they begged him to tour Rhode Island, New Hampshire, and Connecticut to rally the party faithful.

Lincoln's first stop was Providence, Rhode Island. He initially struggled with how to present the gist of the Cooper Union speech after it had been published widely in regional newspapers. Rhode Island gives me an opportunity to dive into the controversial growth of Brown University and the port of Newport, both built on the backs of slave-trading money. The North cannot be absolved from the spread of slavery.

Lincoln traveled next to New Hampshire, ostensibly to visit his son Robert studying at Phillips Exeter Academy after miserably failing the Harvard entrance exams. But Lincoln was besieged with requests to give speeches even before he arrived, leading to expeditions into Dover, Concord, Manchester, and back to Exeter to regale large crowds with his Cooper Union–inspired views. I visit all these locations, noting original buildings, statues, and Lincoln's growing exhaustion from "the unrelenting toil" of convincing party leaders to vote for Republicans.

I track Lincoln's steps as he says goodbye to Robert and makes his way to Hartford, Meriden, and New Haven, Connecticut, where his standard speech expanded to incorporate new issues and anecdotes. His logical and stoic Cooper Union speech now included stories of snakes and tumors. He addressed a shoemakers' strike to promote the true condition of Northern laborers in contrast to Southern slavery. He saw his first "Wide Awake" club and began to attract enormous crowds of supporters on special trains between rally sites. Today, Hartford remembers Lincoln's visit with a sculpture park. While in Connecticut's capital I visited the homes of Mark Twain and Harriet Beecher Stowe and explored their roles in the Civil War. In New Haven I discovered the Lincoln oak on Yale's campus and the grave of Eli Whitney, whose cotton gin is almost single-handedly responsible for the spread of cotton and slavery.

By the time Lincoln was cajoled into speaking in eastern Connecticut, Seward's people had begun to take notice of the competition. Historian Michael Burlingame joins me in eastern Connecticut, where Lincoln made a brief stop in New London before giving a speech in Norwich bookended around Woonsocket, Rhode Island. I add Lincoln (the city) and Cranston to my itinerary to explore how the smallest state celebrates its connection to our sixteenth president. By this time in his tour Lincoln was getting substantial press, which had stimulated William Seward and his handler Thurlow Weed to saturate newspapers with Seward's own speech conveying suspiciously similar themes. Seward was the expected Republican nominee but began to see Lincoln as a potential nominating convention threat—hence Seward's furtive attempts to shoehorn Lincoln into a vice presidential slot.

But Lincoln continued to make headlines. As he desperately tried to break the expanding demands on his time in New England, Lincoln worked his way to Bridgeport, the home of my college alma mater and of showman P. T. Barnum. Barnum would later introduce Lincoln to Tom Thumb, the diminutive star of Barnum's traveling sideshows. I stopped at the still-existing speakers' hall, numerous relevant memorials, and the Gutzon Borglum studio to revisit Lincoln's presence and legacy.

Lincoln never made it to Maine or Vermont, but both states play important roles in the Lincoln legacy. Vice President Hannibal Hamlin was a prominent Mainer, as were other key people in Lincoln's administration. While Lincoln never visited Vermont, his wife Mary and their

INTRODUCTION

children did during and after the Civil War. Their only surviving child, Robert, built his home called Hildene in Manchester, Vermont. Hildene provides an opportunity to discuss Lincoln's legacy, including the continuation of African-American struggles for a semblance of civil and human rights. I visit several sites, talk with experts, and stop at West Point and the Lincoln Depot in Peekskill, New York—where Lincoln stopped on his way to his 1861 inaugural and again in 1865—this time in a casket as his assassinated body made its way back to Springfield, Illinois, for burial.

My long treks on the road mirror Lincoln's travels by rail. Fully exhausted, Lincoln rounded out his 1860 New England tour back in New York, where he again visited influential preacher Henry Ward Beecher's Plymouth Church in Brooklyn. He also toured the House of Industry at Five Points in Manhattan before hopping on the Erie Railroad for his trip back to Illinois. Arriving home, he discovered he missed additional New England opportunities for speaking and photographs but was glad to be home to his family and law practice.

All these New England journeys revealed to Lincoln the unrelenting path to civil war. The 1848 trip was a prelude to his personal and professional greatness. The 1860 trip was a prelude to the Civil War. Join me and a variety of national and local experts as we follow in Lincoln's footsteps and explore how we can apply the lessons he learned to today's resurging existential crisis.

Part I

1848—STUMPING FOR TAYLOR

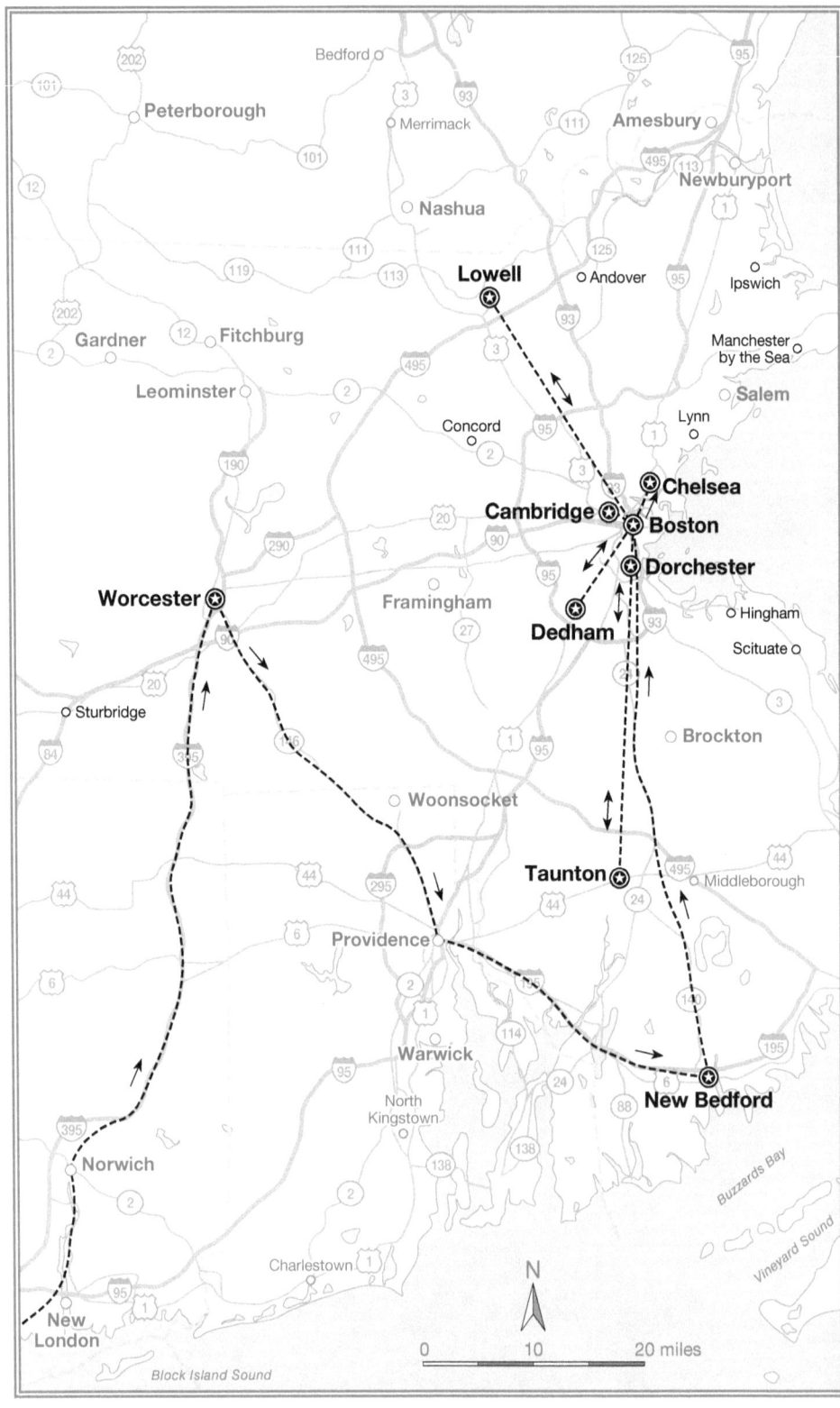

CHAPTER ONE

Zachary Taylor, the Whig?— New England Beckons

A SENSE OF AWE ENGULFS ME AS I CONTEMPLATE THE CARVED EFFIGIES of great Americans standing guard in Statuary Hall of the US Capitol. The hall is an amazing doorway to the past, with sculptures representing heroes from every state. Each state chooses who to honor and most choices seem universally correct. The first to enter, for example, was Revolutionary War hero Nathanael Greene, installed over 150 years ago by his native Rhode Island. Greene represents the state along with its founder Roger Williams, notwithstanding the inconvenient fact that Greene later moved to the South to run Mulberry Grove outside Savannah, Georgia, a slave-labor rice plantation that was, ironically, awarded to him for his war service.

New figures were added to Statuary Hall as states entered the Union, but no removals occurred until 2003. In the two decades since, replacements have been made as sensitivities evolved and new heroes emerged. Kansas was the first state to swap out a statue, replacing nineteenth-century former governor George Washington Glick with war hero and president Dwight D. Eisenhower. Other changes were also non-controversial, as was the case when Lincoln-friend James Harlan (whose daughter married Robert Lincoln) was removed in 2014 to make way for Iowa's great modern-day agronomist, Norman Borlaug. But beginning with the protests spurred by the murder of George Floyd in 2020, the public has questioned whether they could do better finding people more representative of modern values. A few states chose to remove Confederate-linked statues for a more diverse array of political and community leaders representative of their native states. Ohio, for example, exchanged their proslavery nineteenth-century governor William Allen for Ohio-born inventor Thomas Edison. Virginia retracted its statue of Robert E. Lee (in full Confederate general regalia, no less) and plans to install one of Barbara Rose Johns, the civil rights leader who initiated one of the cases fused into *Brown v Board of Education*.[1]

I have come to Statuary Hall to help inaugurate a small room off the gallery—now the rear of the majority party's Whip office—as the Lincoln Room. Statuary Hall in Lincoln's time in Congress had been the House of Representatives, and that side room served as a congressional post office. Lincoln was known to hang out there, telling irreverent jokes to entertain colleagues and using his franking privileges to mail his constituents in Illinois. The Lincoln Group of the District of Columbia, of which I have held leadership roles for over a decade, helped facilitate a bipartisan resolution to designate the room in memory of Lincoln. Today I joined a handful of people for the dedicatory ceremony before taking a private tour of the room, now featuring photos, paintings, and busts of Lincoln.

As congresspeople and other dignitaries gathered for the ceremony, I went in search of the brass plaque embedded in the marble floor indicating the location of Lincoln's tiny desk, one so small he could not sit at it without stretching his unnaturally long legs into the aisle. I finally locate the plaque at the rear of the room, the area once designated for first-year congressmen. As one of the newest Whig members of Congress when he arrived in 1847, Lincoln was not expected to contribute much to the discussion even though he had been the Whig leader during his four terms in the Illinois state legislature. Here in the bigger fishpond of the US Congress, minnow freshmen were expected to sit in the back of the room, keep their mouths shut, and vote the way the party told them. Lincoln duly performed the first and last of those three but was less successful at holding his tongue when he felt an injustice had been perpetrated upon the American people. By December, he told his law partner William Herndon, he planned to "distinguish" himself with a little speech. A week later, the lanky Illinoisan with the homely

The author in front of the Lincoln Room, US Capitol

visage and awkward movements raised his unexpectedly high-pitched voice to introduce a series of resolutions demanding that Democratic president James K. Polk identify the exact spot where Mexican troops had crossed into US territory. Disbelieving the president's tale of Mexican intrusion, Lincoln wanted to know "whether the spot on which the blood of our citizens was shed . . . was or was not within the territory of Spain (i.e., Mexico)."[2]

Brass plaque in Statuary Hall, US Capitol

There were two problems with this venture into congressional speechifying. First, the "spot" he so demanded to know was complicated. Mexico and Texas disagreed on where the previously specified border stood—the Nueces River was the border according to Mexico, while Texas claimed it was at the more southern Rio Grande. The second problem was that the Mexican-American War was popular with the majority of the American people, especially those who believed the United States had a manifest destiny to expand its landholdings to the Pacific coast. Despite the energy Lincoln put into his presentation, his resolutions were roundly ignored, both by President Polk and the Democratic Party–dominated House of Representatives. Unfortunately for Lincoln, his constituents back home in Illinois did not ignore it. Even Herndon grumbled in letters to Lincoln that it was a big mistake to speak out against the war. Lincoln quickly gained the derogatory epithet "spotty Lincoln" in his adopted hometown of Springfield, and his speech may have hurt the chances of the next Whig nominee for the rotating House seat he would soon vacate.

The present-day ceremony had still not begun while we anxiously waited for the keynote speakers to arrive for the dedication, so my mind raced off to that time when Abraham Lincoln had stood at the podium in these very House chambers on July 27, 1848. His topic—the presidential question. Despite the negative reaction to his spot resolutions, Lincoln was an effective speaker and thus was called upon to help convince people that Zachary Taylor was the correct choice as the Whig nominee for president. Lincoln had strongly supported the nomination of Taylor over the aging Henry Clay, the latter previously Lincoln's beau ideal of a statesman. Lincoln felt honor-bound to make the best case.

Like many Whigs, Lincoln, the one who had so bitterly questioned the rationale for the onset of hostilities with Mexico, realized that winning the next presidential election would mean signing on the great military hero of that war. It was General Zachary Taylor and his troops that first put pressure on Mexico at the beginning of the war, and Taylor's definitive win over Mexican president and general Santa Anna at the Battle of Buena Vista led to the war's end. Taylor was the only person the public was interested in having as the next chief executive. If the Whigs did not get Taylor to run for them, the Democrats would.

The move was decidedly hypocritical. Whig leaders had rightfully gained a reputation in opposition to the war, even though Whigs like Lincoln continued to vote for weapons and resources for the troops. Most Whigs felt the war was a cynical attempt to gain more land onto which Southern leaders could spread slavery. The esteemed John Quincy Adams, who after his single term as president had toiled nearly two decades in Congress fighting the Slave Powers, was one of fourteen House "irreconcilables" who voted against the war declaration prior to Lincoln's arrival in Congress.

Further complicating matters was that Henry Clay had offered a fervent antiwar speech in Lexington, Kentucky, which Lincoln witnessed on his way to Congress. Lincoln recognized that the anti-expansionist speech would condemn the Whigs to oblivion if they picked Clay instead of Taylor. Ever the vote counter, Lincoln wrote a friend that "Mr. Clay's chance for an election, is just no chance at all," going on to enumerate which states Clay could not carry. Based on his read of public sentiment, Lincoln noted, "in my judgment, we can elect nobody but Gen. Taylor."[3]

It took a while for the Whigs to talk Taylor into becoming their nominee. He was a Southerner and a slaveholder but nevertheless was not a fan of expanding slavery into the western territories, now doubled in size. With both parties vying for him to lead their ticket, Taylor at first said he would only agree if he could do so "untrammeled with party obligations or interests of any kind," the sort of divine elevation that George Washington had enjoyed after the Revolutionary War.[4] Both the Whigs and Democrats quickly disavowed him of that politically naive delusion. Outgoing President Polk went so far as refer to Taylor as "well-meaning" but also "uneducated, exceedingly ignorant of public affairs, and, I should judge, of very ordinary capacity."[5] Still, the public wanted him, both parties wanted him, and he had to pick one. He agreed to sign on with the Whigs, finding them slightly less objectionable than the conservative Democrats of the South. Now it was time to sell him to the Whig party faithful.

Looking down at the brass plaque in Statuary Hall, I could picture Lincoln awkwardly taking the floor that July, intent on countering those questioning just how whiggish Zachary Taylor was given his largely apolitical history. Lincoln was also determined to question the consistency of the Democratic candidate for president, Michigan senator Lewis Cass.

Wait a second. The name Cass jumped out at me because I had just walked past him in Statuary Hall. Circling back, I found him in stately white marble towering over the folding chairs laid out for the ceremony. Wearing a swallowtail coat popular at the time, his tall, stout frame is even more imposing perched on a four-foot-high pedestal, his hand resting on an open book balanced upon a styled column. When Cass's statue was dedicated in 1889, the then-current Michigan senator Thomas Witherell Palmer said of Cass that "no public man . . . has filled so many places in the economy of life." Checking afterward, I discovered that the Cass statue was the work of Daniel Chester French, sculptor of the grand Lincoln Memorial statue. I will revisit French's New England roots later.

On the surface Cass appeared to be an ideal presidential candidate. While portly and a bit long of tooth—he turned sixty-six years old during the 1848 election year—he possessed a stellar résumé. Born in Exeter, New Hampshire, Cass served briefly as US representative in Ohio before President Thomas Jefferson appointed him a US marshal. When the War of 1812 broke out, Cass took command of the 3rd Ohio Volunteer Regiment, leading them on a series of small military raids around the Canadian border. He resigned from the Army less than two years later and was appointed by President James Madison as the governor of Michigan Territory, a position he held for the next eighteen years. He then served five years as US secretary of war under Andrew Jackson, followed by six years as US minister to France. After his return Michigan selected him to represent them in the Senate, until he resigned in 1848 to run for president. Lincoln's job was to dissuade the public from supporting him. One way of doing that was to challenge his policy inconsistencies. The ever-thorough Lincoln found some.

Senator Cass had voted for internal improvements but then reversed himself to agree with Polk's veto of the same legislation. By accepting the Democratic nomination, Cass approved of their platform that was adamantly against those internal improvements. Lincoln pointed out the duplicity of such positions, further arguing that at least half the Democrats in Congress were for improvements but out of political expediency would vote for a candidate who would eliminate them. We have seen this sort of malleable gamesmanship in modern Congresses where one party's members vote as a bloc against infrastructure projects (today's internal improvements), vociferously labeling them socialism, then rushing home to brag to constituents how they brought infrastructure money to their districts—the very funds they had voted against.

In contrast, assured Lincoln, the Whig candidate's principles were secure. General Taylor—once a general, always a general—would simply sign whatever the Congress voted to pass, postulating that congressmen represented the people. Lincoln added that Taylor would not exercise the veto power except in cases of clear violation of the Constitution. Taylor himself made this clear to irascible Georgia congressman Robert A. Toombs, telling him that "if Congress sees fit to pass" the Wilmot Proviso banning slavery in any of the new territories grabbed from Mexico, he "will not veto it." This was the main Whig argument that Taylor was one of them—the people get to decide policy through their elected representatives in the House. Congress would pass bills, and Taylor would sign them like a good Whig. Sure, his plantations enslaved three hundred African Americans, but he thought it impractical to expand slavery into the western territories, in part because the climate was not conducive to producing copious quantities of plantation-based cotton and sugar. Certainly not an antiracist position (or even a climatically accurate one), which is why many Southern Whigs who were wealthy plantation owners convinced themselves that Taylor would look out for their interests. To Northern audiences, Lincoln noted that Taylor's running mate, Millard Fillmore from Upstate New York, would balance the ticket. The Taylor/Fillmore ticket may not have been ideal for either geographical section, but it seemed close enough to satisfy most of the party. The people, after all, wanted a war hero for president. That meant General Taylor.

Having boosted Taylor's Whig credentials and questioned the consistency of Cass's principles, Lincoln turned to denigrating Cass's own supposed war hero status. Democrats rightfully claimed the Whigs chose Taylor solely to counter the prevailing narrative that Whigs had not supported the war with Mexico. In contrast, Democrats argued, Cass was a true war hero for his feats of daring decades earlier in the War of 1812.

Zachary Taylor circa 1848
PUBLIC DOMAIN, WIKIMEDIA COMMONS

Lincoln could not resist calling that claim to task. He noted that since the election of President Andrew Jackson, whose 1812 hero status helped gain him two terms in office, the Democrats had firmly grasped those military coattails to run the next five elections trading off the name "Old Hickory." Even Polk was some sort of "Little Hickory," Lincoln argued, and now the Democrats were again trying to ride Jackson's coattails with Cass, who they claimed was of a true "Hickory Stripe." Relying on his repertoire of biting wit and humor, Lincoln said that Cass "*in*vaded Canada without resistance, and he *out*vaded it without pursuit." Hardly akin to Jackson's more courageous war record. Referring to his own service in the Black Hawk War in which he saw no fighting action, Lincoln humorously recalled that the only bloodshed he saw was the "good many bloody struggles with the musquetoes; and, although I never fainted from loss of blood, I can truly say I was often very hungry." He ended by mocking the attempt to make Cass something he was not: "If I should ever conclude to doff whatever our democratic friends may suppose there is of black cockade federalism about me, and thereupon, they shall take me up as their candidate for the

Presidency, I protest they shall not make fun of me, as they have of Gen. Cass, by attempting to write me into a military hero."

Lincoln was not finished trying to discredit Cass. Disguising a personal attack as humor, Lincoln questioned Cass's character, suggesting that Cass as governor of Michigan Territory and ex officio superintendent of Indian affairs had received separate pay for being in the same place at the same time, as well as being in different places at supposedly the same time. Lincoln raised this, he claimed dubiously, not to impugn Cass's integrity, but to show his appreciation for the "wonderful physical capacities of the man" for such miraculous achievements.

At the end of his hour-long House speech, Lincoln turned serious, returning to the Democratic accusation that the Whigs were hypocritical for nominating the Mexican War hero Taylor as their candidate for president when the Whigs had "opposed the war." Lincoln's (Bill) Clintonesque parsing of words retorted that it depended on what the meaning of *opposed* was. If it meant that Whigs opposed the war because "the war was unnecessarily and unconstitutionally commenced by the President," then it was accurate to say the Whigs had "very generally opposed it." Polk had marched an army (led by General Taylor) "into the midst of a peaceful Mexican settlement, frightening the inhabitants away, leaving their growing crops, and other property to destruction."[6]

But, as Lincoln made clear, the Whigs dutifully voted to provide supplies for the war after it had become "the cause of the country." Moreover, Whigs offered "the services, the blood, and the lives of our political brethren in every trial, and on every field." Great Whig leaders gave themselves to the cause just as much as Democrats. Whig icons Henry Clay and Daniel Webster each lost a son to the war. Lincoln's own state of Illinois sent Whig leaders Marshall, Morrison, Baker (whom Lincoln had named his second son after), and Hardin, with Hardin killed in battle. Of the five highest officers who perished in the struggle at Buena Vista, four were Whigs. So, while Whigs did not disparage the gallant efforts of Democrats who fought, Democrats should not dishonor Whigs who fought just as gallantly.

The period of Lincoln's first session in the 30th Congress had been a whirlwind of personal and national activity. Gold had been found at

Sutter's Mill in January, setting off the Gold Rush that turbocharged the race to make California a state, in doing so reigniting the slavery conflict to be "resolved" by the Compromise of 1850. January also saw the establishment of the Washington Monument project, whose groundbreaking Lincoln attended on the Fourth of July. In February, the Treaty of Guadalupe Hidalgo was signed, officially ending the Mexican-American War Lincoln had railed against. Later that month, Lincoln was present when former president John Quincy Adams, now a congressman representing Massachusetts, suffered a fatal stroke in the House chambers. Wisconsin became the thirtieth state to enter the Union in May. Lincoln's first session of Congress ended on August 14, 1848, and Lincoln was eager to get home to his family in Springfield in the months before the second session would begin.

The Illinois Whig State Committee had other ideas. They appointed him assistant Taylor elector-at-large with the stipulation that he "take the stump, and labor industriously in the cause of 'Old Rough and Ready,' from now until November next."[7] Instead of boarding a train home, freshman congressman Lincoln obediently sat in the "Whig document room" mailing out campaign material. If Lincoln had spent many a day telling jokes in the House post office, now he was using his franking privileges to promote Taylor as the next great Whig leader. He also wrote a letter to Pennsylvania representative Thaddeus Stevens asking for his opinions on who might win the Pennsylvania elections for governor and president. Still, Lincoln was eager to get out of the intellectually claustrophobic drudgery to which he was bound.[8]

The edict to campaign for Taylor did get him out of the Capitol on at least three occasions in August, diligently giving speeches at local venues. At one of them, in front of the decidedly partisan new Rough and Ready Club in Washington, he continued to deride Lewis Cass. Adding to the criticisms given in his July speech, Lincoln related a tall tale of a gambler betting on a cockfight. When it became clear that his bird was losing, the man surreptitiously switched his allegiance mid-fight to the other bird. As Lincoln had indicated in July, Cass had initially favored the Wilmot Proviso, an attempt to secure all the western territory gained from the Mexican War for free white men only, forever protecting it from slavery. When it became clear that the Michigan senator would be the Democratic nominee, Cass had, without explaining why, simply switched his allegiance to the more Southern-sympathizing anti-Wilmot position.

Electing Taylor was critical and there were rumblings that New England was not happy with the choice, so the Whig Party decided to send Lincoln up to Massachusetts to help make the case. Which gets me to the late Wayne Temple, who at 101 was long considered the "Dean" of Lincoln studies.[9] I had the good fortune to meet with Temple several years ago when he was still working as deputy director at the Illinois State Archives. Even in his mid-nineties at that time, Temple was sharp as a tack, as the old New England saying goes, and regaled me with stories about Lincoln's connections with the Illinois & Michigan Canal, a topic I covered in detail in my previous book. The I&M Canal story begins with Lincoln's 1848 trip to New England, which Temple related in his usual homey style. Temple was one of those people who knows everything there is to know about Lincoln, especially those obscure topics overlooked by others, so his views carry significant weight. He noted that Lincoln was approached during the summer by Junius Hall, a prominent Boston attorney and local Whig leader. Hall wanted Lincoln to bring his speaking talents to the state's capital, as well as to Worcester, the site of the Massachusetts Whig state convention, scheduled to begin on September 13. Other sources suggest Lincoln was invited to Massachusetts by William Schouler, editor of the Boston *Atlas* newspaper. Digging closer into Temple's treatise, I saw that in this case he cites Bill Hanna as a source, and since I had just read Hanna's book on the topic, I decided to reach out to the man who knows more about Lincoln's 1848 visit to Massachusetts than even the dean himself.

William F. Hanna wrote *Abraham Among the Yankees*, first published in 1983 by the Old Colony Historical Society in Taunton, Massachusetts, and reprinted in 2020 by Southern Illinois University Press. I have an original signed copy (number 188 of 250!) and used it extensively to determine the path of my road trips through Massachusetts. I contacted Hanna (call me Bill, he insists) and visited him during my New England road trip. A true historian, Bill spent hundreds of hours digging through

New England–based newspapers of the era long before the digital age made such things available online.

Bill and I arranged to meet at Fireside Grille in Middleboro, Massachusetts, not far from where Lincoln had given his speech in Taunton. We met in the parking lot as a chilly drizzle hurried us into the rustic-looking restaurant to find a table. True to its name, there was a raging fire warming up the main dining room, reminiscent of the centuries-old buildings still common throughout New England. The warmth of the room, and the traditional clam chowder, gave me a much-needed boost after exiting the unexpectedly cold April weather, unseasonable even by Massachusetts standards.

Bill fits the stereotype of a small New England college professor with his graying hair, tortoiseshell-framed glasses, and bright blue flannel shirt peeking out from under his L.L. Bean all-weather anorak. We clicked immediately, recalling mutual friends in the Lincoln studies field and our mutual alma mater in southeastern Massachusetts, before settling in for a long discussion about Lincoln's time in New England, on which he demonstrated his astute insight and knowledge.[10]

I asked Bill who invited Lincoln to Massachusetts. Wayne Temple seems to give more credit to Junius Hall, while others claim it was *Atlas* editor William Schouler. Bill clarified that Lincoln had been corresponding with Schouler in August while still in Washington. Lincoln, again with his questionable spelling, wrote to "Friend Schooler" asking for his "undisguised opinion" about Taylor's chances in New England. Schouler's reply was lost, but it was irresolute enough to scare the national Whig Party into action. The party, after all, had told Lincoln to go to Massachusetts to lasso any wayward Whigs. Meanwhile, Lincoln had simultaneously corresponded with Hall, who was begging him to speak at the Whig convention in Worcester. Lincoln told Hall at first that he expected to travel to Boston but was not sure about Worcester, suggesting that Schouler may have already convinced him that a visit to the Bay State's capital city would be useful.[11] By the way, Schouler would later, as adjutant general of Massachusetts during the Civil War, lay claim to having convinced Lincoln to honor the widow Bixby, a Boston resident who supposedly lost five sons in the war. If the name sounds familiar it is because Lincoln's letter to her has become famous both for its compassionate content and its controversies. Almost certainly you have heard the Bixby letter read by the Army officer at the beginning of the Steven Spielberg movie, *Saving Private Ryan*. It is considered a prime example of Lincoln's personal empathy for the sacrifices made by soldiers and families during the Civil War. Only later was it discovered that Bixby had lied about how many sons she had lost to scam the government out of more pension money. Other historians, including Michael Burlingame, argue that it was not even Lincoln who composed the letter but his presidential secretary, John Hay.[12] Whatever the reality, Schouler was instrumental in getting Lincoln involved.

Bill explained that Lincoln had replied to Hall's request for him to give a speech at the Whig convention with the kind of coy humor he had become known for. "As to speech-making," Lincoln replied, "I have the elements of one speech in mind, which I should like to deliver to a community politically affected as I understand yours to be, *provided* always a tolerable portion of that community should intimate a willingness to hear me." He was referring to the speech he had given in July promoting Taylor and diminishing Cass.[13] By this time, Lincoln was already thinking that it was a waste of time going back to Illinois to stump for Taylor, admitting in his letter to Hall that "it is not very probable Illinois will go for Taylor."[14] With that in mind, Lincoln figured he could do some good by going to New England.

Lincoln's purpose for going to Massachusetts was primarily to persuade Whigs to vote for Taylor, even though many New England Whigs were still not convinced Taylor was one of them. Among their reasons for hesitancy were that he was a war hero in a war they opposed on moral and constitutional grounds, he was a Southern slaveholder, and he had given inadequate indication to the party that he would support Whig principles. Some of these concerns were reiterated by Southern Whigs and Democrats, whom Lincoln had little power to convince, but also by Northern "Cotton" Whigs. And yet there was another, more concerning faction. Some Northern "Conscience" Whigs had splintered off into a separate group calling themselves the Free Soil Party, who did not want

Abraham Lincoln in 1846 by Nicholas Shepherd
PUBLIC DOMAIN, WIKIMEDIA COMMONS

to have anything to do with a slaveholder as their party nominee. It was this latter group on whom Lincoln would focus his oratory skills.

Back in Statuary Hall, 171 years after Lincoln took the floor for his Taylor stump speech, Republican representative Darin LaHood and Democratic representative Raja Krishnamoorthi, both of the "Land of Lincoln," took turns at the podium in the old House of Representatives chambers, now Statuary Hall. They had jointly sponsored House

Resolution 1063 officially dedicating the old post office room, now the back of the majority whip's office suite, as the *Lincoln Room*. A new sign above the door made it clear this was, in a sense, hallowed ground. I posed for the obligatory photos with the Illinois congressmen, then filed into the room for a private tour. I also took advantage of the opportunity to crawl through a trapdoor into a secret hideaway where interns of the majority whip would scribble their names on the subterranean wall (including the "Whipterns of 2019").

I was as proud to have been part of the bipartisan designation in Lincoln's memory as I was horrified by the parading of the Confederate battle flag through this same hall during the January 6, 2021, insurrection. Clearly the country had ruptured along ideological lines just as it had back in Lincoln's day. Could we learn from Lincoln's New England trips as he sought to mend the fissures in his time? It was time to hit the road.

Chapter Two

The Party Divided—
Worcester Free Soilers Rebel

Lincoln received a mixed reception as he rose to speak at Worcester City Hall the night before the Whig state convention. "He has a very tall and thin figure, with an intellectual face, showing a searching mind and a cool judgment," the Boston *Advertiser* wrote.[1] The paper added that "he spoke in a clear and cool, and very eloquent manner" and for an hour and a half carried "the audience with him in his able arguments and brilliant illustrations." Acclaim from the *Advertiser* was not surprising given its Republican-friendly tendency to exalt Republican candidates and insult Democratic ones. In that antebellum era, newspapers were fundamentally partisan and often owned by the parties themselves. Think of Fox News versus MSNBC during more recent elections. Notwithstanding the expected praise by more liberal journals, the conservative Democratic-leaning papers were less impressed (the *Norfolk Democrat* called his speech "nauseous"). And then there were the papers supporting the Free Soilers—lukewarm at best, although one Free Soil paper found him "witty."[2] Worcester was the first of ten speeches he gave over the next eleven days, during which he met some of the key political figures of the region.

Lincoln faced a significant challenge. In addition to the more obvious accusations, the selling of Taylor to Massachusetts was complicated by how the nomination battle had transpired earlier that summer at the Whig National Convention in Philadelphia. Not only was the old Whig stalwart Henry Clay passed over, so was Massachusetts's native son,

Daniel Webster, the state's preferred choice despite his failing health. To keep disgruntled Bay Staters on board the Whig train, party leaders offered Massachusetts the vice presidency. The obvious first choice was Charles Allen, great-grandson of Samuel Adams, and admired by many as "the ablest man of his day."[3] Rather than being pleased, Allen took the offer as an insult, giving an impassioned speech at the convention ripping into his own Whig Party hosts:

> *You have put one ounce too much upon the strong back of northern endurance. You have even presumed that the state which led on the first revolution for liberty, will now desert that cause for the miserable boon of the vice-presidency. Sir, Massachusetts spurns the bribe!*

Allen's indignation was ill-timed. The Whigs selected New Yorker Millard Fillmore for vice president, which took on unexpected importance when Zachary Taylor died sixteen months into his presidency.[4]

Worcester was Lincoln's first stop on this New England tour. He left Washington on September 9, 1848, hopping on the Baltimore and Ohio Railroad as far as Baltimore, then changing trains three more times from there to Jersey City, New Jersey, a customary practice in the days of private railway companies laying short stretches of track with different gauges. East of Jersey City loomed the formidable Hudson River, more than a mile wide with Lower Manhattan waiting on the other side, but no bridge. That meant transferring passengers, luggage, and livestock to a ferry for a crossing to a spot in line with today's One World Trade Center and 9/11 Memorial. From New York he journeyed via the Norwich Line of steamships along the coast of Connecticut up to Norwich, and then on to the Norwich and Worcester Railroad to Worcester, Massachusetts, roughly fifty miles west of Boston.[5] It took him three days.

While railroads now use a standard gauge, they are also less prevalent. Amtrak runs from Washington, DC, to Boston, plus there is a Vermonter Amtrak train that runs from Washington, DC, through central Massachusetts all the way to the Canadian border of Vermont. I will see that train in Windsor later, but for now there are not many railway options for me to follow. I am thankful for President Dwight D. Eisenhower's interstate highway project, the mid-twentieth-century equivalent of the internal improvement programs Lincoln had championed in his political lifetime. Since I will be traveling all over New England in search of Lincoln's forgotten tours, I will be relying on my economically efficient Mazda hatchback for my own expedition following Lincoln's trail.

The chilly rain of early morning had stopped, leaving behind a dense cloud cover casting a dreary aura over Worcester the spring day I arrived. Lincoln had been luckier. His arrival was graced by a crisp autumn day and a celebratory atmosphere as delegates poured into the city for the Whig Party Convention. While he was invited, he was not one of the official convention speakers.

Given that Boston had long been the colonial, and then state, capital of Massachusetts, it struck me as odd that Worcester was chosen by the Whig Party for its 1848 convention. While it had been incorporated as a town way back in the early 1700s, it had only officially become a city a mere six months before Lincoln's visit. According to Bill Hanna, however, Worcester had mirrored the rapid growth of the cities outside Boston, expanding in population by over 150 percent in just two decades.[6] Much of the growth was due to a shift from fishing and whaling (prevalent in places such as Gloucester and New Bedford) to shipbuilding and manufacturing, most notably the cotton textile industry.

It was in Worcester that the Declaration of Independence was first publicly read in Massachusetts by Isaiah Thomas in 1776. The city would also become the recurring location for Republican state conventions for decades to come, so it seems appropriate that it hosted the Whig convention in 1848 (the Whigs would evolve into the Republican Party in the mid-1850s). Worcester was also the center of the Free Soil spinoff faction of the Whig Party and Lincoln was here to bring them back into the fold for the 1848 election.

The exact origin of the city's name is unknown, but Worcester means "war-castle," which is intriguing if not mysterious. Even more mysterious, it seems, is how to pronounce the city's name [Hint: It is not *War-sester*, *War-kester*, or *War-chester*]. Most people who at least try to get it right call it *Wooster*, which is close enough. Unless you are local, that is, as I found out when I pulled over to ask a random pedestrian how to find the "Wooster" city hall. After waiting through his quiet stare for what seemed an interminable time, he finally decided I was not making fun of him but merely "not from around here." With a big smile on his face, he offered: "It's pronounced *Wuh'stah*."

At this point I did feel a bit embarrassed given that I had grown up in the state and still carried an erratically revealing mild accent (and I still occasionally say "I had a wicked good time"). But while my residual accent from "upstate" (i.e., northeast of Boston) has some "downeast" Maine and New Hampshire elements, this man's was more Bostonian, with "r"s added or dropped randomly, for example when "Peter" comes out "Petah" and "pizza" becomes "pete-zr." So Worcester sounds like *Wuh'stah*, although if you say "Wuss-ter" you will still get there. One wonders how Lincoln's high-pitched voice with hints of Kentucky drawl and midwestern Indiana/Illinois had been taken in the Bay State. While this was racing through my mind, the man pointed down the block and told me to "bang a u-ey" (that is, make a U-turn) at the next intersection and go back a few blocks. No way to miss it, he added helpfully.

He was right. I found the current city hall towering over Worcester Common, an urban park that was added to the National Registry of Historic Places in the 1970s. The common in Worcester is tiny compared to the more famous one in Boston. The current city hall built in 1898 dominates the view and a small eighteenth-century burial ground sits in the middle of the common itself, which is replete with reminders about past conflicts, including monuments commemorating those lost in World War II, Desert Shield/Desert Storm, and Vietnam. On one corner stands the most prominent memorial, a sixty-six-foot tall, multifigure Civil War Soldiers' Monument consisting of a tapering granite Corinthian column atop a three-tiered granite pedestal featuring bronze statues representing branches of the military—artillery, cavalry, infantry, and navy. Lincoln shows up as a relief bust on the middle tier. On the opposite corner of the common is Burnside Fountain. Originally designed as a watering trough for horses by architect Henry Bacon—he later designed the Lincoln Memorial in Washington, DC—the main basin, now dry, is topped by an unexpected bronze statue of a boy riding a sea turtle, known affectionately by locals as *Turtle Boy*.

The Party Divided—Worcester Free Soilers Rebel

Despite Junius Hall and William Schouler's desperate invitations, Lincoln arrived in Worcester not scheduled to speak at the Whig convention, duties that fell to prominent Massachusetts political leaders Rufus Choate and Senator Robert C. Winthrop. According to Hanna, the local Whig committee had planned for a huge event outside the city hall the night before the convention in hopes of rallying all the Whig supporters in town. But the committee's chairman, Alexander Bullock, was frantic as the night approached. He had invited several prominent Whigs to speak at this preamble meeting, but no one seemed interested. Most likely they were gathering for drinks and cigars with old friends, which left Bullock in a bit of a lurch. Tipped to Lincoln's presence—he was a sitting congressman and had a reputation for his thigh-slapping humor and sure-to-please speeches—Bullock raced to Lincoln's hotel to beg him to speak. Lincoln was happy to accommodate.

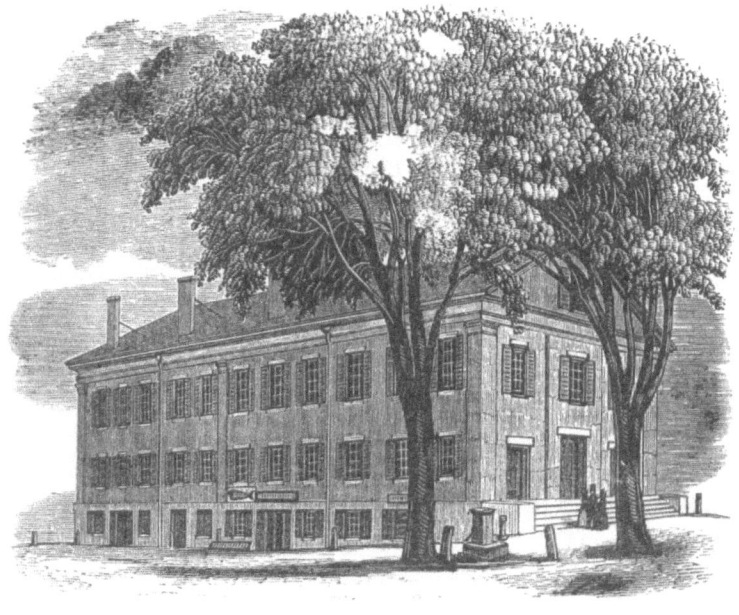

The old city hall in Worcester, Massachusetts, where Lincoln spoke
BY PERMISSION OF MUSEUM OF WORCESTER

Notwithstanding the impromptu nature of the occasion, Lincoln managed to speak for an hour and a half to a large crowd. He repeated the arguments from his congressional speech defending Zachary Taylor as the Whig nominee. Taylor indeed had principles, Lincoln insisted, and offered as evidence a letter Taylor had written to J. S. Allison in Louisville, Kentucky, in which he promised that "the will of the people should produce its own results, without Executive influence." In other words, he would let the people's representatives (i.e., in Congress) pass the laws and he would sign them. He would religiously avoid use of the veto pen unless Congress passed overtly unconstitutional laws. He would be a good Whig, which meant that the president would defer to the wishes of Congress, the "more equal" of the three equal branches of the federal government. Interestingly, Lincoln did not reveal what he surely knew, that the "Taylor letter" had been a campaign document drafted by Whig congressmen John J. Crittenden, Alexander Stephens, and Robert Toombs and issued under Taylor's name. I am sure it was just an oversight.[7]

But promoting Taylor and getting in a few snarky digs about Cass was not the primary reason Lincoln was in Massachusetts. Worcester was the center of the Free Soil movement, which began in Buffalo, New York, in early August but quickly gained a following in central Massachusetts and elsewhere. Bay State politicians that would become household names—Charles Sumner, Henry Wilson, George Boutwell, and Charles Allen among them—quickly formed the state Free Soil Party to protest the choice of slaveholder Taylor as the Whig nominee. The focus of Free Soilers was to restrict the expansion of slavery into the western territories.

To fully understand the Free Soil position, we need to recall the dreaded Mexican-American War that spawned Lincoln's not-so-complimentary "Spotty Lincoln" nickname. Most Whigs were against both the premise of the war (seriously, did Mexico really invade the United States?) and the intended result (imperialistic acquisition of vast new lands upon which to spread slavery). Combined with the upper portion of the Louisiana Purchase that had remained as territory for nearly a half century, the western territories had immediately become a rhetorical battlefield over the rights of Southern slaveholders to bring their human "property" wherever they wanted versus the rights of Northern whites to expand free society west. Enter the Free Soilers, whose name reflects their primary goal—to preserve the entirety of the western territories solely for the settlement of free white farmers, tradesmen, and merchants. The Free Soil Party adamantly opposed the expansion of slavery into those lands, and indeed, opposed the movement even of free Black men. They felt the territories should be restricted to free whites only, and the Free Soil Party split off from the Whigs because they felt the Whigs were too soft on this point. The Whig nomination of Southern slaveholder Zachary Taylor was ample evidence of this fact, and they wanted nothing to do with either the man or the party. Suddenly, former Democratic president Martin Van Buren was the Free Soil candidate running against the Whig Taylor and Democrat Lewis Cass.

This created a problem. No one, not even the Free Soilers, thought that the eighth president could win the popular vote despite being one of the leaders in the so-called Barnburner movement in Upstate New York. It was the Barnburners and residual Liberty Party (another abolition-focused party) who coalesced into the Free Soiler Party Van Buren now represented. Henry Wilson and Charles Allen, the two Massachusetts men who helped organize the state's Free Soilers, were hoping to throw the election into the House of Representatives, where history had shown the man having the most votes did not always come out of the House with the presidency.

Lincoln and other Whig leaders saw this as a looming catastrophe, desperately aware that Van Buren could siphon off enough votes to hand the election to the Democrat Cass just as Liberty Party candidate James Birney had siphoned off enough votes from the Whig Henry Clay to hand the 1844 election to the Democrat James K. Polk. That would be madness. In his Worcester speech, Lincoln explained why a Free Soil splinter group would achieve exactly the opposite of their goals.

First of all, he said, the primary Free Soil goal was to block expansion of slavery into the territories, which is what the Whig Party already adamantly supported. The Boston *Daily Advertiser* noted Lincoln's point—both parties believed that slavery was an evil even though constitutionally they were unable to rid it from other states, but the extension of slavery was under their control. Lincoln claimed the Free Soil party was far behind the Whigs in this regard.

Lincoln had already established himself as a number cruncher and vote-counter when it came to elections. While having no chance of electing Van Buren, the Free Soilers were likely to accidentally get the man they most opposed—Cass—elected instead. In a sense, Lincoln was arguing that voting should be strategic, not simply an exercise in perceived duty and "leave the consequences to God." Rather than throw the election away on principle, stick with the Whig Party that brought you here and work with us to ensure the western territories remain free soil for all.

Was he taken seriously? Not really. The Boston *Atlas* called Lincoln "a capital specimen of a 'Sucker Whig,' six feet at least in his stockings and in every way worthy to represent that Spartan band in the only Whig district in poor benighted Illinois." You can sense the sarcasm dripping from the newsprint. The word *sucker* was a disparaging term for Illinoisans, especially peculiar-looking ones lacking in eastern-style civility, and the Free Soil and Democratic-leaning newspapers used it relentlessly to demean Lincoln's presence in the state. Prominent attorney Edward Pierce panned Lincoln's speech as "not on a high level," mainly because "he labored to prove Taylor was a Whig." As Lincoln toured the state, other papers reiterated their incredulity that Taylor, a Southern slave-holding Mexican war hero, could be passed off as representative of a party who opposed the war and claimed to be the only ones who could protect the western territories from the encroaching freight train of slavery. Even many in the Whig Party cringed at Lincoln's irreverent humor and lack of eastern sophistication, while at the same time welcoming his ability to attract large audiences. Lincoln's western sarcasm and stories also served to broaden the reach of the Whig Party, which was eager to appeal to laborers as well as the more educated "gentlemanly" classes. So, it was no surprise that, as historian Richard Cmiel once wrote, "refined Whig gentlemen, hungry for political victory, found themselves applauding the very invective they had previously condemned." It is hard not to see the same kind of creative rationalization that has allowed today's politicians to admit their own candidate is lacking in social graces, honesty, and expertise, but then vote for him anyway to maintain their party in power.[8]

Levi Lincoln Jr., Worcester, Massachusetts PUBLIC DOMAIN, LIBRARY OF CONGRESS

There were other sites I wanted to see in Worcester, so I headed off on foot from the common in search of the Levi Lincoln house, starting with the corner of Elm and Main Streets where Hanna wrote it was located. Instead, I found a rather imposing bank and several other modern buildings. Thinking I had the wrong address, I checked a 1909 paper by Arthur Rugg. He says the Levi Lincoln residence was at 49 Elm Street, and a quick quarter-mile hike got me to a beautiful brick building that is currently the Chancery of the Roman Catholic Diocese of Worcester. That was not it either. More research took me closer to the goal, a house called the Gov. Levi Lincoln House at 4 Avalon Place, which was listed on the National Register of Historic Places in 1980.[9] Levi Jr. had moved to Worcester after serving as governor of Massachusetts and lived in the unexpectedly modest clapboard house while his more appropriate mansion was being built. The house was originally in an area now called the Lincoln Estate–Elm Park Historic District before being relocated to its more ignominious current location. I would find the mansion later, but not in Worcester.[10]

Meanwhile, it turns out Levi Lincoln and Abraham Lincoln did not simply share a last name; they were distantly related through ancestry that included Samuel Lincoln in Hingham, Massachusetts. Abraham Lincoln found himself intrigued by the family heritage since his knowledge of his ancestry was, at best, murky. I will dig into that in a later chapter, but Levi Jr.'s father, Levi Sr., had been an important figure in early Massachusetts history, practicing law in Worcester in 1775 and functioning as judge of probate to the convention that framed the state constitution. He served in the state legislature and the US Congress and as attorney general for President Thomas Jefferson, where he played a significant role in the events that led to the precedent-setting *Marbury v. Madison* case. After resigning from Jefferson's cabinet, Levi Sr. served briefly as acting governor of Massachusetts. Levi Jr. was no slouch either. After a year as lieutenant governor, he served nine straight one-year terms as governor of Massachusetts, the longest consecutive service as governor to this day.[11] Levi Jr. also had been a leader in both houses of the state legislature and served three terms as US congressman. At the time of Abraham Lincoln's visit to Worcester, Levi Jr. was the city's mayor.

So, it was no surprise that after the convention had finished for the day, in which the main order of business was to nominate George N. Briggs for governor, Abraham Lincoln joined some of the most distinguished men in the state for dinner at the Levi Lincoln house. The event was recalled four decades later by Henry J. Gardner, present at the meal and later governor of Massachusetts in the mid-1850s. Gardner claimed that a who's who of nineteenth-century New England elite were in attendance, including Rufus Choate, George Ashmun, George L. Hillard, Emory Washburn, Alexander H. Bullock, Charles L. Putman, and Stephen Salisbury. Washburn and Bullock would join Gardner in the future Massachusetts governors' club. Hillard and his wife would become prominent abolitionists and secret conductors on the Underground Railroad as it passed through Boston. Ashmun presided over the 1860 Republican convention that nominated Lincoln for president and was the last person Lincoln spoke with before heading out the door to the theater on that fateful last night of his life. Lincoln may have been in awe of the distinguished guest list, because Gardner suggests Lincoln was rather quiet during the event.

Before I leave the party, the one name on the dinner list that intrigued me most was Rufus Choate. Back in the introduction when I was chatting with Ipswich town historian Gordon Harris along the Riverwalk, we could see Choate Bridge, the oldest two-span stone bridge in America, dating back to 1764. The Choate family goes back to the town's founding and one of its prominent members was Rufus Choate, who was born in Ipswich on Hog Island. Choate's house on the island remains to this day and was the setting for the 1996 film version of *The Crucible*. Rufus had served the last four years of his good friend Daniel Webster's Senate term after Webster became secretary of state (Choate later gave back the Senate seat to Webster and returned to his private law practice). While he was a good Whig, Choate refused to join the Republican Party when it organized, thinking it too sectional because it only existed in the North, ignoring the fact that the South would not allow it to exist there. In 1856, he outwardly supported James Buchanan against the first Republican presidential nominee, John C. Fremont. He died the year before Lincoln's election. A grand statue of Choate stands in Boston, sculpted by none other than Daniel Chester French, whom I will come back to later.

As Gardner remembers it, this high-powered dinner took place in Levi Jr's large Greek Revival house on Elm Street. At the time of Lincoln's visit, Levi Jr. was Worcester's mayor, so naturally the house was the center of the city's social scene, especially when like-minded politicians were in town. In researching this book, I found out that the house still exists, just not in Worcester. Passed down through the family for over a century, Levi's heirs sold the property for development in 1949 and moved away. To preserve the house, the people at Old Sturbridge Village agreed to have the entire building moved there. Old Sturbridge Village is the New England version of Virginia's Jamestown, a living museum re-creating life during the 1790s through 1830s. Having visited the village in my long-ago childhood but not since, I decided to make a side trip to Sturbridge—and there it was! Levi's house—now bright yellow with two-story fluted Doric columns painted a glimmering white—was not

The Levi Lincoln Jr. House as it stands today in Sturbridge, Massachusetts

a great fit for the village itself, so it sits just outside the park along historic Route 20.[12] Originally opened as a restaurant, it has gone through a series of small businesses over the years. A Country Curtains store had occupied the property since 1982, but during my visit, Levi's old mansion had been taken over by Lake Road Living, a women's clothing boutique. Paula Bowne, a former paralegal and Texas transplant, was delighted that the Levi Lincoln mansion became available in time for them to open the boutique in March 2020 (yes, just as the pandemic boxed everyone into their homes). A large wooden sign over the entrance says Lincoln House to remind visitors of the building's prominent history.

Being able to visit the building gave me a sense of what Abraham Lincoln must have felt entering the mansion and breaking bread with such distinguished Bay Staters. Gardner disclosed that he visited Lincoln in the White House in 1861, where to his surprise, Lincoln immediately recognized him, saying "You and I are no strangers; we dined together

The Party Divided—Worcester Free Soilers Rebel

at Governor Lincoln's in 1848." Continuing, Lincoln dropped into his trademark self-deprecation:

I had been chosen to Congress then from the wild West, and with hayseed in my hair I went to Massachusetts to take a few lessons in deportment. That was a grand dinner—a superb dinner; by far the finest I ever saw in my life. And the great men who were there too! Why I can tell you just how they were arranged at the table.

Gardner then claimed that Lincoln began reciting the names, starting at one end "and mentioned the names in order," Gardner believed, "without the omission of a single one."

As with all memories recalled decades later, especially after the assassination had created the "Martyr Lincoln," it is difficult to know how much of this is real and how much reflects a need to feel closer to Lincoln. There have been people who questioned Gardner's recollections. Still, the incident does capture two of Lincoln's greatest realities of that period.

First, the self-deprecating humor. Largely unknown outside Illinois, Lincoln was welcomed to Massachusetts not just for "lessons in deportment," but for the entertainment value of his speeches. He was not yet known for his policy chops, and as we shall see, he had not spent a lot of time to that point on what would become the single most driving issue of the nation's history. Second, assuming you take the story at face value, it demonstrates Lincoln's phenomenal memory, a trait I discussed in depth in my previous book.[13]

Lincoln was not quite finished with Worcester. Alexander Bullock, as chairman of the local Whig committee, had asked Lincoln to stick to addressing the Whig positions in general and use "much discretion" to avoid offending those still on the fence about abandoning the Whigs and joining the Free Soilers. Lincoln did try in his city hall speech, but his tendency to brandish humor and sarcasm could be a double-edged sword, entertaining but sometimes bitingly inappropriate. For example, he had taken issue with the Free Soil platform, jocularly proclaiming that it "embraces a few general declarations in regard to other topics [other than slavery], but they are so general" that they called to mind "the pantaloons offered at auction by a Yankee peddler," who described them as "large enough for any man and small enough for any boy." Then the morning after the convention he let his guard down even further. While preparing to leave Worcester, Lincoln made brief remarks at the railroad depot that neglected Bullock's advice. He suggested that enthusiastic antislavery men were better treated in Massachusetts than in his home state of Illinois. "I have heard you have abolitionists here," Lincoln joked: "We have a few in Illinois, and we shot one the other day." The audience knew he was referring to the murder of vocal abolitionist Elijah Lovejoy, whose printing press was destroyed in Alton before a proslavery mob viciously killed him. One can almost hear the gasps as the stunned crowd shook their heads at the callousness of the statement. Lincoln realized his mistake and wisely never repeated it. Perhaps sensing the timing was right to avoid overstaying his welcome, Lincoln boarded a train to the Whaling City, also known as New Bedford.

Chapter Three

The Abolitionists—
New Bedford Whaling and Wailing

If Lincoln thought the Free Soilers of Worcester was the worst challenge he would encounter, he underestimated the radical antislavery sentiment that was waiting for him in New Bedford. Known mostly for its whaling industry, it was also a hotbed of abolitionism. And Lincoln was no abolitionist.

When Lincoln's train from Worcester arrived in New Bedford on the afternoon of September 14, the weather had turned cold and windy. I was in for a similar reception. Having stayed in a hotel in Middleboro after my dinner with Bill Hanna, I drove the half hour to New Bedford in dreary rain, which as it did in Worcester, sputtered out as I parked my car for the day in the Elm Street garage. My goal was the New Bedford Whaling National Historical Park's visitor center, where I hoped to meet up with Judy Roderiques. The center is in a small red brick building with a sandstone facade on Williams Street. Built in 1853, three years after Lincoln's visit to the city, it originally was a savings bank, then it was the Third District courthouse, before it felt too cramped and the court moved elsewhere. After years of various short-term uses, the building became the historical park's headquarters in 1996. Leaving the misty weather temporarily behind, I climbed the granite steps to the heavy front door and found a smiling young park ranger at the front desk. When I asked for Judy, I was told that she would arrive in about an hour. Taking a map, I ventured back out into the gloom to check out the neighborhood.

I had some familiarity with the New Bedford area already. I attended graduate school in nearby Dartmouth at what was then Southeastern Massachusetts University but now is a campus of the University of Massachusetts system. Later in the day I drove over to the unique concrete campus buildings that always reminded me of World War II battleships. It had not changed much in the decades since I walked the halls. As the old college name implies, New Bedford sits in the southeastern portion of the Bay State, roughly equidistant between Newport, Rhode Island, and the Cape Cod Canal as you drive along the coastline. With a population of just over 100,000 today, it is the largest city along the southern coast, although it barely breaks into the top ten cities in the state (for comparison, Boston today is about 650,000 people). That seems large by my standards since my hometown on the North Shore has fewer than 14,000 people. The neighborhood I am visiting, however, carries the aura of a quaint New England seacoast town, with its old buildings and walkable streets.

New Bedford's nickname is the Whaling City, which if unoriginal is historically descriptive. Like Worcester, New Bedford had been around for a long time—it was first settled in 1652—and had been a town since the late 1700s but was only incorporated as a city the year before Lincoln's visit. The first whaling interests started just before the American Revolution, then expanded as whaling families from offshore Nantucket abandoned the island for the deeper harbor on the mainland. British command of the seas largely paralyzed the whaling industry during the Revolutionary War, but once the new United States dug firmly into its independence, the New Bedford whaling industry grew rapidly. Whale oil became the mainstay for lighting most homes, replacing beeswax candles. Its use in machine lubrication helped drive the Industrial Revolution. The oil from both baleen whales (with fibrous mouth plates to sieve plankton from the water) and the waxier oil from toothed whales (with teeth to eat various prey animals) was exceptionally stable and perfect for oil lamps and machinery. The waxy ester oil called spermaceti from the bulbous heads of sperm whales was perfect for candle making. By the time of Lincoln's visit, however, whaling interests were waning, and textile mills were cropping up all over New England, including in New Bedford.

The Abolitionists—New Bedford Whaling and Wailing

My old marine biology days flashed back as I toured the area around the historical park. Across the street from the visitor center was the Custom House, an important facility back in the whaling days and now shared by branch offices of the US Customs and Border Control Agency and the National Marine Fisheries Service, the latter for which I had worked coming out of college. A block away was the New Bedford Whaling Museum and the Mariners' Home built in 1795 and since 1850 housing and feeding poor, unskilled whaling crew back in port from their long voyages. Next door was Seamen's Bethel Church, built in 1832

The Seamen's Bethel Church in New Bedford, Massachusetts

"to protect the rights and interests of Seamen, and to furnish them with . . . moral, intellectual and religious instruction."[1] A young man named Herman Melville joined one of these long-haul voyages in 1839, which led him to write the classic whaling epic *Moby-Dick*. While in the novel Melville writes that "the town itself is perhaps the dreariest place to live in," he added "in the same New Bedford there stands a whaleman's chapel and few are the moody fishermen, shortly bound for the Indian or Pacific Oceans who failed to make a Sunday visit to this spot." Today the Seamen's Bethel Church proudly highlights its whaling heritage and its connection to the giant white sperm whale that became Ahab's—and Melville's—obsession.[2]

One of the more prominent whaling families was led by William Rotch Jr., whose grand mansion and gardens built in 1834 still exist. Having time to spare, I included it on my walking exploration of the area. Now called the Rotch-Jones-Duff House and Museum and open for tours, the large muted yellow house embodies the massive wealth that could be made in whaling. One of the Rotch family ships called the *Dartmouth* was famously relieved of its shipment of tea in a little incident we refer to as the Boston Tea Party. At the time Rotch Jr. was amassing his wealth, New Bedford hosted over eighty registered whaling ships, including brigs, schooners, sloops, and huge square-rigged ships large enough to boil the flensed blubber on board, enabling them to render oil on sea voyages lasting up to four years. Over ten thousand men worked in the American whaling industry, and many of New Bedford's residents shipped out as crew or officers. Other supporting industries also flourished, like barrel making, metalwork, shipbuilding, banking, and insurance. The city also boasted candleworks and refineries, as well as many ancillary crafts and trades. Whaling defined New Bedford until eventually giving way to more modern industries.[3]

After a while I realized my short walk had turned into a long exploration of the city's history, so I hustled back to the park office. This time I found Judy Roderiques on duty behind the counter. She was busy with another patron when I entered the historic building, so the man next to her asked if he could help me. It turns out he was Clifford Roderiques, Judy's husband, who like her was volunteering at the visitor center. I told him I was there to meet Judy. When she heard her name, she looked up with a confused "Do I know you?" look. I quickly introduced myself and how I knew about her. I had seen Judy on a virtual program she did the previous year where she played a local abolitionist woman, Abby Almy, one of "New Bedford's 1850s ladies," interviewing Frederick Douglass, portrayed by the incomparable Nathan Richardson.

Judy had been involved with the historical park since its creation in 1996, first working as a volunteer, then as a national park ranger before retiring and returning to volunteer work. She was a wellspring of information, informing me on both Douglass's and Lincoln's time in New Bedford. At one point she asked me if I saw the melted bell on the Merchants National Bank building, which I had not, but I promised to check it out.

The Merchants' building sits on the site of Liberty Hall, where Lincoln gave his 1848 speech. As with most of the venues Lincoln spoke at that year, Liberty Hall had succumbed to age and alternative land uses. Originally a Congregationalist meeting house, the building had been converted into Liberty Hall in 1839 as a venue for a variety of public meetings. Most notably it hosted abolitionists like William Lloyd Garrison, Frederick Douglass, Wendell Phillips, and Theodore Parker, some of whom Lincoln would engage with in the future, not always favorably. Liberty Hall would burn down six years after Lincoln's visit and be rebuilt. By the end of the century, it would be replaced by a series of bank buildings, with the current one standing since Woodrow Wilson was president. I could clearly see the Merchants' name engraved in the cornice above two massive columns fronting the stately old bank. Unfortunately, the beauty of the building was marred by a "For Sale" sign hanging out front, bringing sadness to the story of Lincoln's visit even though it was not the original building. I wrote it off as history lost.

As Lincoln rose to speak at Liberty Hall, he may have known that it was in this very hall seven years earlier that Douglass first heard firebrand abolitionist William Lloyd Garrison speak. Lincoln's speech was a reiteration of what he had said in Worcester, defending Taylor and his supposed Whig Party principles. While New Bedford had been safe Whig territory and less leaning toward Free Soilerism, they were just as unhappy as the rest of New England with the Whig choice of a Southern slaveholder as their party representative. Newspaper columns barely reported the speech, with the usual partisan biases for what little they did say. One Quaker diarist who attended noted that Lincoln's discourse was "pretty sound, but not a tasteful speech." Talk about your half-hearted endorsements.[4]

Walking around the corner to the Purchase Street side of the old bank, I was able to find the plaque that Judy had told me about. Three feet tall and two feet wide, the plaque featured a bullet point history of the building. At the very bottom of the plaque was an amorphous molten mass of metal about five inches across. Above it there was an inscription explaining that the bell had graced the original Liberty Hall and had been rung in 1851 to warn fugitive slaves that US marshals, in compliance with the Fugitive Slave Law passed the year before, were on their way to New Bedford. The bell melted when Liberty Hall burned down in 1854, and the fragment retained was inserted into the plaque honoring the building.

While Lincoln was touring Massachusetts to support Zachary Taylor's Whig presidential dreams, he was also there to help support congressional and local candidates running for office. In New Bedford, his speech had been preceded by fellow congressman Joseph Grinnell, whom he ran into at the Whig convention in Worcester and who convinced him to come back to Grinnell's home district. Grinnell was facing a difficult reelection campaign and thought Lincoln's jovial presence would help rev up the voting populace. Twenty years older than Lincoln, Grinnell had been born in New Bedford and lived there most of his life apart from his early years as a merchant in New York City and his time in Congress. He had served a term in Congress before Lincoln got there and was reelected three more times. As a merchant, banker, and president of the New Bedford & Taunton Railroad, Grinnell was a pillar of his community and yet another example of Lincoln's consummate ability to hook up with the key movers and shakers of politics. Lincoln stayed in Grinnell's house, which still exists, so I decided to swing by before I left town. What I found was a massive stone mansion with four colossal columns set back from County Street under the protection of a spiked wrought iron fence. I drove up the narrow driveway, finding on the side steps an exhausted care worker wearing scrubs and dragging on a cigarette. The prestigious building is now a home for the elderly, offering "17 affordable one-bedroom apartments, and congregate dining and living space on the first floor for low-income seniors and persons with disabilities." Given that Grinnell lived to a ripe old age of ninety-six, outliving Lincoln by two score years, the current use of his house seems appropriate.[5] Whether Lincoln's presence helped Grinnell's chances was debatable, but Grinnell was reelected to Congress, while Lincoln himself had chosen not to run for reelection.

Lincoln had paid little attention to slavery up to this point in his career. Sure, as a young Illinois state legislator in 1837 he had dissented against a bill that criminalized "anti-slavery agitation." But even there he explained that while "the institution of slavery is founded on both injustice and bad policy," he thought abolitionism increased rather than abated its evils. He thought that while Congress could abolish slavery in the District of Columbia, it did not have the authority to interfere with slavery in the states where it was already present. It was state action, not federal, that ended slavery in the North. His recent spot resolution speech in Congress was more about anti-imperialism than slavery, although others believed Polk had started the war with Mexico to grab more land for slaveholders. Even during this tour of Massachusetts, he focused primarily on convincing Free Soilers that the Whig Party was their best bet for blocking expansion of slavery into the newly gained western territories. Neither the Whigs nor the Free Soilers were actively working to abolish slavery where it already existed.

But it would have been hard to miss the abolitionist sentiment in New Bedford and at his other Massachusetts stops. That gets me to Abolition Row Park, which sits across the street from the Nathan and Polly Johnson House, one of the most consequential houses in town that Lincoln likely never saw but would come to influence his life immeasurably.

Abolition Row Park takes up a small corner at 22 Seventh Street and was only created in 2023. The name comes from the one-square-mile neighborhood that was home to both white and Black abolitionists in Lincoln's time. It was a haven for Black families always wary of

Frederick Douglass statue in Abolition Row Park with the Nathan and Polly Johnson House and Quaker meetinghouse in the background, New Bedford, Massachusetts

slave-hunters working under the authority of the Fugitive Slave Act and part of a network of abolitionists running stations along the Underground Railroad. Massachusetts was a free state, but that did not stop attempts by Southern slaveholders to chase down fugitives seeking a free life, or, as the recent film *Twelve Years a Slave* documented, claim free men as fugitives and ship them south for enslavement. The park celebrates the work of those New Bedford residents who staged dramatic civil rights protests via the Underground Railroad. The space it now occupies replaces two historic houses, one owned by the abolitionist Thornton family that had fallen into disrepair and the other a rooming house destroyed by fire in 2009, the bicentennial of Lincoln's birth. The New Bedford Historical Society purchased the lots and turned them over to the city, which established the space to appropriately remember the historic nature of the neighborhood.

The surface is mostly pavement with a curving pathway representing the Underground Railroad spiraling away from a small wooden gazebo and benches. Granite from a staircase in the rooming house serves as stairs to the gazebo. Another section of granite is inscribed with a Frederick Douglass quotation: "Truth, Justice, Liberty, and Humanity will Ultimately Prevail." Abolition Row's most prominent feature is a spectacular bronze statue of Frederick Douglass. Created by sculptor Richard Blake of Philadelphia, nationally renowned for his artwork of African-American figures, the statue depicts Douglass soon after his arrival in New Bedford. Seated on a spool of sailor's rope, with a cane in one hand and a rolled-up map in the other, Douglass's face carries the intensity of a man struggling to ensure all men could be free.

As Judy Roderiques (in character as Abby Almy) and Nathan Richardson (as Frederick Douglass) explained, Frederick Bailey escaped from slavery in 1838, only ten years before Lincoln's foray into Massachusetts. Working his way by railroad and steamship, he managed to get to New York City, where he stayed in a safe house run by abolitionist David Ruggles long enough to summon Anna Murray, a free Black woman he had met in Baltimore and who helped him escape. There they married and took on the name Johnson. Shortly thereafter they moved to the safety of New Bedford, boarding initially with Nathan and Polly Johnson. Nathan was a prominent African-American resident of New Bedford, where he married Mary (known as Polly) Page, the daughter of a free Black family from nearby Fall River.

Frederick, having originally used his mother's last name of Bailey, then briefly Stanley before settling on Johnson, and finding that Johnson was way too common in New Bedford, wanted a name he could call his own. It was Nathan who suggested the name Douglas (with one "s") based on Scottish Lord Douglas, hero of the narrative poem *The Lady of the Lake* by Sir Walter Scott. To personalize it, Frederick added a second "s," and at twenty years old he became the Frederick Douglass we know today.[6]

The Douglasses lived with the Johnsons for Frederick's first years of practical, if not legal, freedom. With green shutters highlighting its white facade, the three-story Nathan and Polly Johnson House looms across the street from the bench I am sitting at in Abolition Row Park. Next door is the Society of Friends (aka Quaker) meetinghouse; both the Johnson House and the Quaker meetinghouse played important roles in the Underground Railroad. The Quakers were prominent businesspeople in New Bedford, promoting religious and moral business values and, like the Whigs, investing in infrastructure projects such as railroads and steam power while employing workers without discrimination.

Under the protection of the Johnsons, and with training and experience in Baltimore as a caulker—crafting watertight seals on wooden hulls—Douglass sought work at the many shipyards in the city. According to Richardson, Douglass was hired but quickly realized that safety from slavery did not mean social equality. In mere hours, white workers forced him off the worksite, compelling him to find manual labor jobs wherever he could. Even in churches Black parishioners were often relegated to the back row and spoken of condescendingly by the minister. Despite this, Douglass would later write that New Bedford offered at least a semblance of equality in that "the black man's children . . . went to school side by side with the white children, and apparently without objection from any quarter." Nathan Johnson also assured him that "no slaveholder could take a slave from New Bedford; that there were men there that would lay down their lives, before such an outrage could be precipitated."[7]

The Abolitionists—New Bedford Whaling and Wailing

It was in New Bedford that Douglass first started reading *The Liberator*, the abolitionist newspaper started by William Lloyd Garrison. Douglass later wrote that "My soul was set all on fire" by Garrison's passionate call for the immediate abolishment of slavery and investiture of full equality.[8] Douglass would first see Garrison speak at Liberty Hall in 1841, and it was Garrison's people that asked Douglass for an impromptu recounting of his escape from slavery. That encounter led to his heroic speech days later at the Massachusetts Anti-Slavery Society convention on Nantucket. The soft-spoken Garrison followed the imposing baritone voice of Douglass to the stage and a partnership was born. After encouraging Douglass to write the first version of his three autobiographies, Garrison arranged for a speaking tour to get Douglass's very personal account of living under the yoke of slavery out to white and Black audiences in New England. The two men eventually had a falling-out—Douglass came to believe more direct action was necessary, in contrast to Garrison's moral fervor tempered by opposition to violence—but with Douglass's speaking and Garrison's adamant editorials in *The Liberator*, the two sparked a revolution in antislavery thought. Ironically, Garrison and Douglass would both become dedicated supporters of Lincoln late in the Civil War despite opposing his early stance on colonization.

While New Bedford and Massachusetts grew to become hotbeds of abolitionist fever, it was Garrison who fundamentally changed public opinion in the antislavery movement. Garrison was born in Newburyport, a stone's throw from my hometown of Ipswich. On a recent visit to relatives in the town, I stopped by Brown's Square, where a statue of "Garrison the Liberator" dominates the grassy expanse. Not far away on School Street is his recently renovated birthplace house. Originally a successful seaman, Garrison's father hit on hard financial times and abandoned the family when Garrison was only three years old, leaving his mother to raise him under the strict religious morality that later drove his advocacy for Black freedom. He became apprenticed to a printer at age thirteen and while having virtually no formal education became so adept at it that he could compose writing directly as he typeset the *Newburyport Free Press*. Eventually he moved to Boston and in 1831 started his own fervently antislavery newspaper, *The Liberator*.

Statue of William Lloyd Garrison in his hometown of Newburyport, Massachusetts

Most antislavery advocates up to that time (including Abraham Lincoln) favored a gradual emancipation of enslaved people, often combined with some form of colonization. The Northern states had all ended slavery, mostly by gradual means. But while most felt slavery was immoral and wanted to see it end, there was not a strong push for equality of the races. White people had bought into the false concept that whites were a superior race, so the idea of living in political, economic, and social equality with formerly enslaved Black people was anathema to Northern whites (and obviously even more overtly to Southern whites). This incensed the fervently moralistic Garrison, who even other antislavery activists quickly labeled a raging radical. In the very first issue of *The Liberator*, Garrison made his position on ending slavery now and forever clear:

> *On this subject, I do not wish to think, or to speak, or write, with moderation. No! no! Tell a man whose house is on fire to give a moderate alarm; tell him to moderately rescue his wife from the hands of the ravisher; tell the mother to gradually extricate her babe from the fire into which it has fallen; — but urge me not to use moderation in a cause like the present. I am in earnest — I will not equivocate — I will not excuse — I will not retreat a single inch — AND I WILL BE HEARD. The apathy of the people is enough to make every statue leap from its pedestal, and to hasten the resurrection of the dead.*[9]

As much as his fervor repelled some antislavery advocates, Garrison's rhetoric encouraged a growing abolitionist sentiment in the North. That sentiment spread in the 1840s and then especially in the 1850s after the Fugitive Slave Act became law. Among those he inspired were Gerrit Smith, Wendell Phillips, Thomas Wentworth Higginson, and Theodore Parker, all of whom would later vacillate between enemies and allies of Lincoln. Phillips, for example, when Lincoln was later running for president, described Congressman Lincoln's proposed 1848 bill to end slavery in the District of Columbia as "one of the poorest and most confused specimens of pro-slavery compromise." Phillips doubled down by calling Lincoln "the slave-hound of Illinois" because that proposed bill (which he never formally introduced) included language to remove enslaved persons who might rush into the newly free capital from Maryland and Virginia, both slave states.

Another abolitionist forgotten by history is Theodore Parker, a quiet Unitarian minister who became a furious activist against the evils of slavery. Whereas Garrison was the firebrand editor hailing the rallying cry, and Douglass was enthralling the crowds with his personal stories, it was Parker behind the scenes organizing the political path toward abolition. Parker would die on the cusp of the election that put Lincoln in the White House, but not before he had carried on a lengthy correspondence with William Herndon, Lincoln's law partner, acting as a surrogate to allow Lincoln to publicly maintain the more moderate antislavery stance necessary for his political survival in free but anti-Black Illinois.[10] Suffice it to say that Lincoln in 1848 was exposed to much more radical influences than he had seen back home. He was still largely unknown at this point, and there is no evidence that Garrison and the others even were aware of him during this trip, but Lincoln later found himself working to end slavery while balancing his own moderate sensibility versus the increasingly radical abolitionist sentiments of the North.

I had one more place to visit before leaving New Bedford. Behind the Custom House I had seen earlier was Custom House Square, which features a series of wayside exhibits celebrating the 54th Massachusetts Regiment made famous by the movie *Glory* starring Matthew Broderick, Morgan Freeman, Denzel Washington, and other notables. The 54th Massachusetts was one of the first Black regiments formed after Lincoln's Emancipation Proclamation, authorized by abolitionist governor John Andrew. Recruitment was brisk in New Bedford and surrounding towns, hence the prominence of this display. Across the street is a magnificent mural covering the entire side of a building and featuring vignettes with Frederick Douglass, training of recruits for the US Colored Troops, and the heroic battle of Fort Wagner that became the climax of the film. The 54th was led by white colonel Robert Gould Shaw. I will visit Shaw and the 54th Massachusetts again on two more occasions as I tour New England. And since Frederick Douglass is also in the mural, I decided to stop by a similar mural in Lynn, Massachusetts, highlighting its history, including Douglass living there for several years after he left New Bedford.

So far Lincoln had spoken in two cities and run up against two philosophical divisions that threatened the election of Whig presidential candidate Zachary Taylor. Worcester saw him attempting to convince the Free Soil splinter group to stand fast with the Whigs or risk handing the election to the conservative Democratic party. Now New Bedford revealed a severe division between even the antislavery contingents of the party. While most good Whigs were following Henry Clay's moderate lead, including the possibility of sending emancipated slaves (and free people) outside the United States, the more radical factions led by William Lloyd Garrison, Frederick Douglass, and others wanted immediate abolition of slavery. Some of them even wanted full equality! This trip to Massachusetts was turning into more of a trial than Lincoln had anticipated. And now, after a quick stop in Boston, Lincoln was heading into yet another source of division in the Whig Party—the textile mills of Lowell. There he would discover the difference between Conscience Whigs and Cotton Whigs.

CHAPTER FOUR

The Textile Mills—
Lowell and the Power of Cotton

Lincoln was learning that the North had to accept complicity in the growth of slavery. I got a sense of this by following Lincoln to the textile city of Lowell, Massachusetts.

My first stop in Lowell was at one of the few monuments to Lincoln's New England tour that remains today. On the corner of Lincoln and Chelmsford Streets in the old section of Lowell, just a few steps from the Simply Khmer Cambodian restaurant, is a six-foot-tall stone cenotaph bearing a bas-relief silhouette bust of Lincoln, labeled above with "1809–1865" and below, redundantly, with his full birth and death dates. Google Maps tags it as "President Lincoln Memorial," but otherwise there is no indication as to why Lincoln is being honored on what is today a busy intersection bordered by nail salons and pizza places in an obscure part of the city. A large plaque on the back of the memorial gives some indication, documenting that it was "Erected by the School Children of Lowell, February 12, 1909," which was the centennial of Lincoln's birth. At the bottom is quoted "With malice toward none, with charity for all" from his second inaugural address.

Lincoln spoke in old City Hall, which had a second floor designed for public events and housed the first city library in the nation. The brick building still stands, an "Old City Hall Building, 1830-1896" sign embedded in the two upper stories with an Enterprise Bank & Trust Company taking up the first floor. The "new" City Hall that replaced it and in service

Monument to Lincoln commemorating his speech in Lowell, Massachusetts

since 1896 looms over the road two blocks away, a massive stone structure boasting an eight-story clock tower topped by a huge golden eagle. I walked past both buildings on my way to the Boott Museum.[1]

The speech itself was lightly covered by the local press. Basler's *Collected Works*, the ultimate resource for all Lincoln speeches and letters, records only the short article published that night in the Lowell *Daily Journal*, which starts off with "It would be doing injustice to his speech to endeavor to give a sketch of it." The paper did go on to say that Lincoln's speech "was replete with good sense, and sound reasoning, of manner and matter which so eminently distinguishes the Western orators." That "manner and matter" attributed to "Western orators" line was not necessarily intended as a compliment. Bill Hanna identified several other newspaper accounts not saved in Basler. For example, another Whig-friendly paper said Lincoln's speech was "masterly and convincing," while a third noted that "the Whigs of Lowell had one of the tallest meetings on Saturday night that they have yet held," which made me wonder if he was referring to Lincoln's statuesque height, "six feet, four inches, nearly," as he recounted in a short autobiography for his presidential campaign. Not surprisingly, a Democratic-leaning paper declared that "the meeting was vastly inferior" to previous Whig assemblages held in the city. One of the more flavorful accounts came from sixteen-year-old Samuel Hadley, an admittedly Democratic-leaning partisan predisposed to not liking Whigs. Hadley described Lincoln as a "tall man about forty years of age, clothed in dark clothing, wearing a collar which turned over a black silk cravat, over six feet in height, slightly stooping as tall men sometimes are, with long arms, which he frequently extended in earnest gesticulation, of dark complexion with dark almost black hair, with strong and homely features, with sad eyes which now kindled into brightness in earnest argument, or quiet humor, and then assumed a calm sadness." As was so often the case, Lincoln was considered ungainly and homely by many observers, prone to humor to the point of appearing comical, and according to Hadley, "pronouncing words in a manner not usual to New England."[2]

Despite the entertainment value of his speech, Lincoln again "disabused the public of the erroneous suppositions that Taylor was not a

Whig" and attempted to rein in wayward Whigs leaning toward the Free Soil candidate, former president Martin Van Buren. A political poster expressly invited "all the Van Buren converts" to attend.[3] Lincoln reiterated that the Whigs had always led the way against expansion of slavery into the territories, and that Free Soilers should vote for Taylor to avoid inadvertently handing the presidency to Cass. It struck me that third-party candidacies always worked against the goals that third party had set. In more recent times, for example, ultraliberal voters casting ballots for Green Party candidate Ralph Nader carved off more than 2.8 million votes that would have ensured liberal Democratic candidate Al Gore's win in the 2000 election. This in part led to conservative Republican George W. Bush winning the Electoral College despite not winning the popular vote.[4] Closer to the memory of the 1848 voters, it was an antislavery Liberty Party candidate, James G. Birney, who in the 1844 election won just enough votes in New York to keep the antislavery Whig Henry Clay from winning the state, thus giving the election to proslavery expansionist Democrat James K. Polk. Polk quickly started the war with Mexico to bring Texas and substantial new territories for slavery into the Union.

With the 1844 case fresh in everyone's mind, and with everyone's knowledge that the Free Soilers could not win the election, Lincoln argued against splitting the vote in such a way that it would hand the election over to the party whose agenda was the opposite of their own. In other words, voting on "principle" can be shooting oneself in the foot. Voting must be strategic, putting aside minor differences of opinion that can be negotiated in favor of ideological and philosophical principles that follow a path forward rather than backward in our constant quest to form a more perfect Union.

Northerners in the early nineteenth century liked to think that slavery was a Southern problem, a historical memory that permeates the North still today. After all, the large cotton plantations were all located in the South, as were plantations for tobacco, sugar, indigo, and rice, all of which relied primarily on slave labor. Growing up in Massachusetts, I learned that "the North" was against slavery while "the South" was for the continuation of slavery and its expansion into the West. The North,

Northerners exclaimed proudly, got rid of that "peculiar institution" ages ago. Slavery is not us; it is them.

That presupposition is harder to support after a healthy dose of reality-based history. It is true that the Northern states purged slavery early in the republic, at least on paper. Vermont came into the Union as a free state, the fourteenth, but all the original thirteen colonies had legal slavery at the time of the Declaration of Independence. Pennsylvania, New Hampshire, and Massachusetts led the way in the early 1780s to end slavery, followed quickly by Connecticut and Rhode Island. New York and New Jersey banned slavery around the turn of the century, and by 1804 all the Northern states had either abolished slavery outright or put in place a process of gradual emancipation. Sure, there were hundreds of former slaves still indentured without pay as late as 1840, but they were the exception, not the rule, in the North. In contrast, Southern states were expanding slavery, both in numbers and geographically as these states carved up their claimed land westward to the Mississippi River, creating the new slave states of Kentucky, Tennessee, Alabama, Mississippi, Arkansas, Louisiana, and Missouri. The fact that abolition of slavery in the North occurred at the state level, i.e., without federal mandate, reinforced what historian James Oakes calls the "federal consensus," the belief that any abolishment of slavery must be accomplished by the states themselves. In other words, and as Lincoln himself had argued in the Illinois legislature, Congress was powerless to eliminate slavery in the states in which it still existed. Whether slavery came or went was controlled by the individual states. Despite the growing abolitionist sentiment in New England, most of the North understood this restriction on federal power to eliminate slavery.[5]

A greater difficulty was how to manage slavery as the United States expanded, first with the Louisiana Purchase (which led to the Missouri Compromise of 1820) and now in 1848 with the spoils of the Mexican War. Not only was the northern part of the Louisiana Purchase in stasis as federal territory, now added were significant territories in the areas today known as the states of New Mexico, Arizona, Utah, Nevada, California, and parts of Colorado and Wyoming. Should they allow slavery or not? That question was already a factor in the 1848 election and stimulated Lincoln's visit to Massachusetts. It would become an even bigger factor in the 1850s.

So, can the New England states, including Massachusetts, safely say that they are immune from criticism when it comes to slavery? As I discovered during my travels and research, not really. If you examine how the most successful families in New England became wealthy, much of that wealth was derived from some connection to slavery. Early in the nation's history, New England coastal towns prospered as a shipbuilding empire. As we saw in New Bedford, many of those ships were put into service as whalers or by fishermen in the Georges Banks and other productive fisheries off the coast of New England. But many of those ships became the mainstay of the triangular trade, where ships built in Rhode Island sailed to Africa loaded with rum, which was traded for captured Africans, then sailed to the Caribbean (e.g., Cuba, Barbados, and other islands) or Brazil, where captives were sold into slavery on sugar plantations. The harvested sugar would then be processed into molasses for shipment back to New England and the triangular process started another cycle. Other merchandise and supplies may be part of the shipments, but the process was essentially the same right up to the 1808 act that banned international slave trade, although that trade continued illegally up until the Civil War. Before the ban, Newport and Bristol, Rhode Island, were dominating the American slave trade, shipping more than fifty thousand enslaved Africans just in the twenty years between the Constitution and 1808.[6]

I had passed through inventor Eli Whitney's birthplace in Westborough, Massachusetts, after leaving Worcester, and it was Whitney's invention of the cotton gin in 1793 that led to the vast expansion of slavery in the South. While simple in design, the cotton gin could remove the sticky seeds from harvested cotton bolls at fifty times the rate of hand-seeding, thus greatly increasing the efficiency and profit of cotton production. Less enslaved labor was required for de-seeding, but that led owners of large Southern plantations to shift millions of acres to cotton production. As cotton, and the number of enslaved people working it, grew exponentially, New England shifted from rum and slave trading to textile mills for manufacturing clothing from that cotton. After the cotton gin, growers in the interior sections of the South expanded their acreage of the now more profitable cotton and within fifteen years supplied half of Britain's demand.[7] Lowell typified the textile interests of the North, as well as its complicated complicity.

With this background firmly planted in my mind, it was time to visit the Boott Cotton Mills Museum down by the riverfront. Kirk Boott was one of many mill owners in Lowell, and today his complex is under the auspices of the National Park Service as the Lowell National Historical Park. After stopping at the visitor center to get the obligatory map and ranger pep talk, I walked past the aforementioned old and new city halls and historic St. Anne's Church (established in 1824 and where Lincoln worshipped the day after his speech), to the remaining Boott building at Bridge Street and the canal. Most of these mills existed in Lincoln's time and it is likely that he toured one of them on his visit, as he did in other cities. Among the displays was a weave room featuring dozens of power looms cycling their activity. The mill worked by turbines turned by flowing water from the canal before the site was electrified in the twentieth century. The noise from the looms running all at once was deafening, made more unbearable by the summer heat and humidity. Boott and other mill owners had pioneered the idea of women in the workforce, although by the time of Lincoln's visit women were becoming disillusioned by the working conditions, leading mill owners to replace them with newly arrived immigrants from Greece, Poland, Russia, Portugal, and Colombia willing to work for even less pay. That fact reinforced what Ipswich historian Gordon Harris had told me about why Ipswich has such large populations of Greek and Polish residents—they had come to work in Ipswich Mills.

The Boott Museum included exhibits on the experiences of the enslaved men, women, and children who labored in the South to provide the raw cotton that Lowell's mills turned into fabrics. This factory specialized in making three kinds of cloth: shirtings, sheetings, and drillings. Among the enslaved workers' stories were those of Solomon Northup (*12 Years a Slave*), Annie Burton, and Louis Hughes, each providing insight into the violent oppression they experienced. My tour of the Boott Cotton Mills gave a deeper understanding of the complexities of Northern

The Textile Mills—Lowell and the Power of Cotton

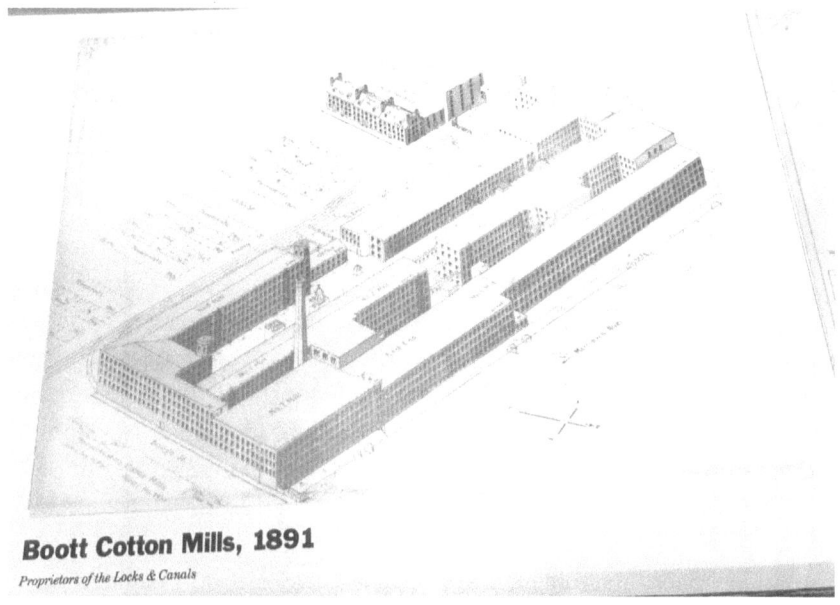

Boott Cotton Mills, 1891
Proprietors of the Locks & Canals

Boott Cotton Mills schematic map, Lowell, Massachusetts

textile production and its relationship with Southern cotton growers. It was time to dig deeper into the people who made this happen.

Lowell is named after Francis Cabot Lowell, who in 1812 returned from an extended trip to England with big plans and secretive designs for a power loom. Lowell joined with other industrialists to form the Boston Associates. Others included Amos and Abbott Lawrence, brothers for whom the city of Lawrence is named, and Nathan Appleton, part of the extended family that holds considerable farmland in my hometown of Ipswich. Boston Associates combined wealthy investors and soon-to-be-wealthy industrialists from forty families to build dozens of cotton mills across New England. They then expanded into a network of banking, insurance, and even railroads to ensure control over all aspects of wealth generation in the North. Lowell was America's first planned city, and the plan was to be a company town focused entirely on producing cotton-based products, with that cotton coming from the slave-labor South.[8]

Northern industry influenced every aspect of the slave-based economy. They built and owned most of the ships, provided captains and crews, insured plantation owners against crop failures and loss of property (including human property), and banks in New York provided the financial credit that plantations needed between planting and selling their crops. Southern plantations avoided growing food crops, preferring to focus on expanding the increasingly profitable cotton acreage. An investigative report published by the *Hartford Courant* newspaper in 2005 noted that planters would "rather buy food at very dear rates than produce it by labor, so infinite was the profit of sugar" and cotton. Northerners filled this void by sending food, both for white planter families and for the growing number of enslaved Blacks. The *Courant* report concluded that "in almost a paradigm of the symbiotic relationship between North and South, Lowell shows how it all came together." Colluding to minimize competition, the dozen textile companies in Lowell made different products, with individual factories specializing in production of, for example, calico prints or fine fabrics or heavy fabric called "drillings." The Lowell mills also made "negro cloth," coarse, cheap wool-cotton blended material for clothing the enslaved laborers who picked the cotton to feed the mills to make the low-quality clothing. The higher-quality textiles produced clothed the rich, both North and South.[9] Ironically, during the Civil War, this reliance on Northern mills for converting raw cotton to clothing meant the South lacked the manufacturing capacity to make uniforms for their own soldiers. They also lacked the food-growing capacity to keep themselves fed.

As Lowell demonstrates, it is important to contrast "slave societies" versus "societies with slaves." I already noted that all the original colonies who became the first thirteen US states had legal slavery at the time of the Declaration of Independence, an especially important fact to remember with the 250th anniversary of that document in 2026. Thomas Jefferson, with whom Lincoln had a complicated relationship, had included a complaint in the draft Declaration condemning Britain for forcing slavery onto the colonies, arguing Britain had "waged cruel war against human nature itself, violating its most sacred rights of life & liberty in the persons of a distant people who never offended him, captivating & carrying them into slavery in another hemisphere, or to incur miserable death in their transportation thither." Alas, delegates to the Continental

Congress rejected this clause because it offended the sensibilities of the delegates from Georgia and South Carolina, not to mention many in the North acknowledged that "tho' their people have very few slaves themselves yet they had been pretty considerable carriers of them to others." To justify the removal of such an obnoxious clause, they argued that "the inclusion of such an indictment would have had a profound impact on the continuing American conversation about rights."[10]

Slave societies are reflected by the plantation-based economies of the American South during the first half of the nineteenth century. Slavery was the center of economic production, with enslaved workers forced to toil under unfathomable cruelty, including whippings, rapes, and separation of families at the whims of the "masters" who "owned" them. That strict hierarchical model extended to all social relations. Slaveholders were the ruling class, dominating every aspect of society with a pseudo aristocratic air. Male slaveholders had ultimate power to do anything they wanted, both within their white households and to keep their enslaved Black workers "in their place." Slaveholders treated those they enslaved with "extreme callousness" because that was how they treated all subordinates, "whether indentured servants, debtors, prisoners-of-war, pawns, peasants, or simply poor folks."[11] The ruling elite in slave societies also controlled the political representation, either by themselves or by installing representatives and senators that would do their bidding, hence why so many duels were fought (or nearly fought) by members of Congress and their supporters. Intimidation at the merest slight kept Southern slaveholders in control of the presidency, the legislature, and the courts at the federal level as well as within their slaveholding states. Threats, violence, and even murder were the tools that kept plantation owners in control of their property (land, wealth, and human) and of the politics of the nation from its beginnings through the Civil War.[12]

In contrast, societies with slaves were exemplified by early Northern colonies and states as they changed their constitutions to eliminate slavery, even if gradually. Slaveholdings in these areas were generally small. Whereas enslaved people and their descendants in slave societies were held forever through generational chattel slavery, the line between slave and free could be more fluid in societies with slaves. Manumission, that is, the ability of individual slaveholders to legally set an enslaved person free, was common and even encouraged in societies with slaves while often blocked by law in slave societies. Slavery in slave societies was thoroughly integrated and essential to the economy, but this was not the case in societies with slaves. In the North, for example, enslaved labor was only a small part of the total labor use. They were marginal to the central economic productive process of society. While there were certainly cases of brutal treatment by Northern slaveholders prior to abolishing the practice, in societies with slaves, there was no presumption of a master-slave relationship as an exemplar of social behavior. Illinois presented Lincoln with a modified "society with slaves" system in which slavery was banned, but the presence and rights of free Black people were also restricted by severe "black laws." Even in New England, where abolitionism was rapidly growing and slavery was disdained, non-whites rarely had social, political, or economic equality with whites.

Prior to the 1850s, the Whig Party was the more liberal of the two major political parties. But, as it is today, that is a bit misleading, with the term *liberal* defined differently depending on whether you are for or against the issue being debated. As we have seen with the modern version of the Whigs, i.e., today's Democratic Party, there is significant variation within the party itself. Some Whigs were more extremely liberal (like the progressive wing of today's Democratic Party), while others were more moderate (Barack Obama and Joe Biden), and still others could be considered more conservative (Blue Dog Democrats, Joe Manchin). Given the mutually beneficial relationship between textile mills and Southern cotton providers, it should come as no surprise that the wealthy members of the Boston Associates consortium and the textile mill owners in Lowell and elsewhere in the Northeast were the more conservative members of the Whig Party. They were called Cotton Whigs. The more adamantly antislavery faction of the Whigs was called the Conscience Whigs.

Lincoln had already encountered the Conscience Whigs. Indeed, they were the main reason he was in Massachusetts. Henry Wilson, a former shoemaker who had grown into a leading state legislator, had, along with Charles Francis Adams, Charles Allen, Anson Burlingame, and Charles Sumner, become disillusioned by what they felt was the lack of Whig commitment to fighting for the end of slavery in the western territories. These men and others denounced the choice of Zachary Taylor and his Cotton Whig allies. Wilson had gone as far as to storm out of the Whig National Convention in Philadelphia, fuming that he would go home and do all he could to defeat Taylor. Forming the Free Soil Party, Wilson was adamant that the Whig dominance of Massachusetts politics must end.[13] To emphasize their focus on blocking slavery expansion into the western territories, the Free Soilers chose as their motto "Free Soil, Free Speech, Free Labor, and Free Men." They were only including white men under that slogan.[14] In a case of strange political bedfellows, it was Henry Wilson two years later as head of the state's antislavery Free Soil Party forming a devil's bargain with the proslavery Democratic Party to form a coalition that put Democrat George S. Boutwell into the governor's mansion and Free Soiler Charles Sumner into the US Senate. Even stranger, all these men later helped form the new Republican Party.

The other faction, the Cotton Whigs, agreed with the national Whig principles of an active federal government and Hamiltonian economic policies empowering individuals to better their condition, along with greater industrialization and government facilitation of education. Where they differed was the emphasis put on the question of slavery. Northern textile mills (and financiers and shipbuilders) relied on strong cotton trade for their livelihoods and wealth. Therefore, they preferred to de-emphasize the slavery issue and often castigated extreme abolitionists like William Lloyd Garrison. Cotton Whigs disdained abolitionist agitation. They needed the cotton, so they turned their eyes askance to its unfairness, immorality, and contradiction to America's founding credo in the Declaration of Independence that said "we hold these truths to be self-evident, that all men are created equal" and endowed with "unalienable Rights including Life, Liberty, and the pursuit of Happiness."[15] Prominent Cotton Whigs included Abbott and Amos Lawrence, Francis Cabot Lowell, Massachusetts governor and polymath Edward Everett, Nathan Appleton, and perennial Whig leader Robert C. Winthrop.[16]

That is not to say that Cotton Whigs in New England were proslavery. Mostly they acknowledged it was wrong, or at least wrong to have in the North, even as they tolerated it in the South. Cotton Whigs did not want slavery to expand westward, but they also told their Southern trading partners they had no intention of ending slavery in the Southern states where it existed. While the Conscience Whigs could be moralistic in their opposition to slavery, the Cotton Whigs refrained from moral argument in favor of a more practical isolation of slavery to the South. Harriet Beecher Stowe, whose *Uncle Tom's Cabin* would create more abolitionist fever than all the William Lloyd Garrison screeds in *The Liberator*, captured the concept well: This was slavery the way Northerners liked it—all the benefits and none of the screams.[17] Around this time in 1848, future senator Charles Sumner wrote to Fanny Longfellow, wife of his friend Henry Wadsworth Longfellow and daughter of textile mill magnate Nathan Appleton, that he could not help but denounce the "unhallowed union" between "the lords of the lash and the lords of the loom."[18] Sumner was quick to make friends, but as this letter shows, he was becoming a staunch abolitionist who was also quick to make enemies.

As he navigated the mill town of Lowell, Lincoln undoubtedly gained substantial insights into the contrasts between the Whig and Democratic parties. The conservative Democrats (again, roughly equivalent to today's Republicans) enjoyed strong party discipline, fervently protecting slavery as a "positive good" that gave owners a constitutional right to move their human "property" wherever they wanted, including into federal territories and even free states. The conservative party claimed to prefer a weak central government, but the reality was that they were happy to have a strong government if it protected slavery and allowed its expansion. In fact, the conservative Democratic Party and its predecessors controlled all aspects of the federal government through the country's history up to the later election of Abraham Lincoln.

In contrast, the Whigs were prone to internal disagreements. The Liberty Party spun off in the 1840s with calls for more direct abolitionist intervention and an effort toward universal emancipation and equality. Led by notables such as the ubiquitous Charles Sumner and radical abolitionist Gerrit Smith, the Liberty Party had little success either against its parent Whig or its ideologically opposite Democrats. Many of its leaders migrated to the new Free Soil Party focused primarily on opposing expansion of slavery into the territories. Free Soilers would have their moment in the sun before they were absorbed into the Republican Party of Lincoln, but in 1848 they were a formidable faction.

There was another division in the Whig Party, and to a lesser extent with the Democrats—that of North versus South sectionalism. This too would become more prominent in the 1850s. The key point to remember during Lincoln's 1848 tour of Massachusetts is that Lincoln's Whigs were a messy, factional party whose disagreements would contribute to its demise in the not-so-distant future. Ironically, the Democrats would later have their own fractioning to hand Lincoln the presidency.

Lincoln continued getting a taste of the divides in the Whig Party—Free Soil spinoffs and the push me / pull me conflicts between Conscience Whigs and Cotton Whigs. He began realizing the internal inconsistencies and commonalities of both factions and the growing recognition that "the slavery question" would become the defining crisis of the ages. Conscience Whigs/Free Soilers, for example, despised slavery, but while most members focused solely on keeping all Blacks (slave or free) from the territories so it would remain open to white settlers, a small segment became more animated about gaining social equality for African Americans.

Similar internal conflicts existed with the more conservative Cotton Whig mill owners dominating the economy in Lowell and other mill towns. Leading Cotton Whigs like Amos Abbott told their Southern plantation suppliers (who were often close friends) that they did not like slavery while also assuring them that the "peculiar institution" would never be interfered with by "sober, honest men." Rufus Choate of Ipswich told a Whig meeting in Boston that while "I would leave to the masters of slavery every guaranty of the Constitution and the Union . . . I deny the morality, I tremble for the consequences, of annexing an acre of new territory for the mere purpose of diffusing this great evil, the great curse, over a wider surface of American earth!"[19] In other words, we will not interfere with slavery where it exists, but it must not be expanded into the western territories. This was essentially the position that Abraham Lincoln took from this point forward. Amos A. Lawrence, son of the Amos Lawrence who had founded much of the cotton textile industry in New England, took it a step further. This Lawrence would become a leading advocate for abolition. And it was this Lawrence, who after a particularly egregious fugitive slave episode in Boston, wrote "we went to bed one night old fashioned, conservative, Compromise Union Whigs & waked up stark mad Abolitionists."[20] Amos A. Lawrence chartered the New England Emigrant Aid Company in the 1850s to fund the westward movement of free-state settlers into the Kansas Territory in an attempt to establish Kansas as a free state without slavery. Some of these wealthy textile industrialists would fund a zealot named John Brown, both in Kansas after the sacking of the free-state capital of Lawrence (named after this same Amos A. Lawrence) and at a small Virginia town called Harpers Ferry.[21]

All this digging into the intricacies of North-South complicity and ever-changing Whig fractionalization convinced me to veer off into another aspect of Lincoln's tour. Back in Worcester he had met a distant relative in Levi Lincoln, but his next few stops would take him near the origins of his family in America. I was off to Hingham.

CHAPTER FIVE

The Ancestors—Boston Burbs and the New England Lincolns

The local Whig committees kept Lincoln busy, with speeches in Dorchester, Chelsea, Dedham, and Taunton over the next four days. The first two are close suburbs of Boston, one south and the other north. Dedham is slightly farther outside the city to the south, while Taunton is closer to New Bedford and Providence and not a townsperson from that city would accept me calling it a Boston suburb. Each of these cities reflected their unique take on industrial towns. All were Whig strongholds with significant numbers of potential Free Soil converts. Lincoln undoubtedly knew little about each venue, merely going where he was asked to speak on behalf of local Whigs in conjunction with the grand goal of convincing Bay Staters that Zachary Taylor should get their vote. Lincoln was already staying at the Tremont House in Boston by this point, using it as a base hotel for his forays into the burbs. Whether his family was with him or not is an intrigue that I will dive into once I get to Boston itself.

How much of this was scheduled in advance is hard to say. Many local organizers heard Lincoln speak in Worcester and feverishly arranged for him to speak in other venues. Hanna points out that on September 16 when Lincoln spoke in Lowell there was already advertising in four Boston daily newspapers hyping his presence on September 18 in Dorchester (Lincoln had spent all day Sunday the 17th relaxing in Lowell). Despite the advance marketing, virtually nothing was reported in the papers after his speech. The same was true the next night in Chelsea, where he spoke at the identical Gerrish Hall where Charles Sumner had promoted the Free Soil candidate the night before. The limited reporting on Dorchester said he spoke to a "full and enthusiastic" meeting, while the sole newspaper report for Chelsea said Lincoln "made a speech which for aptness of illustration, solidity of argument and genuine eloquence is hard to beat."[1] Very little commemoration of Lincoln's visit remains in these towns. Richmond Hall, where Lincoln spoke in Dorchester, still stands but is now a private residence. Lincoln spent the night at prominent lawyer Nathaniel Safford's house a short walk away, but that building is long gone.[2] Chelsea boasts Chelsea Square at Second and Winnisimmet Streets, claiming that the building Lincoln spoke in was Independence Hall, now condominiums.[3]

I was able to find one remnant of Lincoln's visit to Dedham. This time he was met by an entourage at the train station, complete with an earsplitting brass band to lead him to Haven House. Still standing and now called the Dedham Community House, it was built in 1798 for Judge Samuel Haven but owned by newspaper editor Freeman Fisher at the time of Lincoln's visit. The house was designed by famous architect Charles Bulfinch, who also designed the Massachusetts State Capitol in Boston and the intermediate US Capitol rotunda and dome in Washington, DC. Stopping by the renewed Haven House on my travels, I could see why the home was the go-to place for dignitaries visiting the city, including Nathaniel Hawthorne, Oliver Wendell Holmes (both father and son), Richard Henry Dana Sr. (whose son wrote *Two Years Behind the Mast*), and, of course, Abraham Lincoln. I noticed the hex mark on the front door handle designed to keep witches and fire from harming the house. Hex marks and signs are a common sight in this part of New England, especially since I grew up a couple of towns over from the city made infamous by the Salem Witch Trials. Lincoln no doubt admired the high ceilings, French windows, and carved mahogany mantels as he took lunch with his hosts before walking to nearby Temperance Hall to reiterate his pro-Taylor, anti-Cass, and anti–Van Buren talking points. One young journalist, George Monroe, had serious misgivings about the tall Westerner as he escorted Lincoln on the train and to the Dedham

The old Samuel Haven/Freeman Fisher House, now Dedham Community Center, where Lincoln ate in Dedham, Massachusetts

venues, thinking Lincoln looked exhausted, uninspiring, and a little morose. Monroe's attitude quickly changed after Lincoln got rolling in his speech, observing that this awkward, ungainly man soon had the audience under a spell. "I never saw men more delighted," Moore later wrote.[4] This was a typical response to Lincoln's speeches. He started off slowly, looking uncomfortable in his usually wrinkled, ill-fitting suits, then gained strength of voice and oratory as he warmed up to his material. But then, just as he had the audience begging for more, he heard the train whistle blow, and he rushed off to catch the train to Cambridge. To honor Lincoln's visit, a bust of Lincoln, sculpted by Dedham's Alexander Doyle, is on display in the house.[5]

While Lincoln was weaving around Massachusetts, he was coincidentally crossing paths with distant relatives and not that far away from where the Lincoln family tree first planted itself in America. There was also one possible interaction with his mother's side of the family in

Lowell. Because Lincoln spoke on a Saturday night and trains did not run on Sundays, Lincoln spent the weekend touring the city. Things are a bit murky as to who he stayed with, but Hanna suggests it may have been Stedman Wright Hanks, a local pastor at John Street Church and temperance advocate. Hanks was reportedly related to Lincoln via his mother, Nancy Hanks, and had an uncanny resemblance to Lincoln. Hanks had interactions with abolitionists such as William Lloyd Garrison, Frederick Douglass, and others who attended an 1844 abolitionist convention in Lowell. Undoubtedly, Hanks exposed Lincoln to the more radical abolitionist fever that was growing in the Northeast.[6]

When we think of Abraham Lincoln today, we feel like we know a lot about him. He was born in Kentucky, lived his formative years until the age of twenty-one in southern Indiana, then moved to Illinois. His mother was Nancy Hanks, who died when he was nine. His father was Thomas Lincoln, whose own father, Lincoln's grandfather, also named Abraham, was killed in Virginia by Indians. Thomas's older brother Mordecai saved Thomas's life by shooting their father's murderer as he tried to kidnap Thomas. But that is the extent of what Lincoln knew by the time he was making this first visit to New England. When Nathaniel Safford introduced Lincoln to the crowd in Dorchester, he introduced him as one of the "Hingham Lincolns." It is unclear how much of that history Lincoln understood.

"My mother was a bastard," Lincoln supposedly told his law partner William Herndon in a weak moment around 1850, although the veracity of this story is questioned by many Lincoln scholars (sometimes Herndon's statements have significant corroborating evidence, sometimes they do not). Herndon later said that Lincoln was particularly reticent to talk about his mother, but we do know from a more recent study that Nancy Hanks Lincoln was the illegitimate daughter of Lucy Hanks and an unnamed father.[7] According to Herndon, Lincoln alluded to his mother's status in the context of a legal case involving heredity and was making the argument that his own intelligence, logic, and success was likely due to some "Virginia planter": hardly an endorsement of either of his parents' intellectual capacity. With a mother of unknown heritage and an illiterate father who, according to Lincoln's brief autobiography written in late 1859, could only "bunglingly sign his own name," Lincoln became curious about the family tree on the Lincoln side while he was in Congress. More Lincolns arose as he was traveling in Massachusetts.

Remember those "spot resolutions" Congressman Lincoln had introduced in December 1847, the ones questioning President Polk's rationale for starting the Mexican War? While the Democrats unceremoniously ignored them, they were noticed by Massachusetts Whig leader Solomon Lincoln of Hingham. Solomon was about five years older than Lincoln and wrote to Artemas Hale, the Whig congressman for his district. After praising Lincoln's speech, Solomon added that it was "a source of gratification to those bearing his name to know that the old stock has not degenerated by being transplanted. On the contrary, it exhibits fresh vigor in the fertile soil of the West." He also asked Lincoln for further information on his family line.[8]

Receiving the message from Hale, an excited Lincoln wrote back with what little information he had on his heritage [misspellings in the original]:[9]

> *I was born Feb: 12th. 1809 in Hardin county, Kentucky. My father's name is Thomas; my grandfather's was Abraham,——the same of [sic] my own. My grandfather went from Rockingham county in Virginia, to Kentucky, about the year 1782; and, two years afterwards, was killed by the indians. We have a vague tradition, that my great-grandfather went from Pennsylvania to Virginia; and that he was a quaker. Further back than this, I have never heard any thing. It may do no harm to say that "Abraham" and "Mordecai" are common names in our family; while the name "Levi" so common among the Lincolns of New England, I have not known in any instance among us.*
>
>   *Owing to my father being left an orphan at the age of six years, in poverty, and in a new country, he became a wholly uneducated man; which I suppose is the reason why I know so little of our family history. I believe I can say nothing more that would at all interest you. If you shall be able to trace any connection between yourself and me, or, in fact, whether you shall or not, I should be pleased to have a line from you at any time.*

This was Lincoln's first clue he had relatives that could be traced back to Hingham, Massachusetts. Later researchers would track the family back to Hingham, England, which I would get a chance to visit while drafting this book.

Lincoln continued corresponding with his distant relative. Solomon wrote to Lincoln asking for even more information, which Lincoln responded to on March 24. He admitted that he had little additional information on his heritage but would "do the best I can." His grandfather Abraham had, to the best of his knowledge, four brothers: Isaac, Jacob, Thomas, and John. Abraham had three sons, Mordecai, Josiah, and the youngest, Thomas, who was Lincoln's father. Interestingly, after naming his uncle Mordecai's three sons and stating that Uncle Josiah had "several daughters," Lincoln added that his own father, Thomas, "has an only child, myself, of course." That last bit was true at that moment, but neglects to mention that Lincoln had an older sister, Sarah, who died in childbirth at age twenty-one, and a younger brother, Thomas, who died as an infant just weeks after birth. The omission is especially odd given how close he was to his sister, who stepped in for a time as the mother figure between the time when Lincoln's mother died and prior to the stepmother's arrival. Lincoln finished his letter by noting he asked Governor James McDowell of Virginia if he knew any Lincolns there, which set Lincoln on the track of "an old man by the Christian name of David."

He then traded correspondence over the next few weeks with David Lincoln and determined "there is no longer any doubt that your uncle Abraham, and my grandfather was the same man." Lincoln happily provided the info about his own family to David as he had done with Solomon, again referring to his own father Thomas and "I am his only child." Intrigued by what David had told him, Lincoln seemed to have gotten into his head that the family had been Quakers and queried about when he may have emigrated from Berks County, Pennsylvania, to Virginia. Like a modern-day genealogist, Lincoln begged for any additional information on his family going farther back in the family lineage. He also promised to call on David if his travels ever brought him close to where he lived. This seems not to have happened.[10]

The Ancestors—Boston Burbs and the New England Lincolns

Lincoln continued to dig into his family tree long after his visit to New England. In 1854 he corresponded with Jesse Lincoln of Tennessee, who was another nephew of Lincoln's grandfather. He provided what information he knew and queried Jesse for anything additional. Interestingly, Lincoln wrote that Jesse's "current governor, Andrew Johnson . . . told me of there being people of the name of Lincoln in Carter County." Johnson later became Lincoln's second vice president and would succeed him after the assassination.[11] Even as late as spring of 1860 he was trading letters with Richard V. B. Lincoln, who turned out to be a distant relative in Pennsylvania. In his April 6 letter to Richard, Lincoln said he had previously met Austin Lincoln and Davis Lincoln, two sons of a cousin of his grandfather.[12]

I noted before that Lincoln attended the Whig State Convention in Worcester, after which he was invited to a grand dinner at the mansion of Levi Lincoln Jr. Levi was a distant relative of Lincoln's. According to one of the attendees, future Massachusetts governor Henry Gardner, Lincoln joked with his host as to their presumed relationship. After considerable familial banter, Lincoln reportedly said, "I hope we both belong, as the Scotch say, to the same clan; but I know one thing, and that is, that we are both good Whigs." Eight years later, Lincoln received a surprise 110 votes toward the vice presidential nomination for the 1856 election, the very first election with a Republican nominee (John C. Fremont). Lincoln did not come that close to receiving the nomination—the ultimate vice presidential nominee, William L. Dayton, had 253 votes to Lincoln's 110—but Lincoln had twice as much as the next man in the balloting, Nathaniel Banks of Massachusetts, at the time the prominent Speaker of the House of Representatives. When told he had received significant support on the first ballot, Lincoln joked that it must have been "that other great man of the same name from Massachusetts," presumably Levi Lincoln.[13]

All this talk of the Hingham Lincolns called for a visit, so I drove ten miles east of Dorchester to the South Shore area below Boston. I also checked in with Edward Steers Jr., who had recently authored a book called *The Lincoln Tree* about Lincoln's ancestry from "Old Hingham" to

"New Hingham" and beyond. Now an octogenarian, Steers was a research scientist for over three decades at the National Institutes of Health before turning himself into one of the nation's most respected experts on Abraham Lincoln. Best known for his expertise on Lincoln's assassination, his body of work on Lincoln covers a wide range of Lincoln's lesser-known life, most importantly for my purposes, his long-lost ancestry. Much of what I was able to glean comes from his book and my conversations with him over the years.[14]

Hingham is named after Hingham, England, not too far from Ipswich, England, for which my own hometown is named. The new Hingham had been settled by two clerics escaping the unbearable religious oppression of the Anglican Church. Massachusetts Bay Colony of 1637 welcomed them to "worship their God on their terms, not the king's, a form of religious democracy." Among the early settlers was Samuel Lincoln, who was eighteen years old and an apprentice to Robert Lawes.[15] Samuel's two older brothers had already emigrated to New England two years before, and the village of Hingham, according to Ed Steers, quickly became predominantly a Lincoln town, with one-third of the residents bearing the surname Lincoln.[16] That fact in itself makes Abraham Lincoln's task of sorting out his family lineage more than a little tricky.

Following my car's GPS, I was able to locate the Samuel Lincoln House at 182 North Street just before it meets up with the ubiquitous Lincoln Street. From the road the house looks unsubstantial, and a bit run down. In fact, it was run down, or at least run into, in 2021 when a teenage driver attempting to avoid hitting a confused squirrel plunged the front half of her Audi Q7 into the living room of this Lincoln ancestral home. No one was injured in the accident, including the squirrel, and Samuel Lincoln's home had been repaired to look new again. Well, look old again.[17] The house has traditional gray paint and dark red wooden doors common in New England. On the outside wall is a historical plaque—again, ubiquitous in this part of the country—identifying the building as the Samuel Lincoln House, erected in 1650.

Samuel became a successful weaver, made even wealthier by inheriting the estates of his elder brothers in 1644 and 1677. Fathering eleven children, Samuel became a leader in his community, building the home

Historical marker for the Samuel Lincoln House, residence of Lincoln's ancestor, Hingham, Massachusetts

on North Street a short walk to the center of town and the Old Ship Church, the main house of worship in the town and the only surviving seventeenth-century Puritan meetinghouse in the United States. One of the things I like about New England is that it is hard to turn around without running into historically important buildings. My own hometown of Ipswich retains the most First Period houses in the United States, one of which now sits in its entirety in the Smithsonian Institution's National Museum of American History. The Samuel Lincoln House and the Old Ship Church also fit this category, being designated National Historic

Landmarks and listed on the National Register of Historic Places. Not far away is the Old Ordinary, a stunning example of early American architecture built on the main road from Boston for stagecoach travelers to stop "for an ordinary meal" and a drink in the taproom. The Old Ordinary is now operated as a museum by the Hingham Historical Society.

Walking just beyond the Samuel Lincoln House I found … the Samuel Lincoln House. The Samuel Lincoln House at 182 North Street—the one hit by the squirrel-avoiding Audi—is sometimes referred to as the Samuel Lincoln Cottage. A couple of houses away, just around the bend at 170 North Street, is the Samuel Lincoln House, built in 1721. It is in front of this bigger house where a large historical marker explains that Samuel Lincoln was "ancestor of President Abraham Lincoln." The sign also identifies Samuel as "one of the eight early settlers of Hingham bearing that name," purchasing the land in 1649.

Lincoln never got far in his genealogical explorations, but it did not help that the Lincoln family, as was common for lineages of Puritan settlers, were not particularly original in naming their children. Samuel Lincoln's eldest son was also named Samuel, as was his grandson who built the 1721 property. Besides Samuel, other biblical names often repeated over the generations included Abraham, Isaac, Jacob, Mordecai, and a few Thomases. Keeping these names straight is a chore even today.

So, how did we get from the first emigrant Samuel to Abraham Lincoln, the sixteenth president of the United States? Samuel's fourth son was named Mordecai Lincoln, who became a prominent Hingham blacksmith and the direct ancestor (over many steps) to President Lincoln. Not surprisingly, Mordecai's son was also named Mordecai, who had a son named John (kudos for originality), who with his wife Rebecca delivered to the world Abraham Lincoln. This was the Abraham that was killed by Indians in Virginia. Prior to his death, Abraham and his wife Bathsheba had three sons, the ubiquitous Mordecai, Thomas, and Josiah. Thanks to Mordecai's quick action, Thomas was saved from kidnapping and later married Nancy Hanks to create Abraham. And the rest, as they say, is history.

My tour of Hingham's Lincolniana next took me across the street from the two Samuel Lincoln houses to Lincoln Square. On this grassy triangle formed where North Street meets Lincoln Street stands a seated sculpture of Lincoln by Charles Keck. Erected in 1939, a massive bronze Lincoln sits on a stone, leaning slightly forward and looking down at his clenched hands as if deep in thought. The granite pedestal on which it sits carries one of his more famous quotes taken from his second inaugural address: "With malice toward none; with charity for all." It reflects Lincoln's determination to move on from a war that had split the nation over differences in fundamental values (e.g., proslavery versus antislavery). It is hard not to see the same divisiveness in the current era of US politics.

Detail of the Abraham Lincoln statue by Charles Keck, Hingham, Massachusetts

In any case, this statue was what had first drawn me to Hingham, in large part facilitated by a Google Maps project created by two good friends of mine, David Wiegers and Scott Schroeder, both excellent Lincoln scholars, photographers, and fellow road-trippers. Each of them had been independently photographing and collecting information on sculptures for many years as part of their enjoyment of travel and the study of Lincoln. Wiegers had amassed a substantial database and started putting out a calendar of different Lincoln statues each month. His 2020 calendar featured Lincoln statues in foreign lands and since I had traveled widely around the world, I started a series of blogs on my own website highlighting whichever statue Wiegers featured each month. By this time, he and Schroeder had started to compare notes and pondered how best to make the information available. I had been hounding Wiegers for information from his database about statues near where my own road trips were taking me, including Lincoln's two forays into New England. Wiegers recently told me that my frequent inquiries (a nice way of saying pestering) was one of the reasons he and Schroeder embarked on the project to put every Lincoln sculpture online, including full statues, busts, bas-reliefs, and other sculpted artwork. The interactive map includes pins for each statue, plus basic information on who the sculptor was, the type of sculpture, and the date the piece was erected in its current location. As of this writing, the Google Maps–based Lincoln Sculpture Project has around 650 pinned locations and over sixteen thousand views and counting. Admittedly, many of those views were from me as I sought new stops for my New England road trips.[18]

There is one more Lincoln of importance in Hingham, and his house borders the remaining side of Lincoln Square. Benjamin Lincoln's house is a large two-and-a-half-story wood-framed structure with clapboard siding. Built by Benjamin's father, Thomas "The Cooper" Lincoln, the house had passed down through the Lincoln family until the most recent descendants sold it to the Hingham Historical Society in 2020. Like seemingly everything else in this state, the house is a Registered National Historic Landmark.

Benjamin was a celebrity in his own right, separate from any association with President Lincoln, who was only a fourth cousin three times removed through his mother's side. Benjamin served as a major general in the Continental army during the Revolutionary War. Among his many exploits and accolades was that he, as George Washington's second-in-command, formally accepted the British surrender at Yorktown (Cornwallis refused to attend the surrender ceremony, sending his second-in-command, leading Washington to do the same).[19] Benjamin Lincoln went on to serve as Washington's first secretary of war and was prominent in Massachusetts politics for many years. He even led a militia to suppress the infamous, and unsuccessful, Shays' Rebellion in 1787. The guy was accomplished.

The presence of Benjamin Lincoln and all the other Lincolns reminds me that people often assume every Lincoln in city names and parks and buildings is an homage to President Abraham Lincoln. But that is not the case. Many of the Lincoln cities and locations in New England are named after Benjamin (Vermont), or Enoch (Maine), or more broadly after Lincoln, England (Massachusetts). Lincoln, New Hampshire, was named after the Earl of Lincoln. Connecticut never got around to naming anything Lincoln, but at least Rhode Island's town of Lincoln was named after President Lincoln because it was splintered off a neighboring town a few years after Lincoln's assassination. Meanwhile, as Ed Steers pointed out, Hingham was full of Lincolns, and many of them went on to become prominent in their communities. The emigrant Samuel's first son, also Samuel, began the lineage that would lead to three future governors, including both Levi Lincoln Sr. (Samuel's son) and Levi Lincoln Jr. (Samuel's grandson) as Massachusetts governors. Levi Jr.'s brother Enoch Lincoln was a governor of Maine. In addition to his time as governor, as mentioned earlier Levi Sr. served time in Congress and was Thomas Jefferson's attorney general. I cannot help but note the irony of Lincoln trying to credit his ambition and intelligence to some unknown Virginia nobleman who illegitimately impregnated his grandmother, while Lincoln's own male heritage was quite impressive on its own.[20]

Before leaving the area, I drove the six miles of uneven country road to Scituate, where along Mordecai Lincoln Road I located the Mordecai Lincoln Mill and Homestead. This was Samuel Lincoln's son Mordecai, the one who beget the lineage that led to President Lincoln. A Scituate Historical Society marker with the dates 1636–1976 indicates this as "Site of Homestead and Mill Built in 1691-1692 by Mordecai Lincoln, Great-Great-Great Grandfather of Abraham Lincoln."

Lincoln's last stop on the South Shore was Taunton, another town embracing the industrialization wave. Lincoln may have given two speeches that day, one in Mechanics Hall that did not get newspaper coverage, and one in Union Hall, where coverage was less than complimentary. "Mr. Lincoln is a genuine Sucker and is well versed in the political tactics of the Western country," said the *Daily Gazette*, adding that Lincoln's speech "was full of humor."[21] On the other hand, the *Bristol County Democrat* newspaper reporter decimated Lincoln's speech, mocking each of his points in turn and decrying both the veracity and logic of his presentation. The author was Dr. William Gordon, who Hanna describes as "a cantankerous old Free Soiler," which gives you a good idea about how effective Lincoln was in enticing the Conscience Whig/Free Soil contingent back into the mainstream Whig fold and Zachary Taylor's candidacy.[22]

Lincoln had taken the train down from Boston and since there was no late train he spent the night in Taunton, possibly at the home of either Samuel L. Crocker or Francis Baylies. The next morning, he was back on the train to Boston. Before I caught up with him there, I was off to Concord, home of some of the most influential antislavery intellectuals of the era. Lincoln later met some of them in the White House, but how much did they influence his growing awareness of slavery as an issue and abolitionism as a driving force in change?

Chapter Six

The Writers—Concord in the Shadow of the Revolution

The centennial of the Lincoln Memorial dedication was in May 2022. The Memorial is perhaps the most iconic building in Washington, DC, after the Washington Monument. As president of the Lincoln Group of the District of Columbia I had the immense responsibility, and the privilege, of lead organizer for the Centennial celebration broadcasted on national media outlets. I also served as master of ceremonies for that event, which was two hours of re-dedicatory remarks and music. Speakers included renowned historian Harold Holzer, National Park Service director Charles Sams, historian Edna Greene Medford, and a keynote address by Dr. Charlotte Morris, president of Tuskegee University, whose predecessor Robert Russa Moton, had spoken (and been censored) at the 1922 dedication. Broadway and DC music artist Felicia Curry sang selections from Marian Anderson's 1939 groundbreaking event on the Memorial steps. Award-winning stage and screen actor Stephen Lang (you know him as the bad guy in the *Avatar* movies) recited words from Abraham Lincoln. The event was heartwarming and an honor to have had a role in creating.[1]

During the planning process for the centennial, Holzer connected me with Donna Hassler, then the executive director of Chesterwood, sculptor Daniel Chester French's studio in western Massachusetts, and Stephanie Plunkett, curator of the Norman Rockwell Museum in Stockbridge, Massachusetts. The two organizations were collaborating on a special exhibit for the Lincoln Memorial centennial and were looking for additional information. Donna and Stephanie and their teams put together a fantastic exhibition displayed throughout the rest of the spring and summer at the Rockwell Museum. I did not have the opportunity to get up to western Massachusetts to see it then, but to my great fortune they moved the exhibit in the fall to the Concord Museum in eastern Massachusetts in time for me to see it on one of my road trips. The excursion was eye-opening both for the exhibit itself but also for the critical influence of the literary intelligentsia dominating the antebellum era in Concord. These were the writers who influenced antislavery sentiment that prompted Lincoln's growth.

The exhibit itself was called *The Lincoln Memorial Illustrated* and presented a wide variety of Lincoln Memorial–related paintings, cartoons, and other visual artifacts. There were photographs and drawings of key milestones at the Memorial, including Marian Anderson's 1939 musical performance and Martin Luther King's 1963 "I Have a Dream" speech to a crowd of hundreds of thousands. There were drawings by notable political cartoonists commenting on the elections, some congratulatory such as David Fitzsimmons's drawing of the Lincoln Memorial Lincoln with hands raised high after the 2008 election and John Darkow's "thumbs up" to Barack Obama that same year. At the other end of the spectrum was Bill Mauldin's Lincoln weeping with hands over eyes after John F. Kennedy's assassination and Matt Davis's cartoon of the Memorial chair flipped over backward with a shocked Lincoln's feet in the air after the 2016 election. Then there was the patriotic Lincoln flag by artist Anthony Benedetto (better known as singer Tony Bennett) loaned to the exhibit by Bennett's good friend, none other than Harold Holzer. My favorite Lincoln painting was also on display—Norman Rockwell's full-length portrait of a young Lincoln lawyer in a white suit called *Lincoln for the Defense*.[2]

Lincoln's tour of Massachusetts had already exposed him to the fractures within the Whig party—Free Soilers, Conscience versus Cotton Whigs, and the growing abolitionist movement embraced by at least some of the more radical activists. Helping that sentiment to grow was the cadre of influential writers radiating out from Concord, where the

Ralph Waldo Emerson in 1857
by Josiah Johnson Hawes
PUBLIC DOMAIN, WIKIMEDIA COMMONS

spirit of the American Revolution still emanated strongly. These included such tripartite-monikered luminaries as Ralph Waldo Emerson, Louisa May Alcott, Henry David Thoreau, Harriet Beecher Stowe, and John Greenleaf Whittier, not to mention Nathaniel Hawthorne, who somehow did not get the memo about being known by three names.

Of these, Emerson was the most influential at the time. Waldo, as he liked to be called, had become the de facto leader of the Transcendentalist movement that he initiated with his most famous book, *Nature*, and the subsequent essays and a speech called "The American Scholar." Essentially, he argued that immersive appreciation of nature transcends the man-made concept of religion, and true divinity is best discerned by studying nature. It was a mash-up between spirituality and philosophy with a heavy dose of literature based on the idea that people were inherently good, and because society tended to corrupt the individual, people are at their best when they are self-reliant and independent. Transcendentalists believed that knowledge was gained through intuition and experience rather than reason and scientific method. For those of you with a philosophical bent, it was basically the anti-Enlightenment. Emerson not only started a movement, but he also jump-started his literary career with it, and perhaps those of Whitman, Oliver Wendell Holmes (another tripartite scholar), Thoreau, and others in the center of all this metaphysical exploration, Concord, Massachusetts. Whether the concept had staying power is for someone else to determine, but transcendentalism provided a strong moral basis for other reforms, including abolitionism. Emerson later said that "the end of all political struggle is to establish morality as the basis of all legislation," adding that "morality is the object of government."

On the surface, this appears to conflict with Lincoln's belief that "the legitimate object of government is to do for a community of people whatever they need to have done, but cannot do at all, or cannot so well do, for themselves."[3] Lincoln was a strong proponent of rational thinking and, as he said in his 1837 Lyceum speech, "reason, cold, calculating, unimpassioned reason" was the way to solve societies problems.[4] And yet, Lincoln came to profess the immorality of slavery and the necessity of putting it on a path toward its ultimate extinction. At the same time, Emerson's appreciation of nature led him to praise scientific work, e.g., German naturalist Alexander von Humboldt's *Cosmos*, to which Emerson exclaimed in his journal, "The wonderful Humboldt, with his extended center, expanded wings, marches like an army, gathering all things as he goes. How he reaches from science to science, from law to law, tucking away moons and asteroids and solar systems, in the clauses and parentheses of his encyclopaedical paragraphs."[5]

William Herndon, Lincoln's law partner, probably captured the essence of the two men better than anyone, once writing that Emerson and Lincoln:

> *differed widely. Emerson had the genius of the Spiritual and the ideal. Lincoln had the genius of the real and the practical. Emerson lives high among the stars—Lincoln lived low among men. Emerson dreamed, Lincoln acted. Emerson was intuitional, Lincoln reflective. Both were Liberals in religion and were great men.*[6]

But in another letter, Herndon thought there were similarities, noting that Lincoln was "'brim full' of good spirit of the universe," suggesting that "Nature whispered her secrets" to both Emerson and Lincoln and that "they were both interpreters of Nature—one in one line and the other in another," with Lincoln reading the logic of events more than Emerson. The two men approached life from different directions, but each felt personal action was necessary to better their condition and affect change.[7]

Probably more influential to Lincoln was the Lyceum movement that had been launched by Massachusetts farmer Josiah Holbrook in 1826 and blossomed around the nation, most certainly in Concord. Henry David Thoreau and his mentor and benefactor Emerson were leading speakers, both in the Concord Lyceum and elsewhere. Emerson was already well known when he arrived in Concord from Boston, so he was asked to give the Concord bicentennial address soon after he showed up in town. It was Emerson who invited the Alcott family to Concord, led by Amos Bronson Alcott, a teacher, writer, and philosopher who became good friends with Emerson and the Transcendentalist movement. He had four daughters, of which the second, Louisa May Alcott, went on to write a phenomenal semi-autobiographical coming-of-age novel about four sisters during the Civil War, which she called *Little Women*. They all became good friends with Thoreau, the transcendentalist-slash-naturalist-slash-essayist living near Walden Pond, where he would spend most of his days walking in nature and writing about what he discovered.

According to historian Paul Brooks, most of the Lyceum topics were uncontroversial and intellectually esoteric, reflecting a strong desire of educated Easterners to gain wide-ranging knowledge. Technical subjects like mining and hydraulics and physiology were tackled routinely. History was a popular subject, including stories of ancient Egypt and the colonial history of Massachusetts. Even speakers best known for other advocacy spoke on academic topics, e.g., Charles Sumner discussed "The Value of Time" and Thoreau about Scottish essayist and philosopher Thomas Carlyle.[8] Lincoln embraced the Lyceum movement as well, speaking in 1838 on "The Perpetuation of Our Political Institutions" and later, in 1858, on scientific topics in his "Discoveries and Inventions" lecture.[9]

Where the literary intelligentsia of Concord and the political rise of Abraham Lincoln overlapped is when the lyceums veered into the growing antislavery movement. Emerson and Lincoln were both moderate in their antislavery views, believing abolition could only be constitutionally achieved through individual state action, and supporting colonization as a mechanism for avoiding the inevitable racial conflicts of a multiracial society. But Concord became a center of antislavery activity, and the Concord Lyceum became a focal point for conflict between more conservative members and the desire by some (e.g., Thoreau) to bring in more outspoken abolitionist speakers like William Lloyd Garrison and Wendell Phillips. Thoreau defended the right of Phillips to speak a second time in Concord even though he had offended some members on a previous visit. The tension was so high that the more conservative curators resigned. Emerson and Thoreau replaced them. A pleased Thoreau went so far as to publish a long and eloquent letter in Garrison's *Liberator* to celebrate.[10] There is no evidence that Lincoln met any of the Concord writers during his 1848 trip to Massachusetts, but he did meet some of them at the White House during his presidency.

Into this eclectic mix of transcendentalism and antislavery influencers entered Nathaniel Hawthorne, having recently moved into the Old Manse, the Emerson ancestral home he rented from Waldo. Hawthorne was more than a little reclusive but welcomed Thoreau and the others to visit him in the stately home. I had to wonder what kind of host he and his equally shy wife were, especially since Hawthorne often wrote in his journals what he hesitated to say in person. Hawthorne thought Thoreau, for example, was "a singular character," adding that he was "a young man with much of the wild original nature still remaining with him." That sounded mild enough, but not one to hold his pen, Hawthorne also called Thoreau "ugly as sin, long-nosed, queer mouthed, and with uncouth and somewhat rustic—although courteous—manners." Perhaps sensing he was being overly critical, Hawthorne went on to say that Thoreau's "ugliness is of an honest and agreeable fashion and becomes him much better than beauty." That is about as backhanded a "compliment" as one could get, but it came close to the descriptions often lobbed at Lincoln, who was often described as ugly, ungainly, homely, and awkward.[11]

Nathaniel Hawthorne circa 1860–1864 by Mathew Brady
PUBLIC DOMAIN, WIKIMEDIA COMMONS

Thoughts of Hawthorne and the Old Manse put me on a side trip to the historic building at the other end of town, a building that may have witnessed more of the Revolutionary War than it wanted. It was built in 1769 by Reverend William Emerson, who in 1775 inspired—the British would say instigated—his flock to resist the attempt by the British crown to curtail their rights. In March he spouted fire and brimstone to his congregation, calling on them to "Arise! My injured countrymen" to stand up against British tyranny. A month later, on April 19, Reverend Emerson and his family, including son Ralph Waldo Emerson, got a front-row seat for the battle between American Minutemen and British Regulars at Concord's Old North Bridge. It was the "shot heard round the world," as Emerson wrote in his Concord Hymn for the battlefield monument in 1837.[12] Today, I stood on that very bridge next to Daniel Chester French's *Minute Man* statue with a clear view of the second-floor windows of the Old Manse from which Emerson watched the battle. After that revolution, the Old Manse would continue to witness the literary revolutions of

Ralph Waldo Emerson (he wrote the first draft of *Nature* here), Nathaniel Hawthorne, Thoreau, Alcott, women's rights advocate Margaret Fuller, and groundbreaking female scholar Sarah Bradford Ripley.[13] Hawthorne wrote lovingly of the pastoral beauty of the landscape around the home in his *Mosses from an Old Manse*, before reluctantly moving back to his birthplace town of Salem, where he wrote *The Scarlet Letter*. Later he moved to the western Massachusetts town of Lenox (near the current Norman Rockwell Museum and Chesterwood), where he befriended Herman Melville and wrote *The House of Seven Gables* (based on a historic house in Salem). Then he was back in Concord and living at The Wayside, his name for the Orchard House where Louisa May Alcott and her family had lived. I took inspiration from the fact that while he was desperately shy, Hawthorne and his wife, illustrator and transcendentalist Sophia Peabody, managed to befriend a lot of people. Hawthorne even met Lincoln in the White House during the Civil War.

"I have shaken hands with Uncle Abe," Hawthorne wrote from Washington in a letter to his wife on March 16, 1862. A longtime Democrat who had written a glowing biography of his friend Franklin Pierce for president a decade earlier, Hawthorne was pro-Union when the war started, but admitted that he didn't "quite understand what we are fighting for."[14] Heading to Washington but failing to get his own audience with Lincoln, Hawthorne surreptitiously joined a "party of Massachusetts gentlemen" who did have an appointment.[15] True to form, Hawthorne seemed not to have spoken much during the meeting, but afterward wrote a lengthy article for *Atlantic Monthly* so uncomplimentary that the editors chopped out his overly candid personal description of the president. Those omitted lines, which represented about half of the original article, included "in lounged a tall, loose-jointed figure, of an exaggerated Yankee port and demeanor, whom, (as being about the homeliest man I ever saw, yet by no means repulsive or disagreeable,) it was impossible not to recognize as Uncle Abe." The rest of the excised narrative was not much better, describing Lincoln's "rusty black frock-coat and pantaloons," and that "he had shabby slippers on his feet." That was the polite part. While Hawthorne's fiction continues to receive well-deserved acclaim, his commentary on Thoreau and Lincoln showed an acerbic side that belied his inherent bashfulness in public. Maybe it was for the best that he preferred not to talk much in social situations.[16]

Since I have jumped forward to Lincoln in the White House, this is a good time to revisit Lincoln and Ralph Waldo Emerson. William Herndon told his *Herndon's Lincoln* collaborator, Jesse Weik, that he had hundreds of books by various intellectuals and influencers of the time, including Emerson, and that Lincoln "had access to and sometimes peeped into" them whenever he so chose. According to literary historian Robert Bray's analysis, Lincoln had read Emerson's two *Essays* collections from the early 1840s and then later, as president, borrowed *Representative Men* from the Library of Congress. *Representative Men* was a collection of seven lectures Emerson had given prior to 1850, focusing on six "great men" that he believed exemplified the virtues of society. Lincoln would have especially appreciated the treatment of Plato (whom Emerson labeled the "Philosopher"), William Shakespeare (the "Poet"), Napoleon ("the Man of the World"), and Johann Wolfgang von Goethe (the "Writer"). Given his own lifelong struggles with periodic depression, Lincoln particularly related to Goethe's play *Faust*, as interpreted in operatic form by Charles Gounod, in which an intellectual scholar falls into suicidal melancholia before striking a deal with the Devil. Lincoln saw *Faust* performed at Grover's Theatre (now the National Theatre) during his presidency and it probably gave him some insight into the machinations of his overly ambitious generals and Salmon P. Chase. After his son Willie died in the White House, Lincoln dealt with his grief by borrowing a copy of Goethe's *Faust* from the Library of Congress.[17]

Having undoubtedly heard of Emerson's influence in New England, Lincoln may have seen him speak at the statehouse in Springfield in 1853. Lincoln's law office was across the street from the Illinois statehouse, and it seems unlikely he would not have attended, although Lincoln's presence was not mentioned in the diary of good friend and legal colleague Orville Hickman Browning when he noted his own attendance. If Lincoln missed Emerson in his hometown, he did finally meet him in February 1862 when Massachusetts senator Charles Sumner escorted Emerson to the White House. The Smithsonian Institution had launched a lecture series in the red sandstone Castle and among the speakers was *New-York Tribune* editor Horace Greeley (which Lincoln attended) and prominent literary figures like Ralph Waldo Emerson (which Lincoln probably did not attend). Back in 1848, Emerson was opposed to slavery on principle but generally avoided associating too closely with abolitionists, whom he had dismissed as "sour and narrow" with "virtue so vice-like." But by his Smithsonian lecture he was a full-fledged abolitionist himself as he ranted in a rambling speech called the "American Civilization." Like many, he felt the 1850 Fugitive Slave Law was so abhorrent that he declared it was "a filthy enactment," adding, "I will not obey it, my God." After his visit with Sumner and Lincoln in the White House, Emerson, who had supported William Seward for president in 1860, begrudgingly admitted that "The President impressed me more favorably than I had hoped." The "educated, cultured, fastidious New Englander, had not expected much from the rough westerner."[18] Perhaps surprisingly, the White House chitchat with Lincoln included discussion of the infamous slave trader Captain Nathaniel Gordon, who shortly became the first, and only, slave trader ever executed for his actions after Lincoln refused to commute the sentence.[19]

Presidential historian Jon Meacham captures the dynamic between the two men, noting that "all successful men have agreed on one thing, they were causationists." Emerson himself said that "a belief in causality, or strict connection between every pulse-beat and the principle of being ... characterizes all valuable minds." As the United States currently faces an existential crisis as critical as what Lincoln faced, it strikes me that the idea that human actions matter— actions cause more actions cause change—is a message that both inspired Lincoln's decision-making and should drive modern-day Americans in this time of great national upheaval.[20]

Unlike Emerson and Hawthorne, Thoreau died in 1862 having never met Lincoln, but most likely the newspaper-hungry Lincoln had read Thoreau's pieces in Greeley's *Tribune*. Greeley also served as a literary agent promoting Thoreau and making sure his work was published. Lincoln almost certainly read Thoreau's essay, *Slavery in Massachusetts*, published in 1854 and widely disseminated throughout the nation. But according to Robert Bray's analysis, Lincoln seems not to have read the two major Thoreau works we think of today, including *On the Duty of*

Civil Disobedience published the year after Lincoln's Massachusetts tour, and *Walden*, published in 1854. That is a shame because *Civil Disobedience* was Thoreau's protest of the Mexican War just as Lincoln's spot resolutions questioned its rationale. Even more than Lincoln at the time, Thoreau understood the rift developing between the conservative Cotton Whig textile owners and the more liberal Conscience Whig reformers. Thoreau and other abolitionists believed the rights of humanity superseded the right to free enterprise, especially when that enterprise relied on the immoral enslavement of other Americans.

Back on my road trip through Concord, the museum housing the special Lincoln Memorial exhibit also delved into the contributions of more of its favorite sons and daughters. Along with Emerson's writing study, which had been reassembled as he used it, there was Henry David Thoreau's "green desk" (on which he wrote his essays after walking all day) and artifacts from his cabin on Walden Pond. The pond itself is not far away and is now both a State Reservation and a National Historic Landmark. Strolling through the exhibits reminded me that all the press has gone to the more famous personages in the town—Emerson, Hawthorne, Alcott, Thoreau—and less to many of the women who started and led the Concord Female Antislavery Society. Key leaders included the relatives of those famous writers, beginning with Cynthia Dunbar Thoreau, mother of Henry David Thoreau and founder of the society. Two of her daughters (Henry's sisters), Helen and Sophia, were also active participants, as was a neighbor, early childhood educator Mary Rice, who sent President Lincoln a petition signed by 195 schoolchildren asking him to "free all the little slave children in this world." Also active was Emerson's wife, Lidian Emerson, and their daughter, Ellen. Another founding member was Mary Merrick Brooks, a driving force of the movement who worked closely with fervent abolitionists Garrison, Douglass, Wendell Phillips, Harriet Tubman, and others. There was even one African-American member of the society, Susan Robbins Middleton Garrison, who signed petitions protesting slavery and hosted the renowned abolitionist sisters Angelina and Sarah Grimké for tea.[21]

This also happened in my hometown, and historian Gordon Harris told me about the Ipswich Female Anti-Slavery Society led by some of the wives and daughters of the more prominent (i.e., wealthy) scions of Ipswich.[22] Women were not allowed in the all-male American Anti-Slavery Society co-founded by William Lloyd Garrison, so persistent women in both Ipswich and Concord formed their own societies to fight the enslavement of fellow Americans. The Concord Female Antislavery Society coordinated with other such societies to bring speakers such as Garrison, John Brown, and Frederick Douglass to town. Less publicized, but an open secret among like-minded townspeople, was that the society helped run several Underground Railroad stations to facilitate the escape of enslaved Americans into Canada.

The influence of these Massachusetts-based antislavery societies cannot be overestimated. While the men were making the headlines, it was these female antislavery organizations doing the grassroots work inspiring local abolitionist sentiment and coordinating the escape routes for enslaved men, women, and children on the run. While it is unclear how much Lincoln was assimilating all of what was happening on his 1848 tour, he no doubt was hearing about these organizations and these inspirational writers from his Bay State hosts as he moved around the eastern part of the state.[23]

Just before leaving Concord, I received an email from Harold Holzer on a separate matter. When I tapped from my phone where I was, he told me not to miss Sleepy Hollow Cemetery and the Melvin Memorial, a Daniel Chester French tribute to three brothers who died in the Civil War. Sleepy Hollow has a section called "Authors' Ridge," so I was off to yet another cemetery. Following the remarkably well-signed directions around the meandering cemetery roads, I was able to find the ridge. I hiked up some well-worn steps embedded in a rise of land to find a series of gravestones in a line across the top. True to its name, this was the final resting place for Concord authors Henry David Thoreau, Nathaniel Hawthorne, Ralph Waldo Emerson, Louisa May Alcott, plus sculptor Daniel Chester French is not far away along with a host of other influencers of the nineteenth century. Like most writers I am drawn to the homes and graves of the great writers of the past (e.g., Hemingway's houses in both Key West, Florida, and outside Havana, Cuba), so seeing all these in one town is inspiring. There must be something in the water because

Marker for Authors' Ridge in Sleepy Hollow Cemetery, Concord, Massachusetts, showing the locations of gravesites for Henry David Thoreau, Nathaniel Hawthorne, Louisa May Alcott, and Ralph Waldo Emerson other writers admired and read by Lincoln, including Henry Wadsworth Longfellow and John Greenleaf Whittier, had close connections to the Concord intellectual community. In modern times, Concord can boast having been the home of presidential historian Doris Kearns Goodwin (whose *Team of Rivals* about Lincoln's Cabinet inspired the Steven Spielberg movie *Lincoln*) and her husband, Richard Goodwin, speechwriter for John F. Kennedy, Lyndon Johnson, and Robert F. Kennedy.

I was hesitant to leave Concord, in part because of the writing auras I hoped to absorb, but it was time to head to Boston. Much of my time had been moving from place to place in my car, but my plan for Boston was to do what Lincoln did and take the train. Little did I know that I would also be following in Lincoln's literal footsteps walking around the city. My last stop in Concord was a historic cemetery, so it seemed altogether fitting and proper that my first stop in Boston would be an even older historic cemetery. I was off to the "Hub of the Universe."

Chapter Seven

The Hub of the Universe— Boston and Cambridge

I am finally going to Boston. Leaving my car in Ipswich, I boarded the railroad that in my younger days—and at the time of Lincoln's visit—was called the Boston & Maine Railroad but is now part of the Massachusetts Bay Transportation Authority system (known by everyone as the "T"). Since Lincoln did a lot of walking in Boston, I chose to walk the nearly one-mile distance from North Station to my first stop—the Granary Burying Ground.

If the Sleepy Hollow Cemetery in Concord was considered old, the Granary is considered ancient. Established in 1660, the cemetery is relatively small in area but grand in the number of markers squeezed into it (2,300), grander in the number of people buried there (over 5,000), and grandest in the importance of its inhabitants to the origin of the United States. Passing through the wrought iron gate brought me to the artistic grave markers of patriot Samuel Adams and the lesser-known but no less fervent patriot James Otis. John Hancock is best known for his flourishing (and very large) signature on the Declaration of Independence, and this is reflected in his elaborately embellished obelisk tomb. Paul Revere has two markers: a large one placed in the nineteenth century next to the smaller, older slate marker. There is a grave marker for the victims of the Boston Massacre. And impossible to miss in the center of the burying ground is a large obelisk marking the grave of Benjamin Franklin's parents (Ben is buried in Philadelphia).[1]

Tremont House hotel circa 1834, where Lincoln stayed in Boston, Massachusetts
PUBLIC DOMAIN, WIKIMEDIA COMMONS, MECHANICAL CURATOR COLLECTION

The Granary is a block from where Lincoln stayed at the Tremont House hotel (now replaced by a bank headquarters) and no doubt he would have strolled into it to capture a sense of the American Revolution. He also likely stopped into the Kings Chapel and its Burial Ground, directly across the street from the Tremont.[2] In a cemetery even older than the Granary, Lincoln could glimpse at the grave of John Winthrop, the first governor of Massachusetts, and Mary Chilton, the first woman to step off the *Mayflower*. There is also Joseph Tapping's headstone, one of the best known and beautiful stones in the city with its skeleton and Father Time battling over the eventuality of death.[3]

I should make clear that Lincoln had been using Boston as a base from which he traveled to each of the venues around the eastern part of the state, primarily with the growing railway network but occasionally by carriage. He checked into the Tremont House on September 15 after arriving that morning from New Bedford. Unlike what Lincoln was used to in the western states, Tremont House set the standard for luxury in the era and was located on the corner of Tremont and Beacon Streets just a few blocks from the famed Boston Common. A massive four-story, granite building in the neoclassical style, the Tremont was the first hotel with indoor plumbing and running water (water was pumped using steam power to a tank on its roof, then gravity fed to the taps). It was designed by Isaiah Rogers, who also designed the Astor House in New York City, where Lincoln would stay on his later visit. Another notable feature of the hotel was the four Doric columns supporting the front portico. When the Tremont was demolished in 1895, wealthy businessman and politician Stephen Salisbury III arranged for two of them to be transported to his hometown of Worcester. During my own visit to Worcester, I stopped by Institute Park, where the two gray granite columns are located at the Salisbury Street entrance. Interestingly, rose-granite spheres now top both columns and no one seems to remember when they were added; they were not part of the Tremont design.

There are two intriguing mysteries about Lincoln's stay in Boston. The first is whether Mary and the kids were here with him, and the second is whether and/or where a much-quoted interchange with William Seward ever happened. This is a good time to deal with Mary.

Mary and their two children, five-year-old Robert and two-and-a-half-year-old Eddie, accompanied Lincoln on his trip to Boston. Or maybe not. Some historians say she was there, some say she was not, while most ignore the question altogether. What we know for sure is that Mary had been in Washington with Congressman Lincoln for some length of time, but boredom and conflicts with other tenants of the boardinghouse convinced her that a visit to her family homestead in Lexington, Kentucky, was better for all parties. There is correspondence between the couple suggesting she planned to return to Washington in the late summer, and she would have jumped at the chance to visit New England, something she did often during the Civil War. No specific documentation confirms this happened, but there was a semi-plan for her to travel with a male acquaintance (women were not generally allowed to travel unaccompanied) who was heading to Philadelphia, at which point she would have gone back to Washington to meet Lincoln for the trip north.

That is where things get dicey. The only evidence that Mary went to Boston with her husband is a letter she wrote in 1867 in which she rather indignantly declared that artist Francis B. Carpenter, who had spent six months in the White House during the war painting his *First Reading of the Emancipation Proclamation*, was trafficking in falsehoods when he recently stated Lincoln and Seward had met each other in Boston. As we will see later, she was wrong about that part. But in that letter, she explicitly states that "After Congress adjourned in Sept. of that year, Mr. L[incoln,] accompanied by my two little boys & myself, visited B[oston] & remained there 3 weeks, detained by the illness of our youngest son, whom we lost a year afterwards."[4] According to Mary, she stayed in Boston at the Tremont during the entire time (which was ten days, not three weeks) that Lincoln was stumping around much of eastern Massachusetts, often spending the night with local dignitaries.

There is disagreement among Lincoln historians on this point. Wayne Temple writes that Mary was in Boston, and Eddie's lingering illness gave Lincoln the opportunity to take on even more speaking gigs. Jason Emerson, who has written extensively about both Mary and Robert Lincoln, states the same but goes further by adding reference to a statement by Herndon reported by Emanuel Hertz in his 1938 book, *The Hidden Lincoln*. What Herndon wrote in a short essay focused on Lincoln's boat patent is "As Mr. Lincoln was returning from Congress, with his wife and child, and after passing through some of the States of New England, he entered Canada and was at Niagara Falls." Most other biographers either never mention her or presume she was there based on her letter. I put the question to Bill Hanna—the researcher who dug deeply into the newspaper reports of Lincoln's 1848 trip to Massachusetts and whom others often cite. Like most good researchers, he does not definitively rule out her presence but asserts that in all his extensive research of that time there is no record of her presence. No newspaper mentioned her. No letter writer mentioned her. None of Lincoln's escorts mentioned her. Not even Lincoln mentioned her. Given that Eddie was sick, perhaps significantly enough to give Lincoln more time to stump for Zachary Taylor and local politicians, one might expect at least someone to have inquired about the health of his son. But nada. So, was Mary there or not? I lean toward Hanna's position but acknowledge she could have been there, very quietly, caring for her sick son.[5]

Whether Mary was there or not, Lincoln gave the first of his two Boston speeches at the Boston Whig Club. According to the report in the Boston *Atlas* (edited by William Schouler, the man who invited him), Lincoln carried on his usual theme of defending Zachary Taylor as the Whig nominee. Lincoln, the *Atlas* said: "in a speech of an hour and a half, which for sound reasoning, cogent argument and keen satire, we have seldom heard equaled." They went further, saying that Lincoln "pointed out the absurdity of men who professed Whig principles supporting Van Buren, with all his Locofocoism, while the Whigs were as much opposed to the extension of slavery as were the Van Buren party." The competing Boston *Herald* gave a hint of the satiric edge of Lincoln's speech, saying that he "compared [Van Buren] to a man having a gun which went off at both ends—that he would kill the object in view and those who supported him, at the same time." In other words, vote for Whigs, not Free Soilers, which would be tantamount to suicide by handing the state to the Democrats.[6]

After reminiscing about Lincoln's speech, I decided to exploit the bright, warm day and follow the path Lincoln likely walked to nearby Boston Common, which even then was an oasis only a block away from his hotel. Standing on its north side is the Massachusetts State House, its gold dome gleaming in the sunlight. It was that dome that Oliver Wendell Holmes Sr. (the physician, poet, and polymath, not his son, Jr., who became the Supreme Court justice) was writing about when he indirectly inspired the city's—and the state's—most enduring, if not slightly ostentatious, nickname. One of the so-called fireside poets that included William Cullen Bryant, John Greenleaf Whittier, James Russell Lowell, and Henry Wadsworth Longfellow, all of whom Lincoln had read, Holmes tells a story in *The Autocrat of the Breakfast Table* about the "Boston State-House" being the "Hub of the Solar System." The nickname caught on and expanded to include the entire city of Boston as "The Hub of the Universe." It was considered arrogant and offensive at the time by other cities, but today Boston is still known as "The Hub" and the nickname remains a source of pride for Bostonians. The Boston

Bruins professional hockey team logo even features a spoked wheel with a large "B" at its hub.[7]

Edging my way through the ongoing renovations and security checks, I meandered around the inside of the State House to find a bust of Abraham Lincoln crafted by sculptor Leonard Volk in Doric Hall, which I had found reference to on the Lincoln Sculptures Project. While there I found a large standing Lincoln portrait painting, some Ambrose Burnside testimonials, a full statue of Civil War era governor John Andrew, and a bust of John Hancock.[8] Sticking my nose into the State Senate and House chambers (they were not in session) and wandering around the building surprisingly did not set off any warning bells, after which I exited just in time to see one of Boston's famous Duck Boat tours drive by.

I picked the right (or perhaps wrong) day to visit, because now about a hundred people were gathered outside where only a dozen had been when I went in. This was immediately after a Texas judge banned an abortifacient drug that had been on the market for decades and proven safe. One of the many protest signs read, "Keep Your Bans Off Our Bodies." News cameras were capturing the moment, so I moved in for a closer look and found the Massachusetts governor Maura Healey, US senator Elizabeth Warren, Congresswoman Ayanna Pressley, Massachusetts attorney general Andrea Campbell, and Boston mayor Michelle Wu taking turns at the microphone. This was the second time I had seen Mayor Wu that day as earlier I had stumbled upon a ceremony at Boston City Hall in which Wu and other staffers were memorializing state representative Melvin King. King was a longtime leader in the city's civil rights history and had passed away a few weeks before. Seeing such political activity today reminds me that more than a century and a half after the Civil War, the fight for civil and human rights continues, and just as it did at the beginning of our nation, Boston seems to be leading the way.

Stepping back from the crowd, I found the Robert Gould Shaw monument directly across the street from the State House. Erected in 1897, the large (eleven-by-fourteen-foot) bronze relief sculpture by Augustus Saint-Gaudens is the first monument to honor African-American soldiers during the Civil War. Unfortunately, it also has been

Robert Gould Shaw and the 54th Massachusetts Regiment, Boston, Massachusetts
BY PERMISSION OF MELISSA A. WINN

a target of vandalism in 2012, 2015, 2017, and especially during the 2020 protests following the murder of George Floyd. On the other side of the common, just past a spooky Edgar Allan Poe statue (complete with raven) was another Lincoln statue that had come under attack. The *Emancipation Memorial* by Thomas Ball depicted Lincoln, hand outstretched, standing over an enslaved man (patterned after a freedman named Archer Alexander) rising from slavery. This was a copy of the original that stands in Washington, DC. The Boston version was removed by the city in 2020 because the design was discomforting to some modern sensibilities. Only the pedestal remains as the city has not decided what to do with it. Meanwhile, my own Lincoln Group of DC successfully protected the original in Lincoln Park, a mile from the US Capitol, where it still stands despite ongoing controversy.

Strolling around Boston Common as Lincoln likely did, I see many statues and memorials that would not have been there in 1848. Among them is a new installation celebrating the love between Martin Luther King and Coretta Scott King called *The Embrace*, whose enigmatic design has received mixed reviews. There is also a large Soldiers and Sailors Monument, the local Boston fan favorite *Make Way for Ducklings* (five ducklings following their mother that are routinely dressed in occasion-specific celebratory garb), *Triton Babies* statues, and more traditional statues of George Washington, abolitionist Wendell Phillips, Colonel Thomas Cass, commander of the 9th Regiment Massachusetts Volunteer Infantry killed in the Civil War, and Revolutionary War hero Thaddeus Kosciuszko. There is also the famous Frog Pond and the starting point for the Freedom Trail. I even made a short stop at the place where everyone knows your name (especially if your name is Norm) on the corner of Beacon and Brimmer Streets, made famous by the television show, *Cheers*. That September morning of Lincoln's 1848 visit included a large hot-air balloon named the *American Eagle* launched by a Dr. Morrill.[9] Lincoln no doubt was impressed and would embrace the idea of hot-air balloons in the Civil War.[10]

But it was time to get back on the Lincoln trail, so I walked to Park Street station on the other corner of the common and hopped on a Red Line train to Cambridge, home of Harvard. Lincoln had rushed back to Boston by train from Dedham, then walked across town to Causeway Street (where North Station is now) to catch the train on the other side of the river. Lincoln researcher Scott Schroeder, co-collaborator of the Lincoln Sculptures Project, was able to identify the railway station that Lincoln arrived at in Cambridge. It turns out the rail lines are now the Porter Street Red Line station on the T, just one stop past Harvard Square.[11] Whereas my day was getting hotter, Lincoln experienced a sudden rain shower as he made his way to Cambridge City Hall, where he again spoke to disaffected Whigs questioning the appropriateness of choosing the Southern slaveholder Taylor to represent their party. Brass marching bands had started to announce his entrance into events, and a hearty three-cheers was a common refrain at the end.

Like Beacon Hill, Cambridge is synonymous with learned and cultured society. Harvard is the oldest institution of higher learning in the United States, founded by Puritan clergyman John Harvard in 1636.

Lincoln's son Robert attended Harvard throughout most of the Civil War. The number of dignitaries studying at Harvard is too numerous to list, but it includes both Presidents Adams, Charles Sumner, Ralph Waldo Emerson, Henry David Thoreau, Oliver Wendell Holmes Jr., and many others who would influence or cross paths with Abraham Lincoln. Cambridge also hosts the Massachusetts Institute of Technology (MIT). MIT was founded in 1861, which was incredibly bad timing because two days later the Confederate army attacked Fort Sumter, and the war came. MIT went dormant immediately as many of its students enlisted in the volunteer army. It resurrected in 1865 with new funding under the Lincoln-signed Morrill Land-Grant College Act "to promote the liberal and practical education of the industrial classes."[12]

A short walk from the Harvard Square station took me to Harvard Yard, where I paid tribute to the statue of John Harvard while youthful elites leisurely strolled across the grass on this sunny day. Just outside the main gate is a seated statue of Charles Sumner, the often-irascible abolitionist founder of the Liberty Party, then Free Soil Party, before becoming Massachusetts senator as a Republican. He and Lincoln would become strong allies as well as antagonists in the fight for the end of slavery. A block or two farther north on Massachusetts Avenue is the expansive Cambridge Common, where I was on the hunt for yet another Lincoln statue. This standing Lincoln has him in the center spire of a tall monument to those who fought in the Civil War. Called *Lincoln the Man*, it is another creation of Augustus Saint-Gaudens.

Before I leave Cambridge, I must discuss Dawes Island. Not as fancy as the name sounds, this is literally a traffic island, its triangular shape formed by the intersections of Massachusetts and Garden Street as you approach Cambridge Common and the Lincoln statue. It is named for William Dawes, the more important but generally forgotten to history colleague of Paul Revere. Revere was well connected economically and politically—further enhanced by being name-dropped in Henry Wadsworth Longfellow's poem, *Paul Revere's Ride* (you will recall the line, "The midnight ride of Paul Revere"). Meanwhile, Dawes was the first of several men who, in April 1775, rode their horses valiantly to alert Minutemen of the approach of British regulars prior to the battles of

Statue of Charles Sumner outside Harvard Yard, Cambridge, Massachusetts

Lexington and Concord. Dawes Island boasts a series of stand-alone markers explaining the roles of Dawes, Revere, and others. Bronze horseshoes line the edge of the island to represent Revere's path through the area. A large bronze raised plaque shows the route Dawes took from Hanover Street, Boston to Lexington, which was much longer than the route taken by Revere. While the plaque is a more recent installation, Lincoln would have seen the large tomb marker for William Dawes in King's Chapel Burying Ground immediately across the street from his Tremont House hotel. Lincoln had long cherished the heroes of the Revolutionary War and the leadership of the Founders (he later would say in a speech given in Philadelphia's Independence Hall, "I have never had a feeling politically that did not spring from the sentiments of the Declaration of Independence"), and this visit to Cambridge and Boston likely helped inspire that sentiment.

Lincoln had one more speech to give in Boston, where he would meet the man who became his most important political collaborator—and rival—William Seward. That meeting has its own intriguing mystery.

After making the trip out to Taunton, Lincoln returned for his September 22 Boston speech, which almost did not happen. The Free Soil people, knowing that the Whigs were planning a huge political meeting, had rented out all the available meeting spaces. That forced the Whigs to schedule their rally for outside in Court Square between the old city hall and the courthouse. Then a deluge hit, with heavy rain making it impossible to hold a rally outside. Luckily, according to Bill Hanna's investigatory digging, a Dr. Cotton released his hold on the Tremont Temple, a half block across the street from where Lincoln was staying.

In retrospect, the Tremont Temple was a perfect location to boost Lincoln's awareness of the growing importance of slavery to our national survival. Formed a decade before as the Free Baptist Church, it was the first integrated church in America. I visited the current building, which was an enlarged rebuild following a series of fires in the years since Lincoln's visit. The facade reminds me more of a Jewish temple, but it remains the Tremont Temple Baptist Church that hosted speeches by abolitionists like William Lloyd Garrison and Frederick Douglass.[13] For the Whig event, the Boston *Atlas* listed the speakers as William Seward (the keynote), "Abram Lincoln" (despite inviting him as a sitting congressman, the papers still could not get the spelling of his name right), textile industrialist Abbott Lawrence, and Richard Fletcher (former congressman and first president of the American Statistical Association formed in Boston).

Lincoln, who spoke after Seward, by now had become accustomed to his standard talking points attempting to explain why Zachary Taylor, "a man who owns ... two hundred men, women, and children" (as the Democratic-leaning Boston *Post* put it), was the best person to fight the "slaveocracy." Nathaniel Hawthorne later described Lincoln as having "an unmistakably Yankee look" that James Schouler thought made him seem "kinsman" to eastern men unfamiliar with Lincoln's "fifey and shrill" voice. This was his last speech on the Massachusetts trip, and he was less about trying out new material than absorbing new insights for the future.[14]

William Henry Seward in 1848 was already an accomplished lawyer, a former state legislator, a former New York governor, and about to

William Henry Seward circa 1848 PUBLIC DOMAIN, WIKIMEDIA COMMONS

be elected US senator. He was an established Whig leader and a vocal opponent of slavery, which was why he was the headliner for the evening. The comparison of the ungainly westerner with his odd southern-western drawl and unmanageable hair against Seward's erudite eastern formality and stiffness must have been profoundly amusing to the largely learned Boston elite. Whereas Lincoln was forced to argue the inconsistency of Taylor's Whig credentials, Seward spoke in loftier terms of "providence" and not "bow[ing] before the aristocracy of the South," which a splinter vote for the Free Soil third party would assure.[15] Seward argued that "all Whigs agree—that Slavery shall not be extended into any territory now free—and they are doubtless willing to go one step further—that it shall be abolished where it now exists under the immediate protection of the General Government."[16] He "believed in the force of moral power" and that "the time would come . . . when the free people would free the slaves in this country. This has to be accomplished by moral force," adding the caveat that "it has to be done without injustice," by which he meant compensation to slaveholders.[17] This was radical stuff for 1848 and would come back to haunt his chances for the presidency years later, but that night in the Tremont Temple climaxed with the admittedly partisan crowd giving three hearty cheers for "Old Zach," three more for Governor Seward, and three more for Mr. Lincoln, according to the *Atlas*.[18]

While the *Atlas* lauded Lincoln's speech as "powerful and convincing . . . which was cheered to the echo,"[19] Seward seemed less impressed. Two decades later, after the Civil War and Lincoln's life had ended, Francis Carpenter (the painter Mary Lincoln called a liar) reported Seward's recollection of that night. In Seward's memory, Lincoln gave a "rambling, story-telling speech, putting the audience in good humor, but avoiding any extended discussion of the slavery question."[20] Then there was the story that Lincoln told Seward the day after his 1848 remarks: "I have been thinking about what you said in your speech. I reckon you are right. We have got to deal with this slavery question and got to give much more attention to it hereafter than we have been doing."

Therein lies the second mystery of this trip to Boston. Did Lincoln really say this? It does not help the story's credibility that there are two versions. One says that Lincoln and Seward had this conversation the following evening as they shared a room in Worcester, which clearly never happened. Seward's biographer, Walter Stahr, confirms that Seward was in Springfield, Massachusetts, that night while Lincoln was on his way home via railroad and had already reached Albany, New York. Another version says the conversation happened immediately after the speech at the Tremont House hotel, which is at least possible. The bigger problem, which Stahr adamantly points out, is that Lincoln was already fully aware of the importance of the slavery question. He was stumping for Taylor in Massachusetts expressly because of that very question and the split it had already caused in the Whig Party. Lincoln had spoken out against slavery as early as 1837 in Illinois, and his views and speeches generally paralleled Seward's, although perhaps they were not as morally high minded. Stahr also notes that historians today who refer to this incident often do so by referencing the "memoir" of William Seward edited by his son Frederick over four decades later. But Frederick Seward clearly cribbed the story from Francis Carpenter's work. So, we do not really know if Lincoln ever said this. To me, it seems unlikely.[21]

Ulysses S. Grant wrote in his deathbed memoirs that he believed the "Southern rebellion" was "largely the outgrowth of the Mexican War," which he felt was "one of the most unjust ever waged by a stronger against a weaker nation."[22] This agrees with Abraham Lincoln's view, who stated in 1848 that he thought the Mexican War was unnecessary and unconstitutional. Writing that year to his law partner William Herndon, he stipulated that a president could act to repel an invasion, but to:

Allow the President to invade a neighboring nation, whenever he shall deem it necessary to repel an invasion, and you allow him to do so, whenever he may choose to say he deems it necessary for such purpose—and you allow him to make war at pleasure. . . . If, to-day, he should choose to say he thinks it necessary to invade Canada, to prevent the British from invading us, how could you stop him? You may say to him, "I see no probability of the British invading us" but he will say to you "be silent; I see it, if you don't."

He went on to warn Herndon that:

> *Kings had always been involving and impoverishing their people in wars, pretending generally, if not always, that the good of the people was the object. This, our Convention understood to be the most oppressive of all Kingly oppressions; and they resolved to so frame the Constitution that no one man should hold the power of bringing this oppression upon us. But your view destroys the whole matter, and places our President where kings have always stood.*[23]

How prescient Lincoln was in 1848.

Abraham Lincoln finished his tour of Massachusetts and made his way by railroad and steamship home to Springfield, Illinois. In a few months he would return to Washington to finish out his single term as a US congressman, unaware that he would not hold political office again for another twelve years. The Free Soilers did capture a significant percentage of the popular vote in the 1848 presidential election, but Taylor still won, at least for a while. Lincoln was quickly forgotten in Massachusetts, the entertainment value of his presence rapidly fading once he left the state. But Massachusetts had given him new insights into the "slavery question" and the internal conflicts it created within the party and within the nation. Over the next dozen years slavery would become the singular driver of conflict in the United States, pitting progressives against conservatives, antislavery against proslavery, union against disunion. This interregnum was one of the most acutely divisive and adversely significant extended decades in our national history. It would change the direction of our country, and it would change Lincoln into the man Americans routinely vote for as the greatest American president.

Interregnum: 1848–1860

Lincoln had been sent to Massachusetts to convince wayward Free Soilers to stick with Zachary Taylor and the Whig Party. The obvious question comes to mind—did Lincoln's dozen speeches have any effect on the results? I posed that question to Bill Hanna. He had studied Lincoln's 1848 tour of Massachusetts in detail, and he continued to research the topic for many years after his book was published. Did Lincoln matter?

"Not a bit. He was totally inconsequential," Bill told me. "He had no effect on the election and there was no long-term memory of him." When Lincoln came back to New England twelve years later, newspapers never mentioned his previous trip.

I also chatted with researcher Jeffrey Boutwell, who agrees that Lincoln's impact was negligible. Not only did he not swing Free Soilers back into the Whig fold, but their leaders also struck a devil's bargain with the Democratic Party, forming a coalition to break the Whig hold on Massachusetts. Democrats George S. Boutwell and Nathaniel Banks conspired with Massachusetts Free Soil cofounder (and future Republican senator) Henry Wilson to win enough votes in the 1850–1851 state election. The coalition then placed Boutwell into the governor's chair, unseating George N. Briggs, the man Lincoln came to support in 1848. They then chose Charles Sumner, another founder of both the Liberty and Free Soil parties, to become US senator.[1]

Massachusetts had been a reliable Whig state for many elections. In 1840 they gave Whig William Henry Harrison a large popular vote majority over incumbent president Martin Van Buren (then running as a Democrat). In 1844, the state gave a majority to Whig Henry Clay over Democrat James K. Polk, although a third candidate, James G. Birney of the Liberty Party, snagged a significant percentage of the popular vote. Birney took enough of the vote in New York State that year to give the election to Polk, thus defeating the Liberty Party's purpose. This was why the Whigs were so worried about the Free Soil Party in 1848. Zachary Taylor won only a plurality of the vote in Massachusetts, with Van Buren (now as a Free Soiler) coming in second, beating out the Democrat Lewis Cass but causing consternation among the Whigs. Nationally, the Free Soil Party received over 10 percent of the popular vote, making the Taylor win too close for comfort. If Lincoln's trip to Massachusetts did any good, it was to keep it from being even closer than it was. More significant was what Lincoln learned about the importance of party cohesion. The Whig Party fielded another general in 1852 with Winfield Scott, who won Massachusetts in a race again made tighter by a Free Soil candidate but lost in an electoral landslide to New Hampshire Democrat Franklin Pierce in the national election. The Whigs fell apart soon after.

When Lincoln got home after the second session of his term in the US House of Representatives, he settled into his other full-time job of being a lawyer. After failing to get a land office appointment for an Illinois colleague, he tried to secure it for himself, also unsuccessfully. Finally, the Taylor Administration offered him the territorial governorship of Oregon, soon expected to evolve into a US Senate seat when Oregon became a state. Mary Lincoln shot down that idea. She had already sacrificed plenty moving from a privileged upbringing to being the wife of a now unemployed politician. The social scene in Springfield was limited enough; no way was she shipping out to the wilds of the Pacific Northwest. Given that Oregon did not become a state for another ten years, she made a good choice to put her foot down. So, from early 1849 until his nomination for the presidency in May 1860, Lincoln was back to being a lawyer on the frontier.

But the most consequential decade of our history was just getting started. It did not help that Zachary Taylor, the odd fit for the Whig Party, died sixteen months into his presidency. His vice president, New Yorker Millard Fillmore, suddenly was president. In keeping with the bad luck Whigs had with presidents and their seconds (the only other Whig elected president, William Henry Harrison, died a month after taking office), Fillmore was more at odds with his own party than the opposition.

Taylor's demise was a political nightmare. Despite the concerns about how a Southern slaveholder would handle the increasingly contentious debate over the new territories taken from Mexico, Taylor was staunchly against the extension of slavery. Fillmore, not so much. The transition helped set off a cascade of laws and events that put the country on a path to ultimate conflict. One recent researcher captured the idea perfectly, titling his book, *Decade of Disunion*.[2]

If there was anything that epitomized the jumbled mess of party priorities of this period, it was the set of laws known as the Compromise of 1850. Henry Clay, the "Great Compromiser" who had negotiated the Missouri Compromise in 1820 (creating the slave state of Missouri and spinning off the northern counties of Massachusetts into the new state of Maine), was at it again. The end of the Mexican War had immediately thrown the nation into turmoil. Should slavery be allowed into the new territories? Was the Missouri Compromise (which had barred slavery from the northern portions of the Louisiana Purchase land) still in force? The urgency of these questions intensified when gold was discovered in California, spurring rampant migration west as eastern settlers sought the mother lode. Clay, who was a singular Whig leader and Abraham Lincoln's "beau ideal of a statesman," proposed a massive omnibus bill with a slate of compromises that would settle every contentious issue: California's rapid ascension to statehood (gold can move mountains), the fate of the southwestern territories, the slave trade in the District of Columbia, and more. But Clay was showing his age. Already declining in health and influence, the once-great Whig was forced to turn over the project to a first-term senator from Illinois—Democrat Stephen A. Douglas. Douglas showed both his youthful stamina and wily political acumen by splitting the omnibus bill into five separate bills, then negotiating such that each bill could build support to pass with different coalitions. The final separate bills (still collectively called the Compromise of 1850) ensured: California immediately became a free state; Texas would cede some of its disputed western border in exchange for debt relief; governments were established for the New Mexico and Utah territories with no restriction on whether

Interregnum: 1848–1860

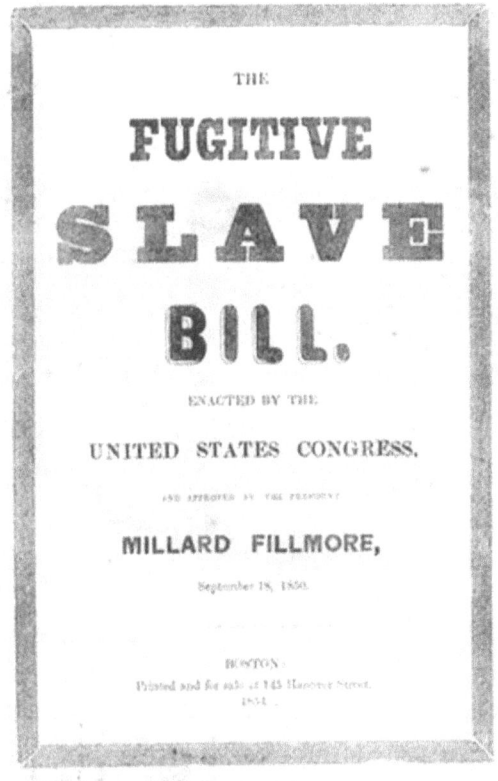

Fugitive Slave Act of 1850
PUBLIC DOMAIN, SMITHSONIAN ARCHIVES

any future state(s) formed would be free or slave; the slave trade (but not slavery itself) was banned in the District of Columbia; and an aggressive Fugitive Slave Act was passed to enforce the capture and return of enslaved persons who had escaped into the Northern free states.

Each of these provisions had its detractors, but the Fugitive Slave Act became the catalyst for the violence and dissension of the next decade. The act was intended to give bite to an otherwise toothless clause in the US Constitution, which simply said that any person held to service or labor who escaped "shall be delivered up," but no mechanism for how that would happen was defined. The Fugitive Slave Act expressly created a federal marshal system and forced state and local authorities to assist in enforcing the law. Citizens in free states who refused to assist or obstructed the capture of fugitive slaves could receive stiff fines or even jail terms. In short, slave states had federal power to force free states and free citizens to help capture and return enslaved "property," with penalties for not doing so. Slave states were impinging upon free states' rights.

This is why Taylor's death was so critical. Taylor had staunchly opposed the Compromise because it virtually ensured the expansion of slavery. After Fillmore assumed the presidency, he went the opposite way, encouraging and colluding with Douglas to ensure the bill's passage, which he promptly signed into law. The law was supposed to resolve all open questions related to slavery for all time. It did the opposite. Northern states were so enraged that many passed "personal liberty laws" attempting to nullify the federal law. These state laws may not have been entirely constitutional, as the Southern states promptly argued, quite ironically given that the South had tried to do the same in 1830 to reject tariffs. Despite the promises of the Compromise supporters, slave states led by South Carolina continued to talk of secession.

Perhaps a sidebar here is necessary. Up to this point, the slaveholding states had controlled the federal government since the beginning of the nation. Up through Zachary Taylor, ten of the first twelve presidents had been slaveholders in some capacity. The only exceptions were the two Adamses from Massachusetts, each of whom served only single terms.[3] The three-fifths compromise in the Constitution (counting three-fifths of the enslaved population toward the total population of a state for purposes of representation) ensured that Southern states, which were generally less populated than the Northern states, had undue control of what happened in Congress. An aristocratic culture centered on brutality to maintain the "master-slave" hierarchy led to significant intimidation tactics to bar the abolitionist movement. Because most presidents had been slaveholders, Supreme Court appointees tended to be either slaveholders themselves or protective of Southern slavery. The repeated threat of secession was a cudgel wielded by slave states to maintain the slave power over the federal government.[4]

Any perceived resolution of the slavery question promised by the Compromise of 1850 was negated in 1854 when Stephen A. Douglas—yes, the same man who pushed through the 1850 laws—decided to upend the status quo by introducing what became known as the Kansas-Nebraska Act. This Act repealed the Missouri Compromise, thus opening all the remaining territories to the potential for slavery. The decision was to be left up to a vote by the people, who through "popular sovereignty" could decide to allow or not allow slavery within the borders of any new state. Passage of the Kansas-Nebraska Act "aroused" Lincoln back into politics.[5]

That is not to say that Lincoln was completely out of politics even though he was focused on building a highly successful law practice. He was routinely enlisted to make speeches supporting the Whig Party. He promoted candidates for Illinois and federal offices, and commonly sparred with the Illinois senators, Stephen A. Douglas and James Shields. Forty-five years old in 1854, Lincoln told a friend that "I was losing interest in politics, when the repeal of the Missouri Compromise [in the Kansas-Nebraska Act] aroused me again."[6] Lincoln became a Whig leader opposing the expansion of slavery. While in his 1848 tour of Massachusetts he spoke mostly about the practical reasons why slavery should not be extended to the territories, but by 1854 he began to rail against the immorality of that "peculiar institution." In what has become known as the "Peoria Speech," Lincoln passionately railed against the Nebraska bill:

> *This declared indifference, but as I must think, covert real zeal for the spread of slavery, I cannot but hate. I hate it because of the monstrous injustice of slavery itself. I hate it because it deprives our republican example of its just influence in the world—enables the enemies of free institutions, with plausibility, to taunt us as hypocrites—causes the real friends of freedom to doubt our sincerity, and especially because it forces so many really good men amongst ourselves into an open war with the very fundamental principles of civil liberty—criticising the Declaration of Independence, and insisting that there is no right principle of action but self-interest.* [7]

In today's parlance, Lincoln was "woke." While he previously thought slavery was on a path to its ultimate extinction, the Kansas-Nebraska Act made clear that was not the case. From this point forward he worked to keep slavery from expanding into the territories. To do so, he would have to get back into political office.

But in what party? "Always a Whig in politics," Lincoln wrote his friend Jesse Fell, but then to his closest friend, Joshua Speed he admitted that "others say there are no Whigs."[8] Lincoln had already seen the crevices splitting the Whig Party in 1848, with Cotton versus Conscience and splinter groups like the Free Soilers. The Kansas-Nebraska Act fissured the party between North and South over slavery.

Out of the dust came a new political party calling themselves Republicans. They were cobbled together from Northern Whigs and the antislavery elements of the Free Soilers, Democrats, Know-Nothings, and abolitionists. Their focal issue was to block the expansion of slavery into the western territories. While individual abolitionists largely joined the Republicans, the party platform did not call for the abolishment of slavery in the states in which it currently existed, just preventing its expansion. Lincoln, like most of the Republicans of his period, believed the Constitution precluded any arbitrary federal abolition of slavery in the slave states. The Southern slave states would have to abolish slavery through state action, just as every Northern state had done soon after the Constitution was ratified. Keeping slavery out of the western territories would put pressure on the slave states to abandon the loathsome practice.

To get back into politics, Lincoln ran for the US Senate in 1855 during the last sputtering of the Whig Party. He lost. He ran again in 1858 against his old antagonist, Stephen A. Douglas, under the new Republican Party banner. He again lost. But the now famous "Lincoln-Douglas Debates" generated national attention.

Meanwhile, Kansas was becoming a war zone. Slave states sent slaveholders into the territory trying to establish enough of a footprint to claim Kansas as a slave state. They employed intimidation tactics, fraudulent voting from Missourians sneaking across the border, and the sacking of Lawrence, Kansas (named after Amos A. Lawrence, now a rabid abolitionist), where free state settlers had set up their own state government. Bleeding Kansas, as it came to be known, caused the deaths of myriad settlers in a fight between slavery and freedom. This was where John Brown first

SOUTHERN CHIVALRY — ARGUMENT versus CLUB'S.

The caning of Charles Sumner by Preston Brooks on the floor of the US Senate in 1856, unknown artist PUBLIC DOMAIN, WIKIMEDIA COMMONS

received public notice. In retaliation for the sacking of Lawrence, Brown and his followers hacked to death five of those implicated in the earlier violence. This period of bloodshed would continue for the rest of the decade.

Then the crisis got worse. The day after the sacking of Lawrence, on May 22, 1856, South Carolina congressman Preston Brooks brutally beat Massachusetts senator Charles Sumner nearly to death with his gutta-percha cane on the Senate floor. Brooks felt Sumner had impugned the reputation of Brooks's relative, Senator Andrew Butler, in an epic antislavery speech called the "Crime Against Kansas." Sumner would not return to health and the Senate for three years. Whereas Northern politicians had been the subject of intimidation from Southern slave powers for decades, voters back home began pressuring them to start fighting back for Northern states' rights. Tensions continued to ramp up as Northern abolitionist feeling shifted from marginalized radical to mainstream public sentiment.

As tensions increased and Democrat James Buchanan, a doughface[9] from Pennsylvania, was inaugurated president, the Supreme Court stepped in to further inflame the situation. The 1857 Dred Scott decision, written by Chief Justice Roger Taney of Maryland, declared not just that Dred Scott (a former slave suing for his freedom) must remain enslaved, he could never be a citizen and thus "had no rights which the white man was bound to respect."[10]

The year after Dred Scott was the Senate campaign pitting Abraham Lincoln against incumbent senator Stephen Douglas. While Douglas won the election (state legislatures voted for senators then, and the state had gerrymandered the districts to ensure Democratic control), Lincoln's debating skills and deft rhetoric put Douglas in the position of endorsing what became known as the "Freeport Doctrine." In short, Douglas insisted over the next two years that popular sovereignty allowed states to reject slavery, in conflict with the slaveholding states adoption of the Dred Scott precept that no territory or state could keep a slaveholder from bringing his enslaved people anywhere he wanted. The debates put Lincoln on the national map. He had adeptly defined the positions of both the Republicans and the Democrats. More critically, he helped drive a wedge between the Northern Democrats who supported the likely 1860 presidential nominee, Stephen A. Douglas, and the Southern Democrats who declared that the Illinois senator was insufficiently protective of slavery.

Meanwhile, John Brown was back, and he had a plan. Brown had been courting the eastern antislavery and abolitionist elite. He received support from a range of New England leaders, including the group known as the Secret Six: Theodore Parker, Gerrit Smith, Thomas Wentworth Higginson, Samuel Gridley Howe, Franklin Benjamin Sanborn, and George Luther Stearns. Others that supported him in one fashion or another were Henry David Thoreau, William Lloyd Garrison, Harriet Tubman, and Frederick Douglass. Many provided funding and weapons, while some balked when they heard, or at least sensed, the details, and felt the plans were too radical or suicidal. The raid was a disaster; people were killed and the desired slave uprising failed to materialize. John Brown was caught, found guilty in a military tribunal, and summarily executed (in one of those twists of history, then–US colonel Robert E. Lee commanded the military and John Wilkes Booth was a spectator at

Interregnum: 1848–1860

John Brown on the way to his hanging in 1859, Thomas Hovenden (artist) and Frederick Juengling (engraver)
PUBLIC DOMAIN, LIBRARY OF CONGRESS

the execution). But while Brown's intention to spark a slave revolt failed, it reinforced the pathological fear of Southern slaveholders that a massive slave uprising could topple their white supremacist societal structure.

This series of events during the 1850s demonstrated to the South that they were losing control of federal political and social power. With the addition of Oregon, Minnesota, and finally Kansas, there were nineteen free states to fifteen slave states by the beginning of 1861 and strong likelihood that most or all the new states being carved out of the western territories would be free. Abolitionist sentiment was increasing rapidly in the North, whose inhabitants were steadily fighting back against Southern assaults on free states' rights. All this made it clear to the ruling class of the South—primarily large slaveholders and their minions—that sooner or later the free United States would have enough political might to pass a constitutional amendment abolishing slavery. Despite South Carolina senator James Henry Hammond's 1858 assertion that "Cotton is King," the idea of Southern secession, combined with acquisition of Caribbean and Cuban land for expansion, became a desirable option for Southern leaders seeking to maintain a slaveocracy.

These were the political conditions setting the stage for the 1860 election. Now firmly back into politics, but still without a political office, an increasingly activist Lincoln found himself invited to New York to give a speech.

Part II

1860—STUMPING FOR HIMSELF

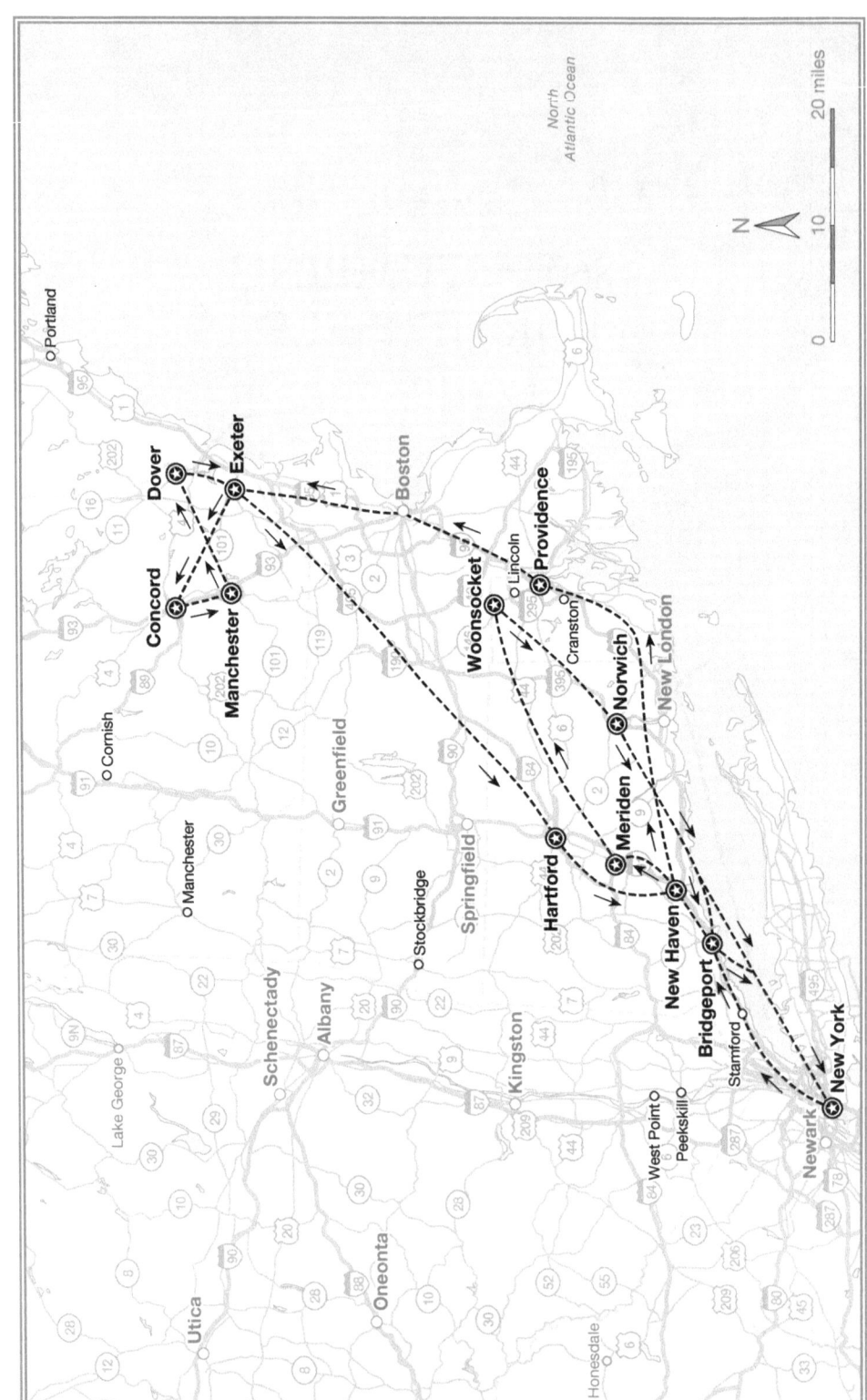

CHAPTER EIGHT

The Speech of a Lifetime—Cooper Union

To Hon A Lincoln, will you speak in Mr. Beechers church Brooklyn on or about the twenty ninth (29) November [1859] on any subject you please pay two hundred (200) dollars

—JAMES A BRIGGS

SO READ THE PUNCTUATION-CHALLENGED TELEGRAM THAT MADE Abraham Lincoln president.[1]

Notwithstanding Briggs's invitation, Lincoln did not speak at Mr. Beecher's Plymouth Church in Brooklyn on November 29, or at any time thereafter. Subsequent negotiations between Lincoln and Briggs moved the date to February 27, 1860, and they agreed the speech would be on a political topic. Only after he arrived in New York did Lincoln find out the venue had been moved to Cooper Union in Manhattan.

To find out why, I sat down with researcher Tom Link at the Lincoln Forum, an annual gathering of hundreds of Lincoln scholars held in Gettysburg, down the road from where Lincoln gave his famous Gettysburg Address. Tom has enthusiastically focused on Lincoln's time in New York and has spent considerable effort following Lincoln's paths around both Manhattan (home of Cooper Union) and Brooklyn (home of Beecher's church). Beecher is Henry Ward Beecher, son of famous evangelist preacher Lyman Beecher and brother of Harriet Beecher Stowe. Beecher himself was a notable Congregationalist clergyman and pastor of Plymouth Church in Brooklyn. A strong opponent of slavery, he raised money to purchase enslaved people from captivity and set them free, as well as sent rifles in boxes marked "Bibles" (garnering the nickname "Beecher's Bibles") to Kansas in aid to Free Soilers fighting against slavery occupation. Plymouth Church had sponsored a series of antislavery speeches by prominent men and Lincoln's reputation had blossomed after the widely disseminated Lincoln-Douglas Debates of 1858.

Lincoln's delay from November to the end of February had pushed it too far away from the series, which led to changes in sponsorship and venue. According to Tom Link, that was a good thing for Lincoln. The continuing wintery weather made the icy East River challenging to maneuver by boat for the crowd expected to attend (it would be almost twenty-five more years before the Brooklyn Bridge was built). In the months since the initial invitation, the original organizers transferred sponsorship to the Young Men's Central Republican Union, who decided the Great Hall of the newly opened Cooper Union for the

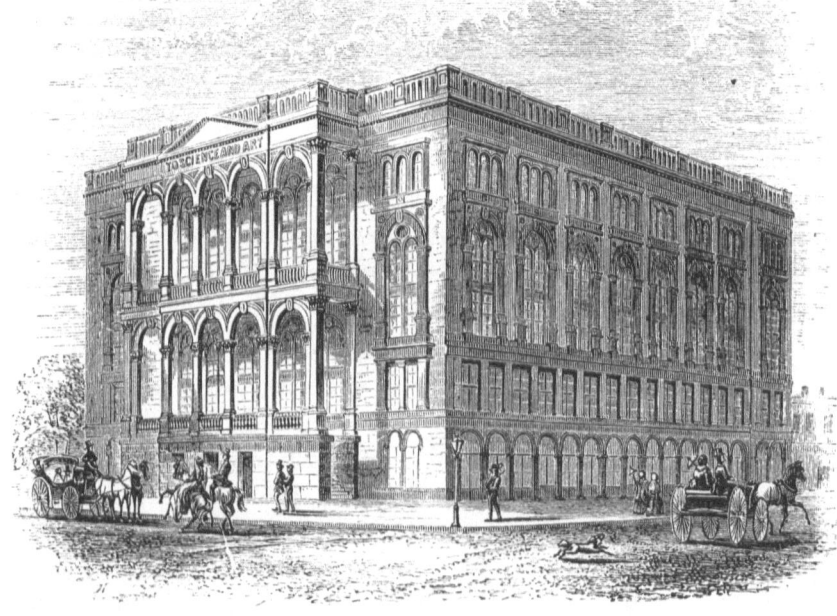

COOPER UNION.

Cooper Union circa 1870, from *Miller's New York Guidebook*
PUBLIC DOMAIN, WIKIMEDIA COMMONS

Advancement of Science and Art, a school located in Lower Manhattan, was a better venue. About 1,500 people attended the event on a snowy night to hear from the former congressman and recent debating star, Abraham Lincoln.

The first time I saw Cooper Union I was on my way to see an off-Broadway play about Nikola Tesla for which I had advised the cast, director, and writer. The main building, called the Foundation Building, is an imposing Italianate brownstone commanding an entire quadrilateral block nestled between Astor Place and East 7th Street. The science-loving Lincoln must have appreciated the technologically advanced structure for its time, complete with a shaft anticipating a commercial elevator before it was invented. Inside there are several lobby galleries that today display artwork from the school's students. The basement is home to the Great Hall where Lincoln spoke, a large room featuring vaulted sandstone arches and sixteen simple round columns below a high ceiling, giving the room the impression of a church nave. As Cooper Union speech expert Holzer points out, "the architectural message was clear: This was a cathedral of knowledge and wisdom." Andrew Freeman, in his 1960 book about Lincoln's New York visit, notes that the auditorium had two thousand red upholstered swivel chairs, and the hall was illuminated by twenty-eight glass chandeliers, "each with six gas burners." The Great Hall would go on to host luminaries of the time like Frederick Douglass, Mark Twain, and Susan B. Anthony, as well as a raft of modern dignitaries and at least a half dozen US presidents. Everyone wants to speak at the historic venue, including Holzer, who has appeared there several times, once with celebrated actor Sam Waterston to re-create Lincoln's address.[2]

It was to Holzer that I ran for more information on Lincoln's Cooper Union speech. After all, his book, *Lincoln at Cooper Union: The Speech That Made Abraham Lincoln President*, is considered the definitive treatise. I have known Holzer for a dozen years and have always marveled at his boundless energy and productivity. Besides authoring, coauthoring, and editing something like sixty Lincoln books and many hundreds of articles, he served ten years as cochair on the U.S. Abraham Lincoln Bicentennial Commission appointed by President Bill Clinton, served another six years as chair of its successor foundation, and continues to serve as chairman of the Lincoln Forum. When he is not on television or giving presentations, he is picking up awards like the Lincoln Prize and receiving the National Humanities Medal from President George W. Bush.

Holzer points out that Lincoln was well aware of how important his speech would be to the Republican Party's chances in the 1860 election, and to him personally as he began to see himself as a possible beneficiary of that opportunity. To understand why, we need to know that Stephen A. Douglas had been actively promoting his concept of popular sovereignty in anticipation of gaining the Democratic presidential nomination. Douglas himself knew that Lincoln was a challenge to him, admitting that he was "full of wit, fact, dates—the best stump speaker, with his droll ways and dry jokes, in the West."[3]

Lincoln spent months preparing for the speech, pouring through historical and legal records such as the Articles of Confederation, the Constitution, and the Federalist Papers to enumerate the actions taken by the Founders of the nation. As a starting point he took a lengthy treatise called "The Dividing Line Between Federal and Local Authority" that Stephen A. Douglas published in *Harper's*, one of the most widely read magazines in the country. In short, Douglas defended his popular sovereignty idea by arguing that the Founders created a country "divided into free and slave states, with the right of each part to retain slavery as long as it chooses, and to abolish it whenever it pleases." Those Founders, according to Douglas, believed they could not abolish slavery where it existed, nor ban it from the territories, adding that only the local people could make decisions regarding the presence or absence of slavery. To think otherwise was to violate "the great principle" of self-government.

There are some obvious problems with this line of argument. Slavery was present in all the colonies and by the time the Founders were framing the Constitution it remained in some form in almost all states. The Founders did not create a country half slave and half free, they simply acknowledged slavery's existence, and even then, hid it ("like a wen" [boil], Lincoln said) by not using the words *slave* or *slavery* in the Constitution. Douglas's argument also conflicted with the Dred Scott decision, which, contrary to Douglas, said local authorities had no power to keep slavery out of the territories. Douglas was also wrong that the framers of the Constitution believed the federal government could not bar slavery in federal territories, as they had done exactly that in the Northwest Ordinance and the Missouri Compromise, notwithstanding the Dred Scott decision irrationally declaring those actions void.[4]

Nevertheless, Douglas went on tour campaigning for popular sovereignty and in Columbus, Ohio, used a phrase that he would come to regret:

Our fathers, when they framed the Government under which we live, understood this question just as well, and even better, than we do now.

Walking around Lower Manhattan, I realized that even the 1860 hustle and bustle would likely have astonished western-bred Lincoln. Having crossed the Hudson River from Jersey City to Manhattan, Lincoln made his way to the Astor House, one of the most luxurious hotels in New York City, conveniently located near City Hall and Publishers Row, which housed the city's most important newspapers. New York City had grown by over 50 percent just in the previous decade, with much of the population growth consisting of immigrants from Ireland, Germany, and other European nations. And according to Tom Link, if Lincoln's room was on the ground floor of the Astor House, he would have looked out on St. Paul's Chapel, built in 1766 and where George Washington attended services immediately after taking the oath of office as the first president of the United States.[5] No doubt Lincoln would have investigated the chapel. Today, from a vantage point on Broadway, I can see the new One World Trade Center looming behind the chapel's historic spire. From the other side, standing in the burying ground facing the skyscraper, is a "Bell of Hope" rung every year on September 11 to reflect both mourning and the chapel's role as a refuge during that warm, clear, cataclysmic day in 2001.

Lincoln's day was less devastating but also less warm. The weather was frigid and light snow was falling, but the Young Men's Committee that had taken over sponsorship of his Cooper Union presence took him around Manhattan to see the sights. One stop was Mathew Brady's photographic emporium housed in a temporary studio at 643 Broadway while his new studio was being prepared. Brady was already a celebrity, and having a photo taken by Brady was becoming a necessity for any up-and-coming politician or social climber. This fit well with Lincoln, who had embraced the new technology of photography within a few years of its invention and had tried to have a photograph taken whenever he did anything noteworthy. This event certainly met the requirements and so Lincoln sat for a series of photos, one of the best decisions he had made. Not only was the Cooper Union address itself widely published in the newspapers, but Brady also reproduced one of these photos in the new carte de visite format, enabling thousands of copies to be printed, sold, and broadly circulated. While many historians today refer to Cooper Union as "the speech that made Lincoln president," the Brady photograph accentuated that by putting a face in front of the public at large. To these two elements I would add a third component that worked in synergy to make Lincoln president—publication of the Lincoln-Douglas debates in book form, which Lincoln made happen a month later. And there was his post–Cooper Union tour of New England.

Having expected to speak at Beecher's church to a religiously abolitionist crowd, Lincoln begged away from his tour guides and the many impromptu visitors to lock himself in his hotel room and edit his speech for an audience likely to expect a more erudite discourse. The committee then escorted him by carriage to the Cooper Union venue, which despite the snow was relatively crowded. The focus of the series, now extended by Lincoln's delayed appearance, was twofold. Sure, the organizers wanted to spread the antislavery word, but there was a larger rationale for bringing in outside speakers—they wanted an alternative to William Henry Seward.

James Briggs, the man who sent the telegram to Lincoln, was one of the New York–based Republicans who thought Seward was more liability than asset. Seward had been a party leader for many years and was the presumptive nominee in the months leading up to the Republican convention, but he also had his enemies. His association with political handler Thurlow Weed seemed a bit tawdry to some, and then he gave a speech in Rochester that left a residue of extremism bothersome to the public. I have been to Lincoln conferences in recent years in which a simple utterance of the words "irrepressible conflict" spawns a roomful of eye-rolling and "what ifs" Seward had never said it. Here is the full sentence, which reflects well the intent of Seward's speech:

It is an irrepressible conflict between opposing and enduring forces, and it means that the United States must and will, sooner or later, become either entirely a slaveholding nation, or entirely a free-labor nation.[6]

Was Seward calling for war? The implication was unnerving to some members of the Republican Party, and they held it against Seward even though the concept was not much different from Lincoln's own "House Divided" speech three months previously. In that speech, given as he accepted the support of the Illinois State Republican Convention in Springfield, Lincoln noted that in the five years since the Kansas-Nebraska Act had supposedly put an end to slavery agitation, the opposite had happened. Rather than agitation ceasing, it was constantly augmented, and the national identity was endangered.

In my opinion, it will not cease, until a crisis shall have been reached, and passed.
A house divided against itself cannot stand.

He went on to say that:

I believe this government cannot endure, permanently half slave and half free.
I do not expect the Union to be dissolved—I do not expect the house to fall—but I do expect it will cease to be divided.
It will become all one thing, or all the other.
Either the opponents of slavery, will arrest the further spread of it, and place it where the public mind shall rest in the belief that it is in the course of ultimate extinction; or its advocates will push it forward, till it shall become alike lawful in all the States, old as well as new—North as well as South.
Have we no tendency to the latter condition?

That sounds radical for the times. To my mind, Seward's speech three months later reiterated Lincoln's concept. Yet Seward's speech was held against him far more than Lincoln's was, suggesting that Lincoln's lack of political office and relative obscurity in the East may have saved him from Seward's fate.

Joining Briggs in opposing Seward were political heavyweights William Cullen Bryant (whose poem "Thanatopsis" Lincoln had read) and Horace Greeley, the influential *New-York Tribune* editor with a long-standing feud against Seward and thus eager to see him toppled. Joining them was another anti-Seward man, David Dudley Field, whom Lincoln had met at the River and Harbor Convention in Chicago just before entering Congress, and whose brother Stephen J. Field, Lincoln would later appoint to the US Supreme Court. Lincoln undoubtedly understood this dynamic, which may have spurred how much research he put into developing the speech. These men did not necessarily see Lincoln as their candidate, but felt confident the hero of the Lincoln-Douglas debates could sway others away from the presumed frontrunner. Lincoln could be a spoiler, they were thinking, and someone more experienced like Salmon P. Chase, Edward Bates, or even William L. Dayton, who had beaten out Lincoln to become John C. Fremont's running mate in the 1856 election, could win the nomination.

When William Cullen Bryant stood up to introduce Lincoln, he seemed to acknowledge the obscurity of the speaker. While noting Lincoln was "an eminent citizen of the West" (which on his 1848 trip had been a sign of coming entertainment), he added "hitherto known to you only by reputation." Even in being complimentary, Bryant showed some eastern condescension, saying "These children from the West . . . form a living bulwark against the advances of slavery." He did, however, give credit to Lincoln as "a gallant soldier of the political campaign of 1858," revealing the main reason for inviting Lincoln in the first place—he made a good showing in the Lincoln-Douglas debates.

Bryant was certainly right to assume the eastern audience would find Lincoln's presence an interesting change from the normal speakers. While they gave him a loud burst of applause, many found him ungainly and unsteady. One attendee watched the long-legged Lincoln stand up

Abraham Lincoln photo by Mathew Brady, taken on the day of his Cooper Union speech, February 27, 1860
PUBLIC DOMAIN, WIKIMEDIA COMMONS

from his chair and commented that "the tall figure would never stop rising." Others noted that his new suit seemed not to fit well and "hung on him rather loosely." Despite his reputation as the "Little Giant killer," he hardly inspired the crowd's confidence: "there was nothing impressive or imposing about him," one attendee remembered. I can imagine what the crowd thought when he began speaking, his high-pitched country twang striking the ears of everyone there.

Like Lincoln, I tend to begin any public presentation deeply nervous and lacking full control of my voice and material. But then I start to feel more comfortable, and the presentation generally goes well from there. Lincoln's voice quickly gained its focus and strength, and he was off on a discourse that completely enthralled the assembled gathering for the next hour and a half. Unlike his 1848 Massachusetts tour, Lincoln refrained from much in the way of humor. This was serious business that already, in early 1860, many understood to be a preamble to intranational conflict. Digging into the speech, there are three main sections.[7]

The first section provides a historical accounting of the Founders' beliefs regarding slavery. And by accounting, I mean in the literal sense, counting the votes and statements of the Founders as indications of their views on slavery. Douglas had argued in his *Harper's* article and subsequent speeches that the framers of the Constitution had intentionally created a nation "half-slave and half-free." Since they created such a nation, we needed to listen to them as we (in 1860) reargued the present and future status of slavery. Here is where Douglas offered up the line I quoted earlier in the chapter and will reiterate here because of its importance. Lincoln would repeat this line over and over in the speech to reinforce his point:

Our fathers, when they framed the Government under which we live, understood this question just as well, and even better, than we do now.

Not so fast, Lincoln suggested in Cooper Union's Great Hall. I can imagine the crowd leaning forward to hear Lincoln's expected rebuttal, only to hear Lincoln say:

I fully indorse this, and I adopt it as a text for this discourse. I so adopt it because it furnishes a precise and an agreed starting point for a discussion between Republicans and that wing of the Democracy headed by Senator Douglas. It simply leaves the inquiry: "What was the understanding those fathers had of the question mentioned?"

Defining the framers as those thirty-nine men who signed the Constitution, Lincoln proceeded to track each of those men through their other votes and statements to determine "how they acted upon it—and how they expressed that better understanding." And he named names.

For example, he said that Roger Sherman, Thomas Mifflin, and Hugh Williamson, all signers of the Constitution, had also all voted while in the House of Representatives for the Northwest Ordinance that banned slavery in the territory that would in time become the states of Ohio, Indiana, Illinois, Michigan, and Wisconsin. This showed their understanding that the federal government did have the authority to control the spread of slavery into the territories, contrary to Douglas's assertion.

And on he went, detailing how the framers of our government, who "understood this question just as well, and even better, than we do now," routinely voted to limit the spread of slavery. In short, they did not approve of slavery (even though many were slaveholders) but as slavery was firmly entrenched in the nation's history, they could not see how to eliminate it in one fell swoop. Instead, they opted for a piecemeal approach under the, perhaps naive, belief that slavery would die under its own immoral weight. Lincoln documents this in detail.

In the second section, Lincoln directs his words to the people of the South, who while not present, would certainly read the speech in the newspapers.

You say you are conservative . . . while we are revolutionary, destructive, or something of the sort. What is conservative? Is it not adherence to the old and tried, against the new and untried?

Lincoln notes that being conservative in this case meant adhering to the beliefs of the Founders that slavery was wrong and inconsistent with a nation where "all men are created equal." He knew this was contrary to how most in the South felt. His congressional friend, Georgia congressman and future Confederate vice president, Alexander H. Stephens, in his "cornerstone speech" would denounce the Founders' assumption of equality, calling it "an error."[8]

In this second section, Lincoln addresses charges by the South that the Republican Party was intent on starting slave insurrections, giving as example the recent case of John Brown at Harpers Ferry. Lincoln rejected this argument, saying that Brown was no Republican and no Republican had been implicated in his enterprise. This was not strictly true, as he would no doubt be reminded when he toured New England beginning the next day, as many of Brown's funders were New England abolitionists who counted themselves among the Republican ranks. In any event, he writes John Brown's actions off as "an attempt by white men to get up a revolt among slaves, in which the slaves refused to participate." He admitted, however, that in accordance with "our fathers, who framed the Government under which we live," Republicans agreed that slavery was wrong.

Rereading the Cooper Union speech in the shadow of the Union itself, I came to my favorite quote in which Lincoln summarizes the South's desire to break up the government unless the North submits entirely to a nation "all slave." If the Republicans were to win the election,

> *You say, you will destroy the Union; and then, you say, the great crime of having destroyed it will be upon us! That is cool. A highwayman holds a pistol to my ear, and mutters through his teeth, "Stand and deliver, or I shall kill you, and then you will be a murderer!"*

Adding, in a statement that foreshadows the January 6, 2021, insurrection and the current state of American society:

> *Your purpose, then, plainly stated, is, that you will destroy the Government, unless you be allowed to construe and enforce the Constitution as you please, on all points in dispute between you and us. You will rule or ruin in all events.*

In his third section, the shortest, he asserts that Republicans cannot relinquish their principle that slavery is wrong just to placate the South. He ends with words that have become as famous as his later Gettysburg Address, complete with his own all-caps emphasis:

> *LET US HAVE FAITH THAT RIGHT MAKES MIGHT, AND IN THAT FAITH, LET US, TO THE END, DARE TO DO OUR DUTY AS WE UNDERSTAND IT.*

Despite what Douglas, Chief Justice Taney, and the Southern slaveholders declared, the framers "of our Government under which we live" understood that the federal government had the authority, and the moral obligation, to keep slavery from spreading into the territories in the belief the "peculiar institution" was on the path to its ultimate extinction. Individual slaveholding states needed to work out how they would end slavery, but surely slavery must collapse because of its economic failure and the weight of its own immorality. Greeley's *Tribune* praised Lincoln's speech, saying that it was "probably the most systematic and complete defense yet made of the Republican position with regard to Slavery. We believe no speech has yet been made better calculated to win intelligent minds to our standard."[9]

As one looks back on this speech over 165 years later, we see how Abraham Lincoln and the Republican Party were progressive in their views while remaining true to the Declaration that "all men are created equal." Southern Democrats of the age were conservative in that they sought to preserve an aristocracy-based Southern society where a few rich plantation owners controlled an economy based on inequality. Lincoln's previous sojourn to New England focused on mending the rift within the Whig Party. Now a Republican, his Cooper Union address and subsequent New England trip attempted to drive a wedge between the Northern and Southern factions of the Democratic Party.

Lincoln had one more task before leaving Manhattan. After his speech he had been whisked up the road to the Athenaeum Club for dinner with James Briggs, Hiram Barney, and other officers of the host Young Men's Republican Union. When they finished around midnight, Lincoln headed not for his hotel but for the *Tribune* offices to review the proof sheets of his speech. Lincoln had made it a habit of making corrections (and sometimes massaging his words after the fact) to ensure his key messages would get out. By the next morning, his Cooper Union speech was published in the New York papers, and not long after, by every other paper across the country that felt inspired to crib from the *New-York Tribune*.

In stunning contrast to how he was viewed in Massachusetts in 1848, primarily as entertainment value to bring electoral enthusiasm to the crowd, Lincoln in 1860 expected to be taken more seriously by the audiences in Rhode Island, New Hampshire, and Connecticut he would soon address. The Lincoln-Douglas debates suggested Lincoln was more serious than he appeared, and the Cooper Union address demonstrated unequivocally that he could be a viable force in the upcoming Republican convention. To enhance his chances, Lincoln needed to make a good showing on his second tour of New England. And he already had been asked to speak in Providence, where he would stop on his way to visit his son Robert in New Hampshire.

CHAPTER NINE

The Seward Rivalry Begins—Providence

EVERYONE SEEMED TO BE AWARE THAT LINCOLN WAS ON HIS WAY TO visit son Robert in New Hampshire. John Eddy was first in line, approaching Lincoln with an invitation to speak in Providence, Rhode Island, on his way north. Eddy was a successful Providence attorney and an influential member of the state's Republican Party. The invite may have come even before he arrived because that afternoon the *Providence Daily Journal* was already reporting that the "Honorable Abraham Lincoln of Illinois, will address the Republicans of this city tomorrow evening." Despite having been at the *New-York Tribune* office until the wee hours of the morning after his Cooper Union speech, Lincoln, accompanied by Eddy, took an early train out of New York, changed trains in New Haven, Connecticut, and arrived in Providence by midafternoon.

I already had some familiarity with Providence. When I was a graduate student in southeastern Massachusetts, I lived on the border with Rhode Island and crossed the bridge often to pick up pizza for myself and my fellow graduate student roommate. After I took a job in Washington, DC, I often flew the commuter route between DC's Reagan National Airport and Providence's T. F. Green International on trips to visit family. Now it was time to take my road trip downtown and see if Providence remembered Lincoln's visit in any way.

While most of New England seems to have forgotten Lincoln's visits, I found a large bronze plaque on the side of the Federal Building declaring "Abraham Lincoln, On February 28, 1860, Spoke in Railroad Hall On This Site." The plaque went on to note that Lincoln had spoken

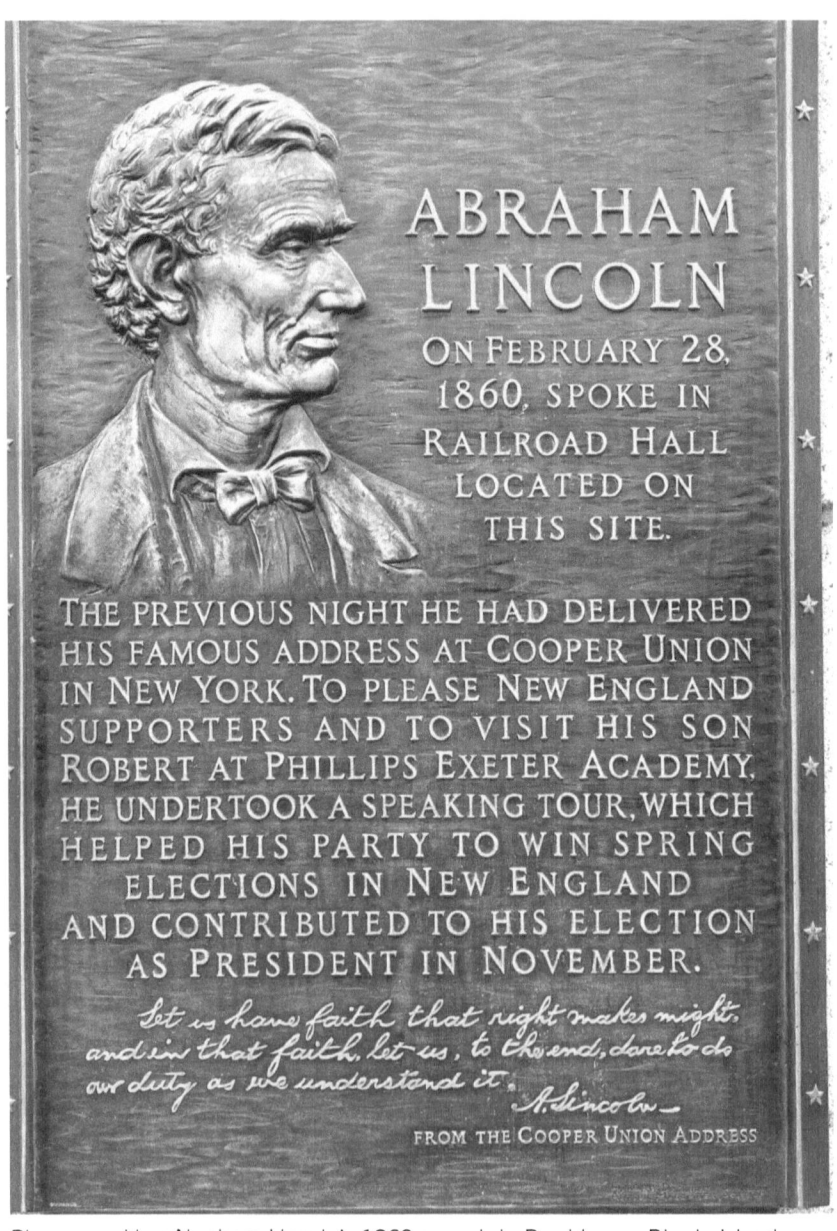

Plaque marking Abraham Lincoln's 1860 speech in Providence, Rhode Island

at Cooper Union the previous night and "to please New England supporters and to visit his son at Phillips Exeter Academy, he undertook a speaking tour, which helped his party to win spring elections in New England and contributed to his election as president in November."

Railroad Hall is long since gone. The current building was built in 1908 as a US courthouse but now serves as the Federal Building housing a historic post office, US District Court for Rhode Island, and a customs house. Massive but beautiful, the Beaux-Arts style building is constructed of New Hampshire granite and complements the Second Empire style of Providence City Hall at the opposite end of Kennedy Plaza. Two groups of allegorical statues sit on either side of the entrances, one representing *Sovereign Power*, the other *Providence as Independent Thought*. The building was added to the National Register of Historic Places in 1972.

The weather was unseasonably warm when Lincoln arrived, contrasting the overcast and chilly weather during my visit. Newspapers were already printing his Cooper Union speech, and Railroad Hall was overflowing with "an audience to welcome and hear the great champion of Republicanism in Illinois."[1] Before I dig into the speech itself, I need to take a step back and address why Lincoln had been invited to Providence in the first place. And for that, I revisit Bill Hanna, the man whose *Abraham Among the Yankees* book became the definitive record of Lincoln's 1848 visit to Massachusetts.

It turns out Hanna also looked at Lincoln's 1860 visit, particularly his time in Providence. I first came across the reference in a paper by Frank Williams, retired chief justice of the Rhode Island Supreme Court, founding chairman of the Lincoln Forum, and one of the biggest Lincolniana collectors in the country.[2] I have spoken with Williams several times over the years, so I looked both at his paper and the earlier one by Hanna, who was nice enough to provide me a copy.

If you remember, Lincoln went to Massachusetts in 1848 because the Whig Party was splitting between its political factions. Conscience Whigs unhappy with the party's choice of slaveholder Zachary Taylor as their nominee formed the Free Soil Party, which threatened to divide the vote enough to deliver the election to the conservative Democratic Party. In a case of déjà vu, the Rhode Island Republican Party was again cleaving along liberal and conservative fractures. Lincoln was getting wedged into the middle of a messy, even hostile, campaign. As usual, the newspapers were highly partisan and took sides in what would become an intense battle for control.

On the one side was the Republican candidate for Rhode Island governor, Seth Padelford. To say that Padelford was radical is an understatement. He was an open abolitionist and had been vice president (and a major funder) of the New England Emigrant Aid Society, the purpose of which was to transport as many as twenty thousand antislavery immigrants from New England to Kansas to shift the balance of power toward a free territory. Even that was mild compared to his purported funding of Hinton Rowan Helper's divisive book, *The Impending Crisis of the South*, which argued that slavery was devastating to the economic potential of non-slaveholders and a death knell to the future of the Southern states. Despite being from North Carolina and a white supremacist himself, Helper became an abolitionist and a pariah in the South. "Helperism" became as charged a political attack as "Black Republicanism" and "Abolitionist," so Padelford's support for Helper was a major sticking point for the more conservative wing of the Republican Party in Rhode Island.

So, the party did what progressive parties always seem to do; it split. The more conservative Republicans in Rhode Island formed a coalition with the Democratic Party, calling themselves the Rhode Island Union Party (or sometimes Union Republicans) to field William Sprague IV as a counter candidate. At only twenty-nine years old, Sprague came from a distinguished family, ran the biggest calico textile printing mills in the world, and self-funded a state militia he commanded when he was only twenty-one.

Since Lincoln had been invited by the state's Republican Party, Seth Padelford was on the stage with him that night in Providence. That put Lincoln in a difficult position. As a rule, he maintained more moderate political beliefs and had adamantly denied he was an abolitionist during the Lincoln-Douglas debates. Despite this history, the local Democratic paper, the *Providence Daily Post*, argued that Lincoln's "abolitionism is unquestioned," citing his "House Divided" speech as evidence.[3] To his credit, Lincoln began his speech with some impromptu humor, rejecting the misrepresentations of the *Post*. As for "Helperism," Lincoln claimed he had never read Helper's book. Whether that statement was credible is debatable. Robert Bray, the researcher who catalogued all the books Lincoln had read, lists *The Impending Crisis* among Lincoln's readings. But Bray also writes a long discussion that, at least to my mind, leaves it uncertain as to whether Lincoln read it or not. Perhaps Herndon had read it, and they discussed it, but Lincoln mentioned Helper in passing when discussing John Brown in his Cooper Union address, so it is clear he was at least aware of it. Whether he was being disingenuous or not about Helper, Lincoln undoubtedly was distancing himself from Padelford's more extreme views even while supporting the party for the governor's election occurring in April. How the audience took Lincoln's prevarication depends on which newspaper you read, with Democratic and Padelford-endorsing Republican papers like the *Daily Post* irritated by "Lincoln's dodging" and more moderate Republican papers like the *Daily Journal* touting Lincoln's "thorough honesty" and "sincere, earnest belief." It is hard not to think about today's viewers of Fox News and MSNBC getting such slanted information that they effectively live in two different info-worlds. Clearly the Padelford people in the room had hoped for more enthusiastic support, with Padelford's manager, Thomas Davis, an ardent abolitionist, stepping on stage after Lincoln to state with irritation that if Lincoln had not read Helper's book, he and Padelford had, and found it excellent.[4]

When the local election was held five weeks later, Sprague beat Padelford by a wide margin, perhaps giving Lincoln confidence that a more moderate position was better for the party than a more radical one. I must assume this was on his mind as the Republican National Convention was scheduled for a few months later in Chicago where the presumptive nominee, William Seward, was considered by many too extreme.

If the name Sprague sounds familiar, it is because after becoming Rhode Island governor, to which he was reelected for two more one-year terms, he also participated in the First Battle of Bull Run, became a US senator, and married Kate Chase, the beautiful daughter of Salmon P. Chase, President Lincoln's secretary of the treasury. Sprague quickly ditched the coalition that got him elected governor, identifying as a Republican throughout his political career. Lincoln would do much the same in 1864, forming a coalition with the War Democrats to get reelected as a National Union candidate that was a temporarily convenient front for the continuing Republican Party.

Across the street from the old Railroad Hall, now Federal Building holding up the plaque honoring Lincoln's speech, is Kennedy Plaza, formerly known as Exchange Place, but renamed after President John F. Kennedy's assassination almost exactly a hundred years after Lincoln's Gettysburg Address. The plaza is the center of the city and Lincoln arrived and departed his various transits of Providence via the Union Depot train station. The plaza has undergone significant changes over the century and a half since Lincoln spoke here and has hosted speeches by Presidents Teddy Roosevelt, Woodrow Wilson, and John F. Kennedy (plus a little magic by Harry Houdini). Today the space serves as a busy bus transfer terminal, but it also has a prominent Soldiers' and Sailors' Monument dedicated to those fighting the Civil War, plus a copy of *The Hiker*, commemorating the American soldiers who fought in the

Exchange Place in Providence, Rhode Island, around the time of Lincoln's visit. Union Depot is to the right and the location of Railroad Hall is in the background.
PUBLIC DOMAIN, WIKIMEDIA COMMONS

Spanish-American War. There also is a revolving series of modern pieces, which on my visit was a large bronze sculpture called *Morphous* by Lionel Smit, featuring a paired set of African heads, touching at the crown but facing opposite. The sculpture "is an exploration of hybrid identity and its ever-changing nature within South Africa's social landscape and evokes a question of time, of past and future, and the balance point" at which the sculptor's home nation found itself a year after Nelson Mandela's death. It is reminiscent of the Roman mythology of Janus, "the double headed deity of beginnings, gates, transitions, time, duality, doorways, passages, frames, and endings." To me it was a reminder that my study of Abraham Lincoln and his times remains relevant in this present time of political turmoil and national identity.

To the northeast of the plaza is a more natural area of trees and open space called Burnside Park, which showcases a large equestrian statue of General Ambrose Burnside. Burnside was born in Indiana but after the Civil War became a three-time governor of Rhode Island (perhaps ironically, succeeded by Seth Padelford) and later its US senator (succeeding none other than William Sprague IV). Most relevant for Lincoln, Burnside was a senior Union general during the Civil War and responsible for some important early Union victories. Lincoln at one point promoted him to major general, and after Burnside refused several times, he eventually took on a short-lived command of the Army of the Potomac. Disastrous defeats at Fredericksburg (where he repeatedly sent his men into a suicidal attack) and the Crater (where poor decision-making led to massive casualties) led to his quick removal. His biggest contribution to society might be that the voluminous bushy facial hair running from his temples to his mustache (but with no beard) gave rise to the word *sideburns*.

Providence is the home of Brown University, which is the seventh-oldest institution of higher education in the United States behind Harvard, William & Mary, Yale, Princeton, Columbia, and the University of Pennsylvania. Like many of the others, there was slavery money involved. Less than a half mile to the other side of the river from Kennedy Plaza, Brown—originally the College of Rhode Island—was established in 1764. There is no evidence that Lincoln checked out the campus on his visit, but since I had spoken several times with Tom Horrocks, former director of special collections at the John Hay Library at Brown, it seemed like a good idea to take a closer look. A Brown alumnus, John Hay, was one of Lincoln's private secretaries and later a distinguished statesman in his own right, including as ambassador to the United Kingdom and then secretary of state under presidents William McKinley and Theodore Roosevelt. He also teamed up with John Nicolay to write the ten-volume biography that helped shape the public's image of Lincoln.

The College of Rhode Island became Brown because of slavery. Originally in Warren, the four Brown brothers—Nicholas, John, Joseph, and Moses—secured the endowment needed to keep the college afloat and expand it. They moved it to Providence and constructed the first building. Joseph Brown became a professor of natural philosophy (what we now know as physics and other hard sciences) and designed the Edifice, now called University Hall, which Nicholas built. Moses was instrumental in moving the school from Warren to Providence. John Brown (no relation to that other John Brown of Harpers Ferry fame) ran the school's finances for two decades, followed by the son of Nicholas for the next thirty years. All this influence and influx of their own money resulted in the name we have known since.

Here is where the slavery bit comes in. Among their other properties, the four Brown brothers owned a brigantine ship named *Sally*, which in 1764 they decided should be put into the lucrative slave trade. Instructing the captain (Esek Hopkins, son of the college's chancellor, Stephen Hopkins, later a signer of the Declaration of Independence) on where and how to trade on the African coast, they provided money and materials for purchasing enslaved people and gave directions for unloading the captives in Caribbean markets. The brothers added specific instructions to acquire four teenage boys for the family's use. The voyage, besides being inhumane and immoral, was a disaster. Competition from other slavers delayed the acquisition of suitable numbers, many of whom died before they even set sail. An uprising en route decimated both captives and crew to the point where only 88 of 196 Africans survived. The results were so brutal that Nicholas, Joseph, and Moses never again invested in the slave trade, although John remained an unapologetic slave trader for

The Seward Rivalry Begins—Providence

many years. After youngest brother Moses became a Quaker and staunch abolitionist, he and John had a messy—and very public—falling-out. As author Nathaniel Philbrick discusses in his book on George Washington's travels to New England, Moses founded the Providence Society for Promoting the Abolition of Slavery, which had John proclaiming "There is no more crime in bringing off a cargo of slaves than in bringing off a cargo of jackasses." John was sure to remind Moses that the textile mills making Moses rich relied on "the labor of the slaves."[5]

Notwithstanding the *Sally* nightmare, the Brown brothers and the ensuing management of the college continued to rely on the wealth of Southern slaveholders to fund the school (as did Harvard, Yale, and the rest). They competed for slaveholder and slave trader families to be on their board of governors and to send their young men to the school, along with substantial fees. Representatives of Brown were sent south in search of financial gifts and students, often dining as enslaved staff waited on them. With all this slave money flowing into Ivy League coffers, it is no surprise that there was little tolerance for antislavery discourse even into the 1840s.[6] Funding from slavery slowed down once the 1808 prohibition of the international slave trade stopped the legal importation of Africans, but some families simply purchased plantations in Cuba to circumvent the restrictions.[7]

The reliance on direct slaveholder money to fund Brown, Harvard, and the other Ivies shifted in the 1800s to an indirect route through expanding textile manufacturing wealth. Remember the Lawrence brothers, the Lowells, and the Appletons from the earlier Boston Associates discussion? What started as textile mills (using Southern slave-grown cotton) quickly expanded into financing and railroads and other endeavors that made the members incredibly wealthy. These industrialists helped colleges and universities to refocus their fundraising and retool academics to teach the technological skills the industrialists needed. John Lowell Jr., for example, son of one of the original textile magnates, Francis Cabot Lowell, bequeathed $250,000 to the Lowell Institute in Boston. Abbott Lawrence, frustrated by the lack of trained engineers and city planners, gave $50,000 to establish the Lawrence Scientific School. In the 1840s, the Lawrence family donated to many smaller schools such as Williams,

Amherst, and Bowdoin to train more engineers. They would get some help in the 1860s when President Lincoln signed into law the Morrill Land-Grant Act funding the creation of scientific and technological training colleges in every state. It would be another century and a half before much of this history would come to light when Brown University commissioned an internal study to determine the extent to which slavery was involved in the early history of the school.[8]

Providence was not the only Rhode Island city built on slave money. Newport, and later Bristol, had been centers of the slave trade even before the capital city. Some of Newport's wealthiest residents were involved in the slave trade, from building ships to funding the voyages to Africa, although most of the slavery connections were more indirect, such as providing food and livestock, barrels and hoops, timber, and shoes to the Caribbean and the Southern states. It was Lopez and Rivera, the largest slave-trading firm in Newport, that donated the lumber for building the Edifice at Rhode Island College, soon to become Brown.[9]

I have a particular affinity for Newport because that is where Isaac Stevens is buried. General Isaac Stevens had been a US congressman and Washington territorial governor and served with distinction in the Mexican War. He once led an expedition to map out a proposed railroad route to the Northwest. Years later, President Abraham Lincoln signed into law the Pacific Railroad Act to create the northern route of the transcontinental railroad, so I liked Stevens already. I had the privilege a few years ago of being the keynote speaker at the annual Lincoln-Thomas Day remembrance at Fort Stevens—which had originally been called Fort Massachusetts until renamed after Stevens's death—part of dozens of fortifications making up the Civil War Defenses of Washington, DC. Today, a large stone on the embarkment marks the location where Lincoln famously, or perhaps infamously, stood in the line of fire during a July 1864 Confederate attack on the fort.

But there is another reason I like Stevens. He fought gallantly at the Battle of Chantilly on September 1, 1862, against Confederate forces led by Thomas "Stonewall" Jackson, only to be killed in battle. I know this because nearly every day I walk through the Ox Hill Battlefield Park (where they use the Confederate name for the battle) a few minutes from

Gravesite of General Isaac Stevens (obelisk) and Hazard Stevens (small stone to the left), Island Cemetery, Newport, Rhode Island

my home. The park takes up a small portion of the overall battlefield, the rest now covered by a shopping center and apartment complexes, but a section of it displays two cenotaphs for Stevens and fellow general Philip Kearny who also died during the battle. Once a year, the local Civil War Round Table plants flags and lays wreaths in their memory. Stevens's stone notes that he died dramatically, "with the flag of the Republic in his dying grasp." But neither general is buried on the site. Kearny is in Arlington National Cemetery, but Stevens is buried in Island Cemetery in Newport, Rhode Island, so I had to stop there. Yes, another cemetery.

Island Cemetery is home to the remains of Newport's most prominent families, many of whom made their money through some connection to slavery. There are several ex-governors, congressmen, and because Newport was a seaport, many former sailors and navy men. Commodore Oliver Hazard Perry is buried here, as is his brother Matthew C. Perry, who helped establish the curriculum of the US Naval Academy and became a leading advocate of modernization that led to him being called the "Father of the Steam Navy." Looking around it is easy to find a Belmont or two, including financier and racehorse owner August Belmont, founder and namesake of the Belmont Stakes, the final race of the Triple Crown. General Isaac Stevens has a tall obelisk, perhaps twenty feet high, reminiscent of the Washington Monument. Its much longer epitaph reiterates the phrasing on the stone near my home, that Stevens "fell while rallying his command, with the flag of the Republic in his dying hand." Next to Isaac's grave is a shorter one for his son, Major Hazard Stevens (listed as Breveted Brigadier General on the stone). Hazard served as his father's aide and was awarded the Congressional Medal of Honor for his service. He lived a long and active life after the war, including as one of the first men to climb to the top of Mount Rainier in Washington State.

Lincoln was likely unaware of this slave-connection history during his visit to Rhode Island. His focus was on repeating the essential ideas of the Cooper Union speech to audiences that had likely read the speech in the newspapers before his arrival. While his 1848 foray into New England had largely been taken as entertainment, the debates with Douglas and his less strident, more serious style seemed to play well with the eastern audiences. The two Republican papers in the area found his Rhode Island speeches to be "logical, but neither elegant nor eloquent" (Cooper Union is primarily an accounting, not an inspirational oratory) and one of Lincoln's "most powerful addresses" met with "immense applause."[10]

As he prepared to leave Providence, Lincoln was approached by Woonsocket businessmen Lattimer W. Ballou and Edward Haris, who coaxed him into returning to Rhode Island after visiting his son Robert in New Hampshire. Lincoln agreed but told them he was already committed to speeches in Connecticut as well. This got me wondering how much of Lincoln's twelve-speech schedule had been prearranged. John Eddy supposedly reached out to Lincoln the day of his Cooper Union speech in New York, but the Providence papers were already advertising his presence before the Cooper Union speech itself, so perhaps there was some correspondence before his arrival. Eddy was not the only one who met Lincoln in New York and invited him farther north. N. D. Sperry, chairman of the Republican State Committee of Connecticut, dispatched a representative to the Big Apple to arrange for Lincoln to speak in various places in Connecticut.[11] This trip was quickly becoming much more than a speech in New York and a leisurely visit with Robert in New Hampshire.

Senator William Seward may have begun to hear the initial feedback from Lincoln's Cooper Union speech, because by February 29, the day after Lincoln repeated the major concepts in Providence, Seward was on the Senate floor with a speech of his own. It is hard to read Seward's speech and not see elements of what Lincoln previously said in his earlier Peoria, House Divided, and Lincoln-Douglas debate speeches. There are also hints of Lincoln's main Cooper Union theme. While Seward's speech is rather long-winded, even for him, he repeatedly refers to the framers of the Constitution and reiterates the gist of Lincoln's argument, that while they could not find a way to eliminate slavery immediately, they attempted to place it on a path toward its ultimate extinction. As Lincoln continued his ever-expanding trek through New England, Seward and his political guru Thurlow Weed would show they were taking closer notice of the gangly guy from Illinois.[12]

CHAPTER TEN

The Robert Visit—New Hampshire

BY THE TIME LINCOLN LEFT NEW YORK HE HAD ALSO COMMITTED TO giving speeches in Hartford, New Haven, and Meriden, Connecticut. In between, he anticipated having a relaxing few days with his sixteen-and-a-half-year-old son Robert, now a student at Phillips Exeter Academy in New Hampshire. Unbeknownst to him, the closest he would come to relaxing would be on the train as he traveled from Providence to Exeter.

One early source of information on Lincoln's 1860 tour of New England was a small pamphlet published in 1922 by Percy Coe Eggleston, whose father had met Lincoln on this trip. But another more comprehensive source also exists for this northernmost portion. Elwin L. Page wrote a fascinating book in 1929 called *Abraham Lincoln in New Hampshire* that focused entirely on Lincoln's trip to the Granite State. Page was a lawyer and associate judge of the New Hampshire Superior Court, who in the 1920s dug through newspapers and archival records of prominent politicians in the state. Page had a particular interest in Lincoln and was a charter member and longtime president of the Lincoln Group of Boston, and I have had the privilege of conversations with the current president, John Rodrigue. My reliable Lincoln-in-New-England resource, Bill Hanna, is also on the board, as well as Tom Turner, who just retired as editor in chief of the *Lincoln Herald* journal, for which I am a columnist and regular contributor. Rodrique and Turner also happen to be longtime professors at Bridgewater State University, where the Elwin Page papers are now held, so it seems fateful to associate with them. Meanwhile, on the bicentennial of Lincoln's birth in 2009, Page's book was reissued and updated by Mike Pride, longtime editor of the *Concord Monitor* newspaper. Pride passed away while I was researching this book, so I have filled in the blanks through ongoing discussions with Hanna, Rodrigue, Jason Emerson, and other current-day Lincoln scholars.

Lincoln was visiting Robert in part to give him a proverbial kick in the backside. Lincoln was largely self-educated, admitting when he was running for president that "the aggregate of all his schooling did not amount to one year," adding "he was never in a college or academy."[1] He wanted better for his eldest son. Unfortunately, Robert failed miserably when taking the Harvard College entrance exams. According to Page, Robert "flunked fifteen out of sixteen" exams, although he suggested somehow this was "through no fault of his own." Robert Lincoln historian Jason Emerson, the modern go-to expert on all things Robert, disputes this number, pointing out that there are no records at

Robert Todd Lincoln in 1865, by Mathew Brady PUBLIC DOMAIN, WIKIMEDIA COMMONS

all of Robert's failure and the incomplete records Harvard retains for that year show only ten subjects were tested. More likely, according to Emerson, Robert was simply overconfident and had not studied hard enough.[2] Confidence never seemed to be lacking in Robert, who in later years liked to claim that his failure to enter Harvard had made his father president. He also supposedly told a friend after hearing of Lincoln's nomination, "Good, I will write home for a check before he spends all his money on the campaign."[3]

So, why Phillips Exeter Academy? Two reasons stand out. First, Robert, having been humbled by his poor showing, approached the president of Harvard for advice on how to better his chances when retaking the exams. Of several preparatory school options suggested, Robert liked Phillips Exeter Academy in Exeter, New Hampshire, the foremost preparatory school in the country, and one that would keep him in the sophisticated East. In essence the school was a farm team, with the expectation that students would go on to Harvard following their studies. But there was a second reason—Amos Tuck. Tuck was a prominent leader in Granite State politics. Initially a Democrat in the state legislature, he broke with the proslavery elements of the party and flirted with the Liberty Party before winning a seat in the US House of Representatives as an Independent, where he met fellow congressman Lincoln. Still searching for a political home, he joined the Free Soil movement around the time Lincoln was in Massachusetts trying to keep them with the Whigs. Tuck had been working to create an independent third party in various forms for years, including the unsuccessful promotion of antislavery independent candidate John P. Hale. When the Free Soilers faded away, Tuck helped unite the myriad factions and founded the Republican Party of New Hampshire. Tuck lived in Exeter and Lincoln liked the idea that Robert would have a family friend to look after him as needed.[4]

Phillips Exeter Academy would give Robert a classical eastern education in languages, mathematics, logic, music, and other liberal arts and sciences useful for an up-and-coming New England gentleman. Robert would later remember the place fondly: "I look back upon my year at Exeter as the most profitable one of my life."[5]

The Robert Visit—New Hampshire

Lincoln traveled by train from Providence to Boston that leap day morning and grabbed a bit of lunch before walking crosstown to the Boston and Maine station at Haymarket Square. This time he continued to Exeter, where he was met on the platform by three emissaries of the Dover Republican Committee. George W. Benn, chairman of that committee, hearing that Lincoln was in the Northeast and working his way to Exeter, had written to "Lincoln, son of A. Lincoln" (aka Robert) asking if his father could "deliver an address upon political topics before the citizens of [Dover] previous to our State election." Robert responded that his father was in Providence and that he would present the request when his father arrived. Before he could do that the Dover emissaries had already accosted Lincoln at the railway station. Suddenly, Lincoln's visit to Robert would include speeches in Concord and Manchester the next day, then Dover and Exeter on subsequent days.[6]

While Lincoln was happy to accommodate New Hampshire Republicans, the unexpected speeches threw off the plans he had previously made to speak in Connecticut. He immediately dashed off a letter to John Candee pleading that "they have got me into such trouble here, that I must postpone your Connecticut meetings," tersely ordering Candee to "fix them as follows." The Hartford speech scheduled for March 2 was moved to March 5, with Meriden and New Haven on the following two days. As we will see, these last two would flip and three additional speeches would be added to Lincoln's schedule.[7]

After spending the night with Robert in Exeter, the next day Lincoln took the train to Concord, the state's capital. Robert went along for the ride, joined by his friend George Latham. Latham also had failed his Harvard entrance exams and was attending Phillips Exeter. The following year when Robert successfully passed and entered Harvard, Latham failed for a second time, prompting a consolatory letter from Lincoln urging him to "let no feeling of discouragement prey upon you, and in the end you are sure to succeed."[8] The two boys (neither had yet turned seventeen) joined Lincoln as he took the trains to the Concord and Manchester speeches, then after skipping Dover to study, saw his final speech back in Exeter.

The heartfelt message to George Latham must have seemed strange to Robert, who had not spent much time with his father growing up and always carried a mix of disconnect and ardor. Lincoln was often away campaigning for other Whigs and serving his term in Congress. Even when he was "home" practicing law, he was usually at the office all day, plus riding the 8th District circuit half the year, three months in the spring and three months in the fall. Robert later wrote a friend that "During my childhood and early youth he was almost constantly away from home, attending court or making political speeches."[9] Still, Lincoln treated Robert (whom he called Bob) with a combination of love and laxity, letting him and the other children run rampant in the office he shared with William Herndon. While Robert would travel extensively with his mother both as a child and as an adult, these train trips to cities outside Exeter were one of the few times the son spent meaningful time with his father. Lincoln was supportive of Robert even with the disappointment stemming from his failure to enter Harvard. And, of course, he paid his son's costs at Exeter (and later, Harvard). Phillips charged $24 a year for tuition (not including books and other expenses), to which Lincoln added $2 a week for room and board at Mrs. J. B. Clark's home and monthly spending money totaling around $150 for the partial year Robert was in Exeter.[10]

My previous trip in Concord occurred around 2011 to visit family. I sat on the steps of the Capitol building and enjoyed the warm sunny day before meeting my brother for dinner at a local Mexican restaurant whose name I do not recall but had both good food and great music. When I revisited the Capitol on the road trip for this book, I realized the Merrimack River passes only a stone's throw from the front steps. Civil War buffs have heard of the Merrimack (sometimes spelled Merrimac) because the river gave its name to the famous ironclad that the Confederate navy called the CSS *Virginia* after building on the hull of the original sailing/steam frigate USS *Merrimack* captured early in the war. The *Virginia*—which everyone in the North still called the *Merrimack*—battled the Union ironclad *Monitor* in the Battle of Hampton Roads, Virginia. The clash ended in a draw and neither ship fought another battle, but the advent of ironclad ships was upon us, and the wooden sailing gunships were quickly phased out.

Like most statehouses, the New Hampshire Capitol stands above the surrounding buildings and is capped by a golden dome. Completed in 1819, this was the actual statehouse that Lincoln had seen on his visit in 1860, a typical Greek Revival building constructed with massive granite blocks; a small portico supported by Doric columns graces the main entrance, which leads into an impressive Hall of Flags inspired by the Charles Bulfinch Massachusetts State House I saw in Boston. In all, there are over a hundred battle flags representing New Hampshire's contributions to the Civil War, Spanish-American War, World Wars I and II, and the Vietnam War. Inside the Capitol are the offices of the state's governor, the General Court, and the House and Senate chambers. It remains the oldest statehouse in America where the legislature still occupies its original chambers.

Going back outside I looked up at the golden eagle standing on the top of the dome. Lincoln would have seen the original gold-painted wooden war eagle during his visit. That eagle is now at the New Hampshire Historical Society a block northwest of the Capitol while a huge "element-proof" peace eagle was installed in 1957.

On the day of my visit, they were having a community event on the Capitol grounds, complete with balloons and face painting for the children and a local band. I worked my way around the crowd to check out the statuary, with Daniel Webster getting the most prominent spot. Most people (including myself) think about Webster as the influential Massachusetts senator, but he was born in Salisbury, New Hampshire, a short distance northwest of Concord. He attended preparatory school at Phillips Exeter Academy and then college at Dartmouth, New Hampshire's Ivy League representative. He later moved to Boston, served twice as a Massachusetts congressman (with Rufus Choate from my hometown of Ipswich serving in between) and twice as US secretary of state (oddly enough, for the successors of two Whig presidents who died after only short terms in office). As much as Massachusetts likes to lay claim to him, New Hampshire never forgot how important he was to their state. Other statues on the grounds include Franklin Pierce, the only New Hampshire native son to become president; a replica of the Liberty Bell; Senator John Parker Hale; and the newest addition, the "first teacher in

Statue of Daniel Webster in front of the New Hampshire Capitol, Concord, New Hampshire

space," astronaut/educator Christa McAuliffe, a Concord resident who died in the Space Shuttle *Challenger* disaster seconds after launch.

Robert and George Latham joined Lincoln in Exeter and the three made their way to Concord where Lincoln spoke that afternoon in Phenix Hall. That building still stands. Today the lower level has a sandwich shop, a handcrafted furniture shop, and the offices of the League of Craftsmen. The building has renovations underway, with plans for a vibrant event venue like what existed when Lincoln spoke. When I was there, signs saying, "Black Lives Matter," "Stop Asian Hate," and "Climate Can't Wait" could be seen in the second-floor windows. My day in Concord had beautiful, sunny spring weather—as evidenced by the celebration going on in front of the Capitol—but a heavy rain pelted Lincoln and the two boys as they made their way to the Phenix.

Lincoln's speech continued the Cooper Union themes, although in much shortened form. He spoke for only half an hour before rushing to catch the train to Manchester, where he gave a much longer speech that evening to an "immense gathering" at Smyth Hall. One point the local newspaper claimed he emphasized was the answer to the question, "What will satisfy the demands of the South upon the subject of slavery?" This was an important point and one that continued to demonstrate the South's uncompromising hostility to even the minor restriction of slavery's expansion. Lincoln and the Republican Party had repeatedly insisted that their goal was simply to restrict the expansion of slavery into the federal territories, not to touch the institution in states where it already existed. This was completely in line with the framers' intentions, as Lincoln so diligently documented at Cooper Union. Sure, Republicans presumed that someday slavery would die under the weight of its own immorality and bad policy, but the continuation of slavery in Southern states was entirely up to them. The federal government would do nothing to ban the South's right to enslave other people within their borders. But even that did not satisfy the South.

No, said Lincoln, to satisfy the South "we must not only let them alone, but we must, somehow, convince them that we do let them alone." This was no easy task. After all, the party had been trying to convince the South from the beginning that they had no intention of forcing the abolition of slavery. As we have seen in the century and a half since the Civil War, entrenched forces are prone to create scenarios that reinforce fears and conspiracies, which further help them rationalize their desire to continue discriminating against other Americans. Lincoln recognized this. With respect to slavery, he noted, the only way to convince the slave powers was for his more progressive Republican Party—and all the Northern free states—to "cease to call slavery *wrong*, and join them in calling it *right*." And this could not be done merely by saying it, it "must be done in *acts* as well as in *words*. Silence will not be tolerated—we must place ourselves avowedly with them."[11]

But what acts would suffice?

> *Suppressing all declarations that slavery is wrong, whether made in politics, in presses, in pulpits, or in private. We must arrest and return their fugitive slaves with greedy pleasure. We must pull down our Free State constitutions. The whole atmosphere must be disinfected from all taint of opposition to slavery, before they will cease to believe that all their troubles proceed from us.*

In other words, the warning he gave in his "House Divided" speech must go unheeded. Free states must no longer be free. We must become not all free, but all slave. We must turn our backs on the principles on which the nation was founded. No, he argued, we cannot do that.

He did, once again, offer concessions to the South. "Wrong as we think slavery is, we can yet afford to let it alone where it is, because that much is due to the necessity arising from its actual presence in the nation." But, he emphasized, we cannot abide it spreading into the territories.[12]

I visited the only memorial of Lincoln in Manchester, a statue gracing the courtyard outside Central High School. That large, seated bronze was sculpted by John Rogers, who is much more famous for his series of inexpensive plaster cast groupings, including the *Council of War* statue I have seen many times in the Smithsonian American Art Museum in Washington, DC. Robert considered *Council of War* to be the most lifelike portrait of his father in sculpture. After checking out the statue I followed Lincoln to Dover, where he went after dropping the two boys

The Robert Visit—New Hampshire

off in Exeter. The train from Manchester had first gone south, switching engines in Lawrence, Massachusetts, before heading back into New Hampshire. Writing to his wife, Lincoln noted that Lawrence was "the place of the Pemberton Mill tragedy." A five-story mill had collapsed there several weeks before, burying many of the workers. Then a fire broke out as rescue operations were underway and killed many of those still imprisoned in the rubble. Final casualties were between 88 and 145 dead and another 166 injured.[13] No doubt Lincoln had this on his mind as he traveled throughout New England. He would refer to factory working conditions when he got to Connecticut.

Lincoln spoke to a large crowd in Dover's City Hall in the evening, finally following through on the promise he made when first arriving in New Hampshire. The Dover *Inquirer* reported that he "spoke nearly two hours and we believe he would have held his audience had he spoken all night."[14] According to observers, he had some notes with him but did not ever refer to them, having given versions of the speech so many times now that he knew his main points by heart. After finishing, he retired to the nearby home of George Mathewson, now called the Lincoln House. Given the opportunity, Lincoln happily compared his height (6'4") to Dover natives Richard Ross (6'2") and Sheriff Edward Barnard, who at 6'7" bragged for the rest of his life that he was "a bigger man than Abraham Lincoln."[15]

The enthusiastic response to his speech in Dover equaled his other stops, and as usual, Lincoln ended with his powerful reminder that Republicans must push through the slander and lies of the conservative South: "Let us have faith that right makes might!"

There was one more stop I wanted to make while in Dover. Remember back at the Capitol building in Concord there was an impressive statue of John Parker Hale? Hale lived most of his life and died in Dover. Following my quirky GPS I was able to locate his house on Central Avenue. The red brick Federal style home is paired with the Annie E. Woodman house next door. Set back between them is the William Damm Garrison house, a small building that with the two residences now houses the Woodman Institute, a museum dedicated to "advance and develop passion for history, science, and the arts." Given Lincoln's strong support for science and technology, I suspect he would have approved.[16] Hale has a magnificent statue in front of the Capitol in Concord, and his portrait hangs next to one of Abraham Lincoln in the chambers of the New Hampshire House of Representatives.

According to journalist Benjamin Perley Poore (one of the Massachusetts men visiting Lincoln in the White House with Nathaniel Hawthorne, as well as later writing *The Conspiracy Trial for the Murder of Abraham Lincoln*), Hale "never failed to command attention." Perhaps not surprising given Hale's independent streak (he changed parties four or five times) and his feverish antislavery and anti-Texas annexation sentiments. It also is not surprising that Lincoln came to rely on him as a Senate ally during the Civil War or that Lincoln appointed him in early 1865 as the nation's minister to Spain. On the fateful morning of April 14, 1865, Hale visited Lincoln at the White House to discuss his appointment. But here is what makes all this intriguing—Hale's daughter, Lucy Lambert Hale, had secretly become engaged to an actor named John Wilkes Booth. Lucy had arranged for Booth to be present on the platform behind Lincoln for his second inaugural address. Within hours after Hale's meeting with Lincoln, Booth would sneak into Ford's Theatre where the Lincolns were watching a comedic play called *Our American Cousin* and fatally shoot the president. When Booth was caught after twelve days on the run, he carried a photograph of Lucy Hale on his person (along with photos of other young women). There is no evidence that Lucy was aware of Booth's plans, and she did eventually marry William E. Chandler, another New Hampshire senator, but the proximity of John P. Hale to all this action is more than a little unnerving.

Lincoln was not finished with his speechifying in New Hampshire. Taking the short train ride back to Exeter late Saturday morning, he checked on Robert and George and felt confident they had properly attended to their studies. That night he gave his fourth speech in the Granite State at Exeter Town Hall, with many of Robert's classmates in attendance to get a gander at "Bob's father." To get a sense of what they thought of Lincoln I spoke with Ron Soodalter, an independent scholar and colleague of mine on the board of the Abraham Lincoln Institute. He told me Robert's elitist friends were not initially impressed. One of them remembered that Lincoln was "tall, lank, awkward; dressed in a loose, ill-fitting, black frock coat, with black trousers, ill-fitting, and somewhat baggy in the knees." They made fun of Lincoln's legs, so long that he "twisted them about under the chair to get them out of the way." Another friend whispered, "Don't you feel kind of sorry for Bob?" One of the girls whined that "Isn't it too bad Bob's got such a homely father."

Exeter Town Hall where Lincoln spoke in 1860, Exeter, New Hampshire

That impression was consistent with other observers of Lincoln when he rose to speak. He often seemed ungainly and unsure what to do with his long arms and legs. His high-pitched voice took people by surprise. And yet, this initial underestimation quickly faded as Lincoln got into his speech. The same student who disparaged Lincoln's looks noted that "Not ten minutes had passed before his uncouth appearance was absolutely forgotten." As Soodalter notes, "there was no more pity for our friend Bob; we were proud of his father," adding that shaking Lincoln's hand after the speech "was one of the greatest privileges of my life."[17]

Before leaving Exeter, I looked more around the town. The Town Hall where Lincoln spoke still exists, a beautiful building facing a gazebo in the middle of an intersection. Outside is a wayside marker touting Lincoln's visit. The Phillips Exeter Academy campus dominates one section of town, its Academy Building and Abbot Hall (which Lincoln would have seen) center the 147 buildings on seven hundred acres. Robert, usually reticent to provide documents and photos, gifted a portrait of his father and two autographed letters to his alma mater in 1909.[18] Not far away is the Squamscott Hotel (later called the Major Blake Hotel) where Lincoln likely stayed for his three nights in Exeter.[19] I was also drawn to a statue in a small park for World War I hero General Steven Gale, mainly because it was a creation of sculptor Daniel Chester French, who lived in Exeter for a time. I was able to find the house where French lived for many years at 34 Court Street.

Following Lincoln's whirlwind tour of the area, Robert, that is, Bob, had yet another full day to spend with his father as the next day was Sunday. "Today is Sunday morning," Lincoln wrote to his wife on March 4, "and according to Bob's orders, I am to go to church once today."[20] But the day off from speaking was not entirely a day of rest. Lincoln had received requests for even more speaking events, many of which he turned down. He wrote to Isaac Pomeroy that he could not possibly give a speech in Newark, New Jersey. "I have already spoken five times, and am engaged to speak five more," he wrote. He went on to say he was also "declining invitations to go to Philadelphia, Reading, and Pittsburgh" because he was committed to helping local candidates in the spring elections in New England. He also wrote to James Briggs, the one who had brought him to Cooper Union, to beg that Briggs make no additional arrangements to detain him further. He was "worn down" and in desperate need to return to his home in Illinois. A few days later he wrote again to Briggs, reminding him he was overbooked and could Briggs "please try to get Mr. Greeley or Gen. Nye, or some good man, to go speak at Keene, N.H."[21]

At this point in his trip, Lincoln was showing the strain from what was becoming a much bigger expedition than he had imagined. Expecting to speak at Cooper Union and then spend a few days with Robert, instead he had been giving speeches nonstop. He was not finished. In his letter to Mary, he wrote that "tomorrow I bid farewell to the boys, go to Hartford, Conn. and speak there in the evening; Tuesday at Meriden, Wednesday at New-Haven—and Thursday at Woonsocket R.I." But he promised her, "Then I start home, and think I will not stop," although he might be delayed in New York City "an hour or two." He was wrong, as he would find himself also speaking in Norwich and Bridgeport before finally getting to New York, then stuck there on Sunday before finally starting home on Monday, over a week after he wrote his letter. Wearily, he wrote:

I have been unable to escape this toil. If I had foreseen it, I think I would not have come East at all.

While he thought his speech in New York "went off passably well," he was finding it difficult to "make nine others, before reading audiences, who have already seen all my ideas in print." Whether he was being disingenuous or truly in angst is somewhat debatable. Given the enthusiasm of the audiences and the many requests for additional speeches, it is hard to believe that Lincoln was not thinking about his chances for the Republican nomination. His appearances at the various venues were often accompanied by voluminous crowds and bands escorting him to and from the halls. Now he was headed for Hartford, where another nascent organization would give him a wake-up call.

Chapter Eleven

The Bedful of Snakes—Central Connecticut

By the time Lincoln made it to Hartford, Connecticut, he was undoubtedly tired of repeating the same old Cooper Union catalog of how the "fathers who framed the Government under which we live" had cast various votes intended to put slavery on a path toward its ultimate extinction. He dropped the vote-counting aspects of the speech and simply repeated that key phrase as a sort of shorthand—five times in his New Haven speech alone—and expanded the speech to include more informal anecdotes. He also addressed a new issue that gave him a chance to rebut a common slave power talking point and define how Northern workers were able to better their condition, an opportunity enslaved men in the South did not have. And if that was not enough, he was the first to be exposed to a new, and soon to be huge, force that promoted the Republican Party as the election season got underway.

Lincoln left Exeter by train on Monday morning, March 5, arriving in Hartford that afternoon and speaking at City Hall that evening. The next six days followed the same pattern, rushing from one city to the next and giving speeches that ran two hours or more at each location. Reports of his speeches in Providence and New Hampshire, plus Cooper Union itself, had been reprinted in the major New England papers along the way, which was why he was generally greeted by large and enthusiastic crowds at each stop.[1]

As usual he was invited not so much for his own benefit but to fire up the crowds to vote for the local politician in need. In Hartford, that was the incumbent governor William A. Buckingham. Buckingham had served many years as mayor of Norwich, where Lincoln would speak in a few days, and had first been elected governor in 1858. Like Massachusetts, Connecticut had gubernatorial elections annually, and Buckingham was up for his third term. How much Lincoln's presence helped is hard to determine—Buckingham was reelected by only 538 votes over another previous governor, Thomas H. Seymour—and reelected yearly through 1865, which was fortuitous for Lincoln as Buckingham was a strong war governor and Seymour was a Peace Democrat willing to give up the Union to end the war.[2]

I have passed through Hartford a hundred times on road trips between my homes in New Jersey and then Washington, DC, and my family home in Massachusetts. Years ago, I worked with a client there, but I had never spent significant time visiting. Not long before I started this project, Hartford created the Lincoln Financial Sculpture Walk at Riverfront, a mile long section of the Connecticut River filled with parks and sixteen statues related to Lincoln on both sides of the river. The sculptures run the gamut from recognizable figures of Lincoln to more abstract designs. There is even a huge bronze Tom Turkey representing Lincoln's supposed first presidential pardon of the Thanksgiving delicacy. Beautifully warm sunny weather gave me the opportunity to check out all the statues, with my two favorites being the first and the last I saw, each anchoring their side of the river.

Lincoln Meets Stowe by sculptor Bruno Lucchesi is a half-size bronze sculpture topping an iron stand. It commemorates the 1862 meeting of Abraham Lincoln and Hartford author Harriet Beecher Stowe in the White House. The meeting occurred, but the story that Lincoln purportedly quipped upon meeting her, "So you're the little lady who started this big war" is probably apocryphal. If he said it, he was referring to her 1852 novel, *Uncle Tom's Cabin; or, Life Among the Lowly*, whose vivid depiction of the realities of slavery sold over 300,000 copies in its first year and helped drive abolitionist sentiment in the North and paranoid backlash in the South. While the Fugitive Slave Act of 1850 clearly outraged the

Statue on Riverfront of Lincoln greeting Harriet Beecher Stowe, Hartford, Connecticut

Northern political elite, Stowe's book helped motivate the growing middle class.[3] While in the city I dropped by the Stowe family home, next door to the Mark Twain house.

Each of the artworks on the sculpture walk had its own mystique and message, although some required careful reading of the accompanying markers to understand. The flat rocks in a metal stand signified equality, for example, while the deep meaning of a mosaic became clear only after reading that it depicts secession, with its cryptic stars and stripes and blocks splitting apart. One of the most beautiful statues was a multi-figure sculpture called *Emancipation* on the bridge connecting the two sides. But my other favorite was near the end of the walk, called *A Welcome Conversation*. A bronze Lincoln sits on a large rock, his face animated and arms outstretched in conversation with an unseen companion, complete with an empty rock for them to join him. I admit that I did exactly that, posing as if deep in discussion of the end of slavery or listening to Lincoln telling one of his Aesopian stories.[4]

Leaving the sculpture walk I took a quick stroll around Bushnell Park, an expansive urban oasis less than a mile from the river. Walking around the Lily Pond I dodged geese and a great blue heron to see a statue of Horace Wells, a dentist often credited with pioneering the use of anesthesia in medicine. I suspect he had nitrous oxide parties because he became rather erratic in his business and personal practices before leaving his wife and son to move to New York, where he became addicted to chloroform and was arrested for throwing sulfuric acid at two prostitutes on his thirty-third birthday. Three days later he slit his own femoral artery to end his life. On a less macabre note, the park also includes Connecticut's immense State Capitol complete with a golden dome. At the time of Lincoln's visit he would have seen the Old State House, still in existence a short walk away and open for tours. Bushnell Park also has a towering Soldiers and Sailors Memorial Arch dedicated to the four thousand Hartford citizens who served in the Civil War, four hundred of which died for the Union cause. Completed in 1886, it is the first permanent memorial arch built in America.

Lincoln was well known to have a repertoire of humorous stories always at the ready. On his 1848 New England tour the audiences expected, and largely got, sharp quips and interesting tales. Researcher Richard Carwardine examined Lincoln's humor and noted that by the time of his 1860 New England tour he largely refrained from humor for its own sake, though he continued to use parables as a form of communication.[5] Back when I was digging into the Cooper Union speech, I mentioned that I had always liked his turn of phrase in the highwayman story, where the attempted robber says, "Stand and deliver, or I shall kill you, and then you will be a murderer!" Lincoln seems to have dropped that story somewhere on his New England tour because it does not show up in the reports of his Hartford and New Haven speeches. Instead, he uses two other stories intended to show the logic of Republicans. There are two lengthy newspaper reports for Hartford and an even longer report for New Haven, all of which relate the stories with slightly different wording, so what follows is my attempt to consolidate and paraphrase the gist.[6]

The first involves venomous snakes, which we can equate with slavery. "If I saw a venomous snake crawling on the road," Lincoln relates, "any man would say I might seize the nearest stick and kill it." The path forward is clear. "But if that snake was in bed with my children," well, the proper course of action is more difficult to discern and "I must be more cautious. If I were to strike out at the snake, I might also strike the children," or worse, "arouse the reptile to bite the children." Adding, "Thus, by meddling with him here, I would do more hurt than good."

In this short parable, Lincoln succinctly captures the Republican position on slavery. The party was entirely focused on keeping slavery from extending into the western territories. Rather than let slavery spread, they would kill it before it spread. But slavery already existed in the Southern states. Lincoln and the Republicans acknowledged what historian James Oakes calls the federal consensus, the understanding that the federal government does not have the authority to ban slavery in states where it is present. "The manner in which our Constitution is framed constrains us from making war upon it where it already exists," Lincoln says. Rather than beat the venomous snake of slavery in bed with existing states, they must leave it alone. For slavery to end in Southern states, each state must take steps to rid it from their borders, just as each Northern state had done early in the nation's history.

The Bedful of Snakes—Central Connecticut

To carry the analogy further, Lincoln explained that it would be foolish to introduce slavery where it does not exist. "If there was a bed newly made up, to which the children were to be taken," Lincoln noted, "and it was proposed to take a batch of young snakes and put them there with them, I take it no man would say there was any question how I ought to decide!" There would be no hesitation what our policy should be: "If the question is to put it in bed with other children, I think we'd kill it."

The lesson from Lincoln's parable seemed to be both obvious and effective, as in both Hartford and New Haven the newspapers reported much cheering and laughter.

But Lincoln had another parable up his sleeve, at least in the Hartford speech. The timeline gets a bit muddled, but he said he met Mr. Cassius M. Clay "in the cars at New Haven one day last week," which would have meant they crossed paths on Lincoln's way from New York up to Providence. During that ride, "in front of us sat an old gentleman with an enormous wen upon his neck." For those not up on their medical anomalies, a wen is a large boil or cyst, often a sign of some significant underlying problem, and that if the man did not have it removed, "it will shorten his life materially." Lincoln noted that the "wen represents slavery; it bears the same relation to that man that slavery does to our country. That wen is a great evil; the man that bears it will say so. But he does not dare cut it out for fear of bleeding to death." Lincoln further questioned whether you would "engraft the seeds of that wen on the necks of sound and healthy men?" No, he argued, the man must endure it in hopes he would eventually see relief. "The wen represents slavery on the neck of this country," he added, making his point that slavery has already diseased the Southern states where it exists and must not be introduced into the territories.

Lincoln acknowledged that the stories are only applicable if men think slavery is wrong. Those who think it right "will look upon the venomous snake as a jewel, and call the wen an ornament." What was the path forward, he asked, answering that "I suppose the only way to get rid of it, is for those who think it wrong, to work together, and to vote no longer with the [conservative Democrats] who love it so well."[7]

After rereading the speeches, I recalled that Harold Holzer once told me that someone on the train from Hartford to New Haven had asked

Lincoln why he was not being more direct in attacking the slave powers. Richard Carwardine may have the answer. He pointed out that Lincoln used parables and humor to reach the common people. His aim was to communicate and convince, not to amuse. While some of his stories might seem trivial to the eastern elite, they spoke more directly to the masses of voters who would make a difference in the election.[8]

As Lincoln was riding with Governor Buckingham away from City Hall, he suddenly found his carriage surrounded by a group of uniform-clad marchers. Regarding the unannounced group with a mix of confusion and amusement, Lincoln had no clue that he had gained his first view of the Wide Awake movement that would quickly grow to several hundred thousand members in support of the Republican ticket—with him as the presidential nominee. The Wide Awakes would help propel Lincoln to the White House.

To find out more about this group, I reached out to Jon Grinspan, a Smithsonian National Museum of American History curator and author of a book named, appropriately enough, *Wide Awake*. Grinspan agreed to meet with me on his work break at the Smithsonian. I had visited the American History museum many times, in part because an entire house from my hometown of Ipswich stands as the exhibit *Within These Walls*. Once located at 16 Elm Street, the house was moved here in 1963 and displayed such that visitors can look in the various rooms and experience the respective lives of five residents over the years. I even had a chance to watch a live performance of the play by the same name written by Ipswich playwright, actor, and director J. T. Turner. Over a cup of coffee, Grinspan told me that the Wide Awakes became one of the most consequential political organizations in American history even though they started accidentally and as the result of a theft. A nineteen-year-old textile store clerk named Edgar Yergason was excited by the forthcoming election campaign and supported Governor Buckingham's reelection. One day he noticed the store across the street had several oil-based torches they were refilling, so in a moment of questionable decision-making, he stole one. Bringing it back to his own shop he discovered a slick of oil staining his new coat. While his coworkers laughed at him, Yergason grabbed a roll

Wide Awake exhibit at the Connecticut Museum of History and Culture, Hartford, Connecticut

of waterproof black cambric and fashioned himself a cape to protect his clothes. Soon the other clerks did the same.⁹

Meanwhile, Cassius Marcellus Clay, the same Kentucky abolitionist politician who Lincoln had discussed wens with on the cars from New Haven, paraded by trailing 1,500 rowdy supporters, having just given an impassioned speech to promote Buckingham's candidacy. Seizing the opportunity, Yergason and the other clerks joined the parade with torches and capes catching the eye of other participants, including an editor for the *Hartford Courant*, who was so impressed he wrote that this Republican Party was finally "Wide Awake." The name stuck and many others showed interest in joining, so they formally organized and decided to go with the *Courant*'s idea and call themselves Wide Awakes.

So where does Lincoln come into this? According to Grinspan, the now fifty or more members had augmented their capes with soldier's caps, and each carried an oil lamp on a long wooden staff. The day after the group officially formed, they went out to support the latest politician speaking on Buckingham's behalf. This time it was Abraham Lincoln. It was this large group of young men wearing a semblance of a uniform carrying torches that surrounded the Buckingham and Lincoln carriage. The men did not say anything, they simply formed an escort and marched Lincoln back to his lodgings. They were so unassuming that Lincoln had no idea how important they would be to his own presidential campaign.

I asked Grinspan just how important that was for the Republican Party. The Wide Awakes "brought enthusiasm and rallied voters," he told me. Buckingham won reelection in Connecticut by only a few votes in early April, but the Wide Awake movement grew exponentially over the next few months. Yergason and his group became the "Hartford Originals" as more chapters split off in Hartford, then Waterbury, then New Haven, then New London, then into Bristol, Rhode Island, Massachusetts, and nationwide (at least in the North).

So how much did Lincoln interact with the Wide Awakes? According to Grinspan, Lincoln seems to have kept them at arm's length. That is not surprising given that the custom of the day was that presidential candidates did not campaign for themselves. Instead, surrogates would speak on their behalf. Later, when Wide Awakes got to Illinois, they swarmed Lincoln's house persuading, or perhaps coercing, him to join their rally. They did the same for Carl Schurz and other surrogates, essentially pressuring them to actively argue against slavery. Even vice presidential nominee Hannibal Hamlin started marching at the head of Wide Awake companies. After the election Lincoln suggested their service was done and strongly discouraged them from coming to Washington to act as a bodyguard, something they had proposed but Lincoln felt was overly antagonistic. Interestingly, Grinspan told me that Robert Lincoln enlisted in the Exeter Wide Awake club.[10]

Grinspan hooked me up with the Connecticut Museum of Culture and History, so while in Hartford I decided to stop by to see the exhibit he helped them develop. I was able to attend a special exhibit talk led by Christina Rewinski and trade emails with Clare Nelson, Sierra Dixon, and Natalie Belanger, all of whom helped me better understand the role Wide Awakes played in the election.

My last stop in Hartford connected the dots from the writers of Concord, Massachusetts, I discussed back in the 1848 tour. Harriet Beecher Stowe lived in Hartford for the last twenty-three years of her life, which is why there is a statue on the Riverfront of her greeting Lincoln. Like the writers from Concord, her *Uncle Tom's Cabin* helped stimulate abolitionist fever in New England. But first I was heading next door to the home of Mark Twain, born Samuel Clemens. Lincoln never met Mark Twain but there are interesting connections. The amateur astronomy buff Lincoln may even have been looking up at the sky during the Leonid meteor showers in 1835 as Twain was born in Hannibal, Missouri. In 1859, Lincoln rode the Hannibal and St. Joseph Railroad to give a speech in Council Bluffs, Iowa, the same railroad incorporated in the office of Mark Twain's father thirteen years before. Both Twain and Lincoln had worked as steamboat pilots, Lincoln on the *Talisman* and Twain writing about his experiences in *Life on the Mississippi*.

The Mark Twain house is a pleasure to visit for writers. The American High Gothic style house with twenty-five rooms resembles, as one biographer put it, "part steamboat, part medieval fortress and part cuckoo clock."[11] I especially liked the top floor room with his tiny writing table crammed into the corner while the nearby large desk went mostly unused because it looked out onto the billiard table that was too much of a distraction.

Lincoln would not have read any of Mark Twain's stories (his first, "The Celebrated Jumping Frog of Calaveras County," was published in 1865, about seven months after Lincoln's assassination). But Twain says his humorous writing style was strongly influenced by another pen-named humorist, Artemus Ward (born Charles Farrar Browne), and the "Jumping Frog" story was published in the *New York Saturday Press* only because he finished it too late to be included in a book Artemus Ward was compiling. This is the same Artemus Ward that Abraham Lincoln so often read to break the tensions of the Civil War. Ward's humor so entranced Lincoln that on September 22, 1862, he read snippets from one of Ward's books to his Cabinet secretaries before settling into the business of the day—the first reading of the preliminary Emancipation Proclamation.

Mark Twain's piloting job ended when the Civil War started, as much of the Mississippi River became part of the war zone. So, what is a writer/riverboatman to do? While it stayed in the Union, Twain's birth state of Missouri was a slave state, so Twain decided to join the Confederate army, if only half-heartedly. His unpaid service lasted only two weeks in 1861 before disbanding. He then left for Nevada to work for his older brother, out of harm's way for the rest of the war, though his brief service for the Confederacy did give him material for another of his humorous sketches, *The Private History of a Campaign That Failed*. Later, Mark Twain published the memoirs of Civil War hero and president, Ulysses S. Grant.

Like Lincoln, Mark Twain was fascinated by science and technology. Whereas Lincoln is the only president with a patent, Twain had three patents of his own: a type of alternative to suspenders, a history trivia game, and a self-pasting scrapbook. Lincoln and Twain would have gotten along well if they had ever met.

Following Lincoln, I was on to New Haven, home then of Yale College, which would award the first PhD in the United States soon after Lincoln's 1861 inauguration.[12] Like Brown, Harvard, and all the Ivies, Yale had some ties to early slavery. In 2017, Yale renamed Calhoun College, which was named after South Carolina's John C. Calhoun—an alumnus, former US vice president, US senator, US secretary of state, US secretary of war, and blatant white supremacist known for arguing that slavery was not only not a necessary evil but a "positive good." That college is now called Hopper College after Grace Murray Hopper, who received a PhD in mathematics and mathematical physics at Yale before becoming a trailblazing computer scientist and culminating a forty-five-year career as a rear admiral in the US Navy.

My main target in New Haven was the Lincoln Oak Memorial in the expansive New Haven Green surrounded by the Yale campus. On this pleasant day the campus was full of people, the vibrancy of the young permeating the atmosphere much like the bands that enlivened Lincoln's every stop. A large oak that had witnessed Lincoln's arrival stood on the green until 2012's Superstorm Sandy toppled the venerable old tree.

Planted in its place now is an aspirational oak sapling, so small compared to the original that it took me fifteen minutes of searching to locate it. At its base is a stone marker noting that it was planted as part of the Founders' Day celebration of the city's 375th anniversary. I also visited the Grove Street Cemetery to see the grave of Eli Whitney, the inventor of the cotton gin. I previously discussed the importance of the cotton gin in expanding slavery, which Lincoln understood and talked about repeatedly. A graduate of Yale, Whitney also invented a process for the machine manufacture of interchangeable parts for muskets, which made him both wealthy and the nation's foremost arms supplier. His massive gravestone includes a scroll on the top and inscriptions extolling his contributions to the "useful science & arts" and that he was "in the social relations of life a model of excellence." I have not seen any evidence that Lincoln visited the grave, or even if he knew Whitney was buried there, but I suspect he would have appreciated the name Eli Whitney, for better and for worse.[13]

The grave of Eli Whitney, inventor of the cotton gin, at Grove Street Cemetery in New Haven, Connecticut

When Lincoln spoke at Union Hall that evening, he appeared to omit the Cassius Clay and wen story (thank goodness) but kept the venomous snakes and added an anecdote that he offered as "another specimen of bushwhacking" by the slave powers. Slaveholders had long argued that Northern free laborers were no better off than Southern enslaved labor. South Carolina senator James Henry Hammond embodied this line of thinking, arguing that the natural order of society is divided between the powerful wealthy and the "mudsill," whose place is to labor for the wealthy. Lincoln disagreed, repeatedly arguing that any "prudent, penniless beginner" could work his way into wealth, and that all men had the right to "better their condition."[14] The timing of Lincoln's tour gave him a perfect example to emphasize his point and counter Hammond's. Beginning on February 22, intentionally chosen because it was George Washington's birthday, about three thousand shoemakers in Lynn, Massachusetts, walked off their jobs. The strike quickly grew to about twenty thousand workers in factories across New England, which the slaveholders used as an example of how Northern workers were even worse off than enslaved workers (who at least were given food and shelter). Lincoln admitted he was not completely up to date on the details but rejected the Southern argument.

> *I am glad to see that a system of labor prevails in New England under which laborers CAN strike when they want to, where they are not obliged to work under all circumstances, and are not tied down and obliged to labor whether you pay them or not!*

He went further to say that "I like the system which lets a man quit when he wants to, and wish it might prevail everywhere." His main argument was that any man should have the opportunity to get wealthy—"I don't believe in a law to prevent a man from getting rich"—but he did want even "the humblest man an equal chance to get rich with everybody else."[15]

Certainly, this opportunity was not available to enslaved men, women, and children held throughout eternity in bondage. The shoemakers' strike ended in April with some pay increases and company recognition of some labor unions, but chattel slavery promised to enchain enslaved families forever. Alas, Lincoln did also appeal to white fears of competition, noting that if the western territories were kept free of slavery, they also would allow white settlers to "strike and go somewhere else, where you may not be degraded, nor have your family corrupted by forced rivalry with negro slaves." Merging this thought with his earlier venomous snake parable, he assured them "I want you to have a clean bed, and no snakes in it! Then you can better your condition."

Reiterating his main points, Lincoln argued that slavery was wrong, and the South would not be happy unless the North stopped calling it wrong and changed free state institutions to treat slavery as right. This challenged the regular fallacy of Southern exhortations of "states' rights." The only states' right they argued for was the right to enslave other Americans based on the color of their skin. Slave states were happy to have a federal government with massive power, for example the Fugitive Slave Law that federalized slave catching, as long as that power reinforced the idea that slavery was right. Slave states tried as hard as they could to void the states' rights of free states to bar slavery from their borders. Lincoln also emphasized that in the North, Black men were considered men, not property, where the South believed the opposite. He noted that Stephen A. Douglas "vilifies me personally and scolds me roundly for saying that the Declaration [of Independence] applies to all men, and that negroes are men." He went so far as to suggest that slave owners knew that slavery was wrong but only pretended it was right so they would not feel so bad about enslaving fellow Americans.

Lincoln had an impromptu meeting with Gideon Welles, editor of the *Evening Press*, who later commented that Lincoln "has been caricatured," but "is an effective speaker, because he is earnest, strong, honest, simple in style, and clear as a crystal in his logic."[16] As president, Lincoln would make Welles his secretary of the navy. But Lincoln had to rush to yet another speech, so he hopped aboard a special train that took him—and three hundred exuberant Republicans—to Meriden, a city about halfway between Hartford and New Haven.[17] I visited the current City Hall, where today there is a plaque commemorating Lincoln's speech.

The actual building that Lincoln spoke in was dedicated only two years before Lincoln's visit, complete with a speech by none other than the Reverend Henry Ward Beecher. Unfortunately, despite considerable expansion in the late 1800s, the building burned down in 1904 and was later rebuilt. Today there is also a tall obelisk to remember the Meriden sailors lost on the USS *Maine*.

Based on his letters of this time, Lincoln probably thought he had finished speaking in Connecticut. He had one more event in Woonsocket, Rhode Island, where he was headed next, after which he was clear to start the long trek home. Again, he would be wrong.

CHAPTER TWELVE

The Vice Presidential Abyss— Eastern Connecticut and Rhode Island

THE SPECIAL TRAIN THAT TOOK LINCOLN AND THE CROWD OF EXUBERant supporters from New Haven to Meriden also took him back to New Haven, where he spent the night. By 7:15 the next morning he was on yet another train toward Woonsocket with a stopover in New London. The Woonsocket speech had been arranged by Latimer Ballou and Edward Harris prior to Lincoln leaving Providence on his way to New Hampshire a week before. Because there were multiple railroads with frequent changes, Lincoln had about a three-hour layover in New London, Connecticut. Nehemiah Sperry of New Haven had telegraphed Julius W. Eggleston (father of the Percy Coe Eggleston who was one of the earliest sources of information on the trip), who belatedly rushed to the train station to meet Lincoln. Unfortunately, by the time he arrived, Lincoln had already begun walking into town on his own, cognizant of the limited time he had to get lunch before the next leg of the trip. Retracing his steps, Eggleston found Lincoln along the route and escorted him to the City Hotel. While Lincoln dined, Eggleston brought a few prominent Republicans out to meet him. Most likely they included Mayor J. N. Harris, former mayor Henry P. Haven, and others.[1]

Percy Coe Eggleston quotes Lincoln as lamenting during those impromptu meetings that he was "not much of a public speaker" and "cannot put on frills and fancy touches," as more erudite eastern speakers might do. Instead, he said his forte is the ability to "demonstrate the strength of our position by plain, logical argument." Eggleston does not cite any source of the quote, but it is consistent with Lincoln's clear, almost scientific analysis and presentation of the material. Eggleston also says that Lincoln passed through New London on his way back from Rhode Island to Norwich, Connecticut, where at the train station he took time to write an autograph for Sarah, the daughter of a respected citizen familiarly known as "Uncle Peter."[2]

Today, New London is best known as a seaport and location of the US Coast Guard Academy. Across the Thames River is Groton, the home of General Dynamics and the Naval Submarine Base. Submarines were part of Lincoln's life too, both the unsuccessful Union submarine *Alligator* and the havoc caused by the Confederate submarine *Hunley*, which was the first to sink a Union vessel before itself sank (ironically, there were more men lost on the *Hunley* than the USS *Housatonic* that it sunk). In any case, after lunch, Lincoln took the New London train to Providence, then from there on to Woonsocket, about fifteen miles north of Providence and just short of the Massachusetts border.

While Lincoln's trip to Woonsocket was somewhat roundabout, my own road trip took advantage of Lincoln-related stops along the way. First up was meeting with one of today's foremost Abraham Lincoln scholars. Not far from New London is Mystic, home of Mystic Pizza (the actual restaurant on which the movie was based), Mystic Seaport (shops and ships), and Mystic Aquarium (one of sixty-one public aquariums I have visited around the world). More importantly, it is the home of Michael Burlingame.

Burlingame taught in the history department of Connecticut College in New London for more than three decades before "retiring" to join the faculty of the University of Illinois, Springfield, where he has been for the last sixteen years. He has written or edited nearly twenty books about Lincoln, including the massive, two-volume, green-covered, *Abraham Lincoln: A Life* he affectionately calls "The Green Monster" because of the boxed set's resemblance to the venerated left field wall of Fenway Park, home of the Boston Red Sox. I have known Burlingame for many years and have the pleasure of serving with him on the Abraham Lincoln Institute board. He agreed to sit down to chat about all things Lincoln.

The Vice Presidential Abyss—Eastern Connecticut and Rhode Island

Picking me up at my hotel, we drove into downtown Mystic to feast at an energetic Italian restaurant called Bravo Bravo. Over a sumptuous plate of pappardelle pasta and glass of white wine, our conversation meandered around our respective backgrounds, book projects, and Lincoln's two trips into New England, much of which stimulated the further digging into resources and topics that appear in this book. Besides the wellspring of knowledge that he graciously shared, he has a reputation for his unbelievable ability to locate and evaluate some of the most obscure sources of information about Lincoln from small libraries and private collections.

With a head full of Lincoln information and a belly full of pasta, I drove up the I-95 highway (Dwight D. Eisenhower's version of the internal improvement programs that Lincoln had so strongly supported) on my way to Woonsocket. I made two stops along the way.

Cranston was once known as Pawtuxet, like the river that runs through it. My main reason for stopping here was to check out the Lincoln statue in Roger Williams Park. After searching for it in the gloomy fog of morning, passing the Museum of Natural History and Planetarium that Lincoln would have loved because of his interest in astronomy, I found the standing Lincoln on a hill overlooking a small traffic circle (or rotary, as we say in New England). Despite Lincoln using Providence as a hub for his travels in the area, this is the only full-size monument to Lincoln in Rhode Island. Sculpted by Gilbert Franklin, it was commissioned by wealthy jewelry manufacturer Henry W. Harvey in memory of his wife, Georgina. The rather unique inscription indicates Harvey's desire "to perpetuate the memory of Abraham Lincoln and to inculcate loyalty and patriotism in the minds of all those who come here for rest and relaxation."

Having paid homage, I hit the road again in search of Lincoln, the town, one of the few specifically named after Abraham Lincoln and not some other Lincoln (like Benjamin or Enoch). Originally settled in the 1600s, the area went through some cleavage and in 1871, just six years after Lincoln's assassination, the town split off from Smithfield and named itself after the fallen president. The small town, which today still only claims about 22,000 residents, was one of many dominated by textile mills running along the Blackstone River, and thus also dependent on slave-grown cotton prior to the Civil War.

The rationale for stopping here goes beyond the town's name. While researching the area for my trip, I came across an article announcing that a new painting was to be installed in the Lincoln municipal building, which houses the town offices, police department, and courtroom. With the fog still hanging close to the ground, I finally located the building on the long road leading into town and dropped in, much to the surprise of the two women staffing the main office. "Can I help you?" the first asked with a confused look on her face (they do not get a lot of out-of-towners dropping in), to which I responded, "Yes, I came to see . . ." (and pointing at the painting that jumped out at me as soon as I entered the room) . . . "that!" By all means, I was told, get a closer look. Which I did. The classical-style painting is by Eileen Mayhew, a Bristol-based portrait artist, who donated her portrait of Lincoln to the town in 2021. The portrait shows a bearded Lincoln sitting at a desk holding a document. In the lower corner Mayhew has painted "After John Denison Crocker, 2011." I did not recognize the name, but I would discover him, and another painting, later on this road trip.

The woman who had let me in to see the painting asked if I had seen the "other painting," to which she directed me down the hall. There, at the head of the town's courtroom, behind the judges' bench, was a full-length modern style portrait of Lincoln, this time standing, posed with one hand on a book and the other holding a rolled-up paper. On the front of the judges' bench was the town shield featuring a fleur-de-lis over a red cross with, appropriately, a large axe like what Lincoln had used so frequently on the frontier. To one side of the front wall there was another tribute to Lincoln, this one a small bronze-looking bust sitting on a wooden shelf that even David Wiegers and Scott Schroeder of the Lincoln Sculpture Map Project had not yet known about. Having grown up in a town even smaller than this, I most look forward to discovering places like Lincoln, Rhode Island, because they are so easily overlooked.

Abraham Lincoln was no longer traveling alone. According to former Rhode Island chief justice Frank Williams, at least four hundred people from the Providence area paid fifty cents each to crowd on the train to his destination. A "Du Dah" band provided entertainment on board and a raucous crowd escorted Lincoln to Harris Hall, named for

Modern painting of Abraham Lincoln in the Lincoln, Rhode Island, municipal building

Edward Harris, one of the men who had arranged for Lincoln's speech. Harris was among the wealthiest men in the state, a self-made man who owned four textile mills in Woonsocket specializing in woolen clothing. He had built the Harris Institute that housed Harris Hall, second only to Railroad Hall in Providence as the biggest auditorium in the state. Between 1,000 and 1,500 people jammed into the hall to hear Lincoln's speech despite the overcast, drizzly weather that matched my own visit to the city.

Lattimer Ballou introduced Lincoln with fanfare, saying that he was "the champion of freedom, and the friend of man," referring to the fame he achieved following his high-profile debates with Stephen A. Douglas. Lincoln's speech was barely covered in the press despite the earlier coverage of his time in New England, although his friendly home-state *Chicago Tribune* later reported that it was "one of his most powerful." He followed closely the modified Cooper Union speech he gave in New Haven, which would be his template for the rest of his time in New England. Following the speech, Eggleston has him going back to Providence but Holzer documents that he stayed overnight at Oakley, the name of Edward Harris's mansion in Woonsocket, leaving the next morning for Providence and change of trains to Norwich, Connecticut, via New London.

Before leaving Woonsocket, I tracked down the old city hall that is part of the remaining Harris Institute building not far from the train tracks. The old stone building included a bronze plaque noting that "Abraham Lincoln on March 8, 1860 Spoke Here in Harris Institute Hall" as part of his post–Cooper Union tour. It goes on to say that "This tour helped his party to win spring elections in New England and contributed to his election as president of the United States." There is even the famous "right makes might" quote from the Cooper Union address.

Following Lincoln's trail, I also visited Norwich, Lincoln's final stop in the eastern part of Connecticut, but as it turns out, not the last stop on his tour. Sitting on the confluence where the Yantic and Shetucket Rivers merge to form the Thames River, Norwich has embraced Lincoln's speech more than most places in New England. The City Hall (built in 1873 to replace the Town Hall in which Lincoln spoke) is one of the most beautiful city halls I saw on this trip, its red brick front and ornate filigreeing typical of Second Empire style. The mansard roof and corner clock tower and belfry overlook Union Square on a sloping hill. Inside the main entrance is a mini-museum featuring a drawing by a local artist, a bronze plaque with the Gettysburg Address, and a large painting under glass that looked familiar. To my surprise, this was the original John Denison Crocker on which Eileen Mayhew had based her painting, the one I saw back in Lincoln, Rhode Island.

The most eye-catching display in the mini-museum, however, is a large six-by-seven-foot, hand-painted silk banner featuring a beardless Lincoln (he did not grow the beard until later that year). The banner was hung at the Wauregan Hotel during his visit. Its text reads "No. 1 Red, White, and Blue, No. 1" over Lincoln's picture and "Norwich" underneath.

Banner in Norwich City Hall commemorating Lincoln's speech in 1860, Norwich, Connecticut

Axes splitting rails are painted to the sides. A circle of thirty-four stars, representing the states of the Union at the time, ring the olive branches that surround the portrait. Within the branches are the Latin words, *In Hoc Signo Vincemus* at the top and *Ubi Libertas, Ibi Patria* at the bottom, which the signage in Norwich translates roughly in context to "In this motto we trust . . . Where there is liberty, there is homeland." The fact that the banner is here is somewhat of a miracle. It disappeared after 1860 until it showed up at Edwin Nadeau's Auction Gallery in 1997. After finding out about it, the city of Norwich scrambled to raise funds to purchase the banner, which it did for $35,750 (including bidder's fee). A bit frayed after all these years, it was sent to the Textile Conservation Center in Lowell, Massachusetts. On January 24, 1999, the banner went on public display for the first time and today remains the centerpiece of the City Hall museum. Since the banner was originally hung at the Wauregan Hotel—where Lincoln stayed that night—I made sure to check out the building in downtown Norwich. After falling into disrepair and being condemned in the 1990s, the massive brick building has now been completely restored to its former glory and serves as an apartment building.[3]

Lincoln was escorted to Norwich Town Hall by the Buck Club, named after Governor Buckingham for his reelection campaign. As was now the norm, the hall was filled to capacity for Lincoln's speech, which again followed along the same lines as what he said in New Haven. At one point he had to stop when the one-hundred-person delegation from Danielson (up the road from Norwich) arrived.

By the time Lincoln left Norwich he must have been exhausted. He had one more stop in Connecticut, but he was also undoubtedly feeling some pressure from the Seward camp. There even seemed to be an effort to pigeonhole Lincoln into a vice presidential role, likely ensuring Seward the nomination.

The question of when Lincoln started thinking of himself for the Republican presidential nomination has been a topic of debate among scholars since 1860. Robert Lincoln in his later years liked to claim that his failure to pass the Harvard exams, and thus his year at Phillips Exeter Academy that spurred Lincoln's 1860 visit, "had made his father president." Robert suggested that Lincoln had not at all considered his own chances for the presidency until after this New England tour.

That claim hardly seems credible. After all, Lincoln had received 110 votes on the first ballot toward becoming vice president in 1856 when John C. Fremont became the first Republican presidential nominee. William Dayton of New Jersey had received 253 votes and ultimately ran away with the vice presidential nomination, but Lincoln's total was more than double the third-place competitor, Nathaniel P. Banks of Massachusetts, who at the time was Speaker of the US House of Representatives. Lincoln had also risen to national recognition for battling Stephen A. Douglas in the 1858 debates, which were widely reprinted in the newspapers and about to come out in book form at the behest of Lincoln himself. Clearly, the 1860 version of Lincoln was not as obscure as many people imagine.[4]

William Seward may have been getting concerned about the visibility Lincoln was receiving on his New England tour. While most of the people introducing Lincoln simply referred to him as the distinguished gentleman from Illinois, there was also a smattering of "our next vice presidential nominee" and even "presidential nominee." In Norwich, for example, the speaker immediately following Lincoln, Deniel P. Tyler, referred to Lincoln as a possible vice presidential nominee:

I care much as to who is to be the nominee for President but more for him who is to be nominated for Vice-President. Would it not, my friends, be "nuts" to us all to find out some day before long, that Stephen A. Douglas, when he goes into the senate chamber of the United States, should see the Vice-President's chair filled by one he so much fears and we and all good Republicans so deservedly esteem? That would be the long and short of the matter of the late Illinois election.

Mainly these introductions were hype to rile up the crowd—even those partisan papers that voiced approval of his speaking tour did not foresee Lincoln as the nominee—but there was at least an inkling that he was a possibility for one of the top roles.

At the beginning of this jaunt, right after the Cooper Union speech, one likely apocryphal story smells a lot like someone trying to get Lincoln out of the way. First reported by John W. Starr in his *Lincoln and the Railroads* published in 1927, the story goes that Erastus Corning, the president of the New York Central Railroad, was so impressed by Lincoln's Cooper Union speech that he offered him the job of general counsel of the railroad with a salary of $10,000 per year, more than three times his average income in the 1850s. Harold Holzer states that there is no evidence of this offer and rather doubts the credibility of the person relating it, James Merwin, a cousin of Corning and friend of Lincoln. Robert Lincoln, always mindful to protect his father's image, said he did "not for a moment believe there is any foundation for the statement."[5] I am also skeptical, but what makes it intriguing is that Corning had intensely lobbied Thurlow Weed when trying to get approval for the railroad consolidation from the state legislature. With Weed's influence, the legislature pushed through the consolidation, making Corning the railroad's first president and deeply indebted to Weed. Thurlow Weed was William Seward's closest political adviser and routinely protected Seward from his perceived enemies. While there is no hard evidence of any Seward influence on Corning to get Lincoln out of politics at Cooper Union, it is not entirely implausible.

Meanwhile, Seward was doing his own speechifying. Two days after Cooper Union, Seward stood up in the Senate chambers, ostensibly to talk about the proposed entry of Kansas into the United States as a free state, and delivered a speech officially titled "The State of the Country." Seward spent virtually no time specifically talking about Kansas other than to place it into the bigger history of the tug-of-war between free and slave states, which he referred to as Labor and Capital states, respectively; one focused on men laboring for themselves, the other on property laboring to provide capital to other men. As Seward was prone to do, he started off with a Victorian grandiosity of speech seemingly designed to express erudition. After a while he settled into merely long and windy, in comparison to Lincoln's more common language. Whether Seward read Lincoln's speech before composing his own is unknown but given the national press coverage it would have been hard to miss.

The Vice Presidential Abyss—Eastern Connecticut and Rhode Island

Seward's speech covered topics more broadly than Lincoln's Cooper Union address, but there were some common themes. Early on he reiterates what Lincoln had said (without attribution) about some believing that slavery is right while the Republican Party believed it was wrong. Whereas the labor (free) state "encourages and animates and invigorates the laborer," the capital (slave) state oppresses the laborer as nothing more than "capital of another man." Using the conceptual language that Lincoln had used, Seward then dives into what the "fathers of the Republic" believed and did. "They generally condemned the practice of slavery," Seward argued, "and hoped for its discontinuance," which they expressed in the Declaration of Independence, the Northwest Ordinance, and by intentionally avoiding the word in the Constitution. The fathers also agreed that "Congress may . . . prohibit the importation of persons after 1808." They also understood they could not abolish slavery where it existed but could bar it from entering the federal territories. All of this sounds a lot like what Lincoln said, although certainly not the detailed argument in which Lincoln presented it.

Having structured the beginning of his speech to address the actions of the fathers, Seward's next section spoke directly to the slave states, just as Lincoln had done. He refuted the accusation of sectionalism, just as Lincoln had done. He addressed accusations that Republicans were a party of "ulterior and secret designs," countering that the Republican Party was merely following the lead of the founders, again, just as Lincoln had done. Seward noted that the party favored a free labor system in which the laborer, "no matter how humble the occupation," was "politically the equal of his employer" and that had an opportunity to rise in economic status. Seward went on to discuss how the South wanted the North to censor themselves, to say slavery was not wrong. Like Lincoln, he addressed the accusation that John Brown was somehow working on behalf of the Republican Party.

Lincoln had ended his speeches in New York and New England with "Let us have faith that right makes might" and encouraged the Republicans in the North to do their duty. Seward's ending was less soaring, but he too argued that all will stand "unmoved, enduring, and immovable" in the right of freedom.

Detail of William Henry Seward's Senate Speech, February 29, 1860
DAVID J. KENT DETAIL OF PUBLIC DOMAIN DOCUMENT, LIBRARY OF CONGRESS

Lincoln's reaction to Seward's speech was perhaps not what one might have expected. Back in Manchester, New Hampshire, Governor Frederick Smyth met Lincoln at the train station and asked him what he thought about Seward's speech, which Lincoln had read in the papers on the train. "I am delighted with it," Lincoln replied, "That speech will make Mr. Seward the next president of the United States." Perhaps feeling the need to pump up their speaker, when introducing Lincoln that night Smyth boldly introduced Lincoln as the "next President of the United States." Later, Lincoln asked Smyth if he meant it, to which he replied that if Lincoln made the same impression at all his stops that he had made in Manchester, he undoubtedly would be nominated. Lincoln supposedly replied "No! no! that is impossible. Mr. Seward should and will receive the nomination. I do not believe that three states will vote for me in the convention."[6]

Again, I question whether this conversation took place, at least in the manner reported. Lincoln was a notorious vote counter. He had meticulously cataloged the electoral votes won and lost by John C. Fremont in the 1856 election and knew which states the Republican Party needed to capture in the fall. While he no doubt believed Seward was the presumptive nominee, he also knew which states Seward would have the most difficulty winning. It was this knowledge that led to his strategy of being "everyone's second choice" at the nominating convention to occur in May. The conversation with Smyth, which was reported by Eggleston with his usual lack of citation, sounds too much like the postelection revisionism all too common by everyone who had a passing interaction with Lincoln before he became famous, all wanting to enhance their own status by association.

What for sure did take place was that Seward's people went after Lincoln. When James Briggs had invited Lincoln to speak in New York, he wrote that they would pay him $200 for the speech, ostensibly still part of the lecture series they had created. Briggs noted it was the standard fee and Lincoln welcomed it to cover the costs of his expanding trip. Meanwhile, the *Chicago Press and Tribune*, a reliable Republican newspaper, began praising Lincoln's Cooper Union speech, to which the entitled Seward took offense. Seward supporters soon began forcefully promoting their candidate as the presumptive nominee. When they later found out that Lincoln had accepted a $200 speaker fee, they attacked him for charging "a price" for a political speech. As we see so often today, facts did not seem to have inhibited feigned outrage and personal attacks. The idea was to demean and dismiss Lincoln as a candidate, even though he had done nothing wrong and had significantly helped the Republican Party's chances in the eastern elections. The attacks were so vicious that Lincoln felt compelled to write a letter to Cornelius McNeill, the editor of the Middleport *Press*, denying it: "It is not true that I ever *charged* anything for a political speech in my life," then went on to explain what had actually happened. Having explained himself, he told McNeill that "I wish no explanation made to our enemies," because "what they want is a squabble and a fuss." So, go ahead and deny the accusation, but do not get pulled into the mud with the pigs.[7]

Meanwhile, Thurlow Weed was doing his part to promote Seward. The newspapers under his control neglected to report that Lincoln had left New York City and was touring New England. Rather than report on Lincoln's speeches, Weed's *Evening Journal* made sure to highlight any praise the New England papers were printing about Seward's

Senate speech. "The hour and the man are both come," one Vermont paper praised in religious tones, completely ignoring the presence of Lincoln in their neighboring state.[8] If Seward was not worried about Lincoln as a possible rival, his people certainly acted like they were.

He had reason to worry. While New England had been a reliable Whig and now Republican stronghold, many important New Englanders were getting anxious about Seward's electability. Fellow senator Hannibal Hamlin of Maine, a good friend of Seward's, expressed his reservations, as did another prominent Maine Republican James G. Blaine. When the nomination convention finally took place in May, New England representatives, assumed by Seward and Weed to be backing them, largely endorsed Lincoln instead.

By the time Lincoln returned to Illinois, a movement had begun among his friends to put forth his name as the Republican nominee. In a response to Lyman Trumbull's request, Lincoln did admit frankly, "the taste *is* in my mouth a little," although he thought that might disqualify him (as if Seward had not been openly angling for the nomination for a year). Still, he was open to the idea but also willing to serve in whatever capacity that helped the party's "common cause." Ever the vote counter, he then went through his analysis of the chances Seward and Bates and McLean had to win the largely Democratic state of Illinois, which Fremont had lost in 1856 and had to be won by Republicans to gain the presidency in 1860. Wary of being seen as campaigning, he ended the letter by begging Trumbull, "Let no eye but your own see this—not that there is anything wrong, or even ungenerous, in it; but that it would be misconstrued." That concern sounds familiar today as all it takes is one poorly phrased sound bite to become a disingenuous meme and destroy a candidate.[9]

It is unclear when the speech in Bridgeport, Connecticut was added to Lincoln's itinerary. He did not mention it (nor Norwich) in his letter to Mary from Exeter, nor did I see any letters after that. But go to Bridgeport he did, and given my own history with the city, his visit gives an opportunity for me to both reminisce and explore those who have sculpted Lincoln and the showman who entertained him.

Chapter Thirteen

The Sculptors and the Showman—Southwestern Connecticut

From Norwich, Lincoln was back on the train to New London, then yet another railroad through New Haven to Bridgeport, where he would give his last speech on this 1860 tour—and the last time he would visit New England.

On the train from Norwich, Lincoln apparently spoke with a local minister named John Gulliver, with whom he engaged in a soul-baring conversation. I say "apparently" because hundreds of people claim to have had conversations with Lincoln in which he revealed his deepest thoughts, something he was not prone to do even with his closest friends and colleagues. His own law partner, William Herndon, once said that "Lincoln never had a confidant, and therefore never unbosomed himself to others." While Herndon thought it likely that Gulliver and Lincoln chatted on the journey, he doubted Lincoln would reveal himself so frankly to a stranger. Still, Harold Holzer notes that Lincoln appears not to have corrected, or even responded to, the pre-publication account Gulliver sent him. There is no way to know if Lincoln even read it. By the time Gulliver published his article, Lincoln was the Republican nominee and deep into the presidential campaign.[1]

Gulliver claims that Lincoln remembered seeing him in the audience in Norwich and invited him to accompany him all the way to Bridgeport. Among the tidbits garnered was that an unnamed Yale professor of rhetoric had heard his earlier speech in New Haven and was so impressed that he "gave a lecture on it to his class the next day." Lincoln was astonished that his speech would receive "commendations from literary and learned men." Gulliver then offered an analysis of his own, telling Lincoln:

> *The clearness of your statements, Mr. Lincoln, the unanswerable style of your reasoning, and especially your illustrations, which were romance and pathos, and fun and logic all welded together.*

Lincoln supposedly told Gulliver that he had "been wishing for a long time to find someone who would make this analysis for me," adding: "It throws light on a subject which has been dark to me." Lincoln then went on to explain in detail how he developed his speaking style.[2]

I have to say that I am with Herndon in expressing my skepticism. Not only were there errors in the stories related by Gulliver, and the fact that Lincoln rarely revealed his history and innermost thoughts to even his close acquaintances, but I also find it hard to believe Lincoln was clueless about his own logical strengths and presentation skills. He had been a lawyer who was adept at convincing juries to find in his clients' favor and was a persuasive politician. This entire trip to New England was to reinforce the detailed reasoning and logic of the Cooper Union address, complete with his use of verbal illustrations and rhetorical highlights to nail home the key points. This is a topic that I discussed in depth in my previous book, so yes, I find it easier to believe that Gulliver extrapolated significantly, although admit that at least some elements probably stemmed from their conversation. After all, it was a long trip.

Bridgeport, Connecticut's largest city, grew quickly in the nineteenth century into an industrial, shipbuilding, and whaling powerhouse. It was a convenient stop for the railroads from New York City northward, and since 1883 has been the northern end of the Bridgeport–Port Jefferson Ferry on Long Island. It was also the home of P. T. Barnum.

I have some familiarity with Bridgeport, having earned my undergraduate degree at the university there many years ago. Not only was I eager to locate the hall Lincoln spoke in, but it was also a chance to visit the university I had not seen for decades.

The first trick was finding the location of Lincoln's speech. Lincoln had spoken in Washington Hall, which was an auditorium in the old Bridgeport City Hall and now called McLevy Hall. This was the city's largest venue, and local advertisements gave ample notice of his arrival. His reputation as a speaker had spread across the region because of the myriad speeches he had already given on this far-ranging swing across New England. Not surprisingly, McLevy Hall was packed to capacity for the event. Lincoln was described by a local newspaper as a "tall, bony, angular, big jointed figure with a towering head and very expressive countenance." Despite the kudos he had been receiving for nearly two weeks in New England, the focus still seemed to be on his awkward appearance, although to their credit, they added that he conveyed "intellectual power."[3] Surprisingly, they did not record the speech itself, perhaps because he was now doing a full two hours of the modified New Haven version of his original Cooper Union speech. Lincoln did receive what was now the ubiquitous standing ovation as he wrapped up his remarks.

McLevy Hall where Lincoln spoke, Bridgeport, Connecticut

McLevy Hall remains in the city and like all such ancient edifices has gone through a series of uses over the years. To find out more I checked in with Carolyn Ivanoff, a retired high school administrator, independent historian, frequent speaker on Civil War topics, and a first-person reenactor (including Clara Barton, the famous Civil War nurse and founder of the American Red Cross). The Civil War Trust once named her as "Teacher of the Year" and she is the author of *We Fought at Gettysburg*, detailing exploits of the 17th Connecticut Volunteer Infantry. She lives in Bridgeport and is a frequent contributor to the Bridgeport History Center. I first came across her when she was giving a presentation to the local Civil War Round Table in Washington, DC, on George Loring Porter, who while born in Concord, New Hampshire, spent most of his post–Civil War life living in Bridgeport. Porter was a newly graduated Civil War surgeon in 1862 and served the war with distinction. Perhaps his biggest claim to fame was when he was assigned the surgeon in charge of the assassination conspirators during their detention and trial and then was put in charge of the disposal of John Wilkes Booth's body. Porter became a huge collector of memorabilia, but his Lincoln collection has since been scattered to private and institutional collectors. Today, at the Bridgeport Brewing Company, you can buy a pint of "Dr. Porter's Stout Beer."

It was Ivanoff who told me that McLevy Hall was gutted many years ago and turned into city offices. By the time of my visit, the city was desperately trying to sell the building but was not getting any takers. The outside of the hall was designed by Alexander Jackson Davis to look like a temple and, although in need of some touch-ups, was still in good shape. It is on the National Registry of Historic Places, so any buyer has to be willing to preserve at least the outside for its historic value. There is a large bronze plaque on the front of the building commemorating Lincoln's March 10, 1860, speech. That is the only evidence of Lincoln's presence in Bridgeport despite the visit occurring just months before he was nominated for president.

Since I was in town, I decided to check out the University of Bridgeport campus. Bridgeport had enticed me out of high school because it had a significant marine biology program. While my hometown was historically important, it was also a seacoast town with a spectacular beach, many square miles of salt marsh, and an incentive to spend time on the waters. Half the families in town owned either a boat or a clam rake. Many had both. With Jacques Cousteau sailing the television airways every week while I was growing up, it was almost inevitable that I go into science for my paying career. To placate my history interests, I continued to pursue Abraham Lincoln on the side. Long after I graduated, this small private school fell into some hard financial times and was kept afloat with a substantial but controversial investment from the Unification Church. I lost connection to the school as I moved on to master's and doctoral studies elsewhere and my science career evolved from marine biology into regulatory science. After all these years I wanted to check out the school, and even more importantly, check out Seaside Park, which serves as a 375-acre, two-and-a-half-mile-long border between campus and Long Island Sound.

I was shocked to reach the edge of campus and find an open dirt area where my dormitory for four years had once stood. By the looks of the fenced-off dirt lot, the demolition had happened within a few weeks prior to my visit. The English and Literature Building in the next lot over was similarly bulldozed. Neither lot belonged to the university anymore, and the changes extended to other areas of campus where roads had been closed off, buildings had been ripped down, and I saw nothing new that had replaced them. I discovered that a few years ago the university was purchased by Goodwin University, although it retained its original name. My old science building remained but the interior had been repurposed with fewer laboratories and constricted science programming. Overall, the campus had shrunk in capacity over the years and the whole place looked a bit run down to my nostalgic eyes. Even though it was a school day, I saw only an occasional student. This was in sharp contrast to George Mason University in Virginia where I pursued doctoral work and the two Ivy League schools I visited earlier on this road trip tracing Lincoln's steps, all of which were vibrant student scenes even between class sessions.

Hoping to regain some sense of excitement I remembered from the old days, I drove off campus to Seaside Park, where I knew there were several statues of interest. The day was overcast and the brisk cold wind coursed through my suddenly aging bones while thrashing the waves into whitecaps, tossing them violently against the rock riprap along the shore.

But at least the statues were still there. One of the first statues I visited was the one and only P. T. Barnum. Yes, that P. T. Barnum.

You can fool some of the people all of the time, and all of the people some of the time, but you cannot fool all of the people all of the time.

Statue of P. T. Barnum in Seaside Park, Bridgeport, Connecticut

The Sculptors and the Showman—Southwestern Connecticut

One of the great mysteries of life is whether this famous quotation usually attributed to Abraham Lincoln was ever uttered by him.[4] Sometimes it is attributed to P. T. Barnum. Maybe neither of them ever said it. But it highlights an unexpected crossing of the paths of these two iconic nineteenth-century men. It all started when Lincoln arrived in New York City to give his Cooper Union address. Lincoln stayed at the Astor House, from which he could see across the street Phineas T. Barnum's American Museum, variously described as "a temple of diversions," the "greatest collection of novelties and amusements," and where "Icelandic giants, Patagonian women, dwarves, sea-serpents . . . and heaven only knows what else" were displayed for public entertainment. There is no evidence Lincoln stopped in for a visit, and then the museum burned down in July 1865 due to a fire in the revolutionary new ventilation system.[5]

Lincoln's last speech on his New England tour here in Bridgeport was given at a venue that is today only a few hundred yards from the "Barnum Institute of Science and History." This Barnum museum with its odd mix of Byzantine and Romanesque stone and terra-cotta construction was not built until 1893, so Lincoln would not have seen it. He might, however, have appreciated the idea behind it. Rather than a sideshow like the New York location, this was designed as a resource library and lecture hall and attracted lectures by the likes of the Wright Brothers and Thomas Edison. Today it includes a city history museum.

I passed the Barnum facility on my way down to Seaside Park, where I found a large bronze statue of P. T. Barnum looking out over Long Island Sound with my old college library at its back. The statue was created by Thomas Ball, whose name should sound familiar because I mentioned him earlier as the sculptor of the controversial Emancipation (or Freedman's) Memorial located in Washington, DC, that came under threats of vandalism during the events of 2020. The threats were so significant that the copy of the statue in Boston was removed by the city for safekeeping. So, why is Barnum such a feature of the park? Mainly because he was a longtime resident and short-time mayor of Bridgeport and provided the initial land and financing to create Seaside Park for the city. The park and Barnum provide a few other connections to Abraham

Lincoln: a huge soldiers' monument for city men who fought in the Civil War; a statue of Elias Howe (inventor of the sewing machine, which Lincoln noted in his "Discoveries and Inventions" lecture); and the William Hunt Perry Memorial Arch, designed by Henry Bacon, the same architect who designed the Lincoln Memorial in Washington, DC.

Barnum had one more act to play for Lincoln. One of Barnum's best attractions was Charles S. Stratton, the three-foot-tall, twenty-five-year-old Bridgeport native who went by the name General Tom Thumb. Stratton was introduced to twenty-one-year-old Lavinia Warren, herself only thirty-two inches tall and billed as "The Queen of Beauty." The two genuinely fell in love and were married on February 10, 1863. Ever the showman, Barnum arranged for their honeymoon tour to pass through Washington, DC, where Barnum finagled an invitation to highlight them at a White House reception. The juxtaposition of the six-foot, four-inch Lincoln with his two diminutive guests must have been eye-catching as they promenaded around the East Room, Lincoln bending down to hold Lavinia's hand "as though it were a robin's egg." Twenty-year-old Robert, home from Harvard, refused to come downstairs to participate in what he considered a spectacle, at least until his father ordered his presence. Nine-year-old Tad, on the other hand, was enchanted. One guest noted in her diary that, "The smallest and greatest men in the nation met," referring to Stratton and Lincoln.[6] As an aside, the Peter Cooper who started the Cooper Union where Lincoln spoke two weeks before had developed a tiny steam engine in 1828 and called it *Tom Thumb* after the miniature English folklore character who was "no bigger than his father's thumb." Barnum used the same inspiration for Stratton, adding the "General" part because of the Civil War.[7]

Lincoln finished his speech in Bridgeport that evening and immediately boarded the nine o'clock train to Manhattan to begin his long-awaited, and much-needed, trip back to Illinois. I will give him some peace to travel while I point my car in the direction of Stamford, Connecticut. Lincoln never visited Stamford, so I was intrigued to find on the Wiegers/Schroeder Sculpture Project map a Lincoln statue in Veterans Park. The hard-surface plaza has several memorials dedicated to the city's fallen and returning warriors from the seemingly ubiquitous wars the country has fought from the Revolutionary War to Afghanistan and the "Global War on Terror."

Holding a prominent position on the front corner of the park and facing a major intersection and the magnificent Old City Hall is a large, seated statue of Lincoln sculpted by John Blair. An exhausted-looking Lincoln slumps forward on a stone bench, his hand resting on the top hat lying beside him. Looking closer, the statue gave me a sense of the familiar. Blair designed the statue to look like one by Gutzon Borglum located in Newark, New Jersey, which makes the statue not only a tribute to Lincoln but a homage to Borglum, who had a studio in Stamford.

That tidbit of knowledge got me off looking for Borglum's old studio, the remnants of which I found on, appropriately, Gutzon Borglum Road and the equally aptly named Studio Road in the northern woods of the city. The studio is no longer there but the house he lived in still stands under the auspices of a private owner. If you have not placed the name Gutzon Borglum yet, he is the sculptor that, besides the seated Lincoln in Newark, carved the gigantic head of Lincoln that now sits in the crypt as you enter the US Capitol. He also sculpted a wonderful statue of Mary Magdalene located in the District of Columbia's historic Rock Creek Cemetery. But he is most famous for the heads of George Washington, Thomas Jefferson, Theodore Roosevelt, and Abraham Lincoln that we know as Mount Rushmore. Both Borglum and Rushmore had their controversies. Borglum had been the original designer of what became Stone Mountain outside Atlanta, Georgia, that monument to the Confederacy that to this day garners conflicting disdain and adoration. Borglum was fired after "creative differences" severe enough that he blasted away the work he had already done and destroyed the clay and plaster models. When he got to Mount Rushmore in the Black Hills of South Dakota, the rocky outcrop already had a name, "Six Grandfathers," and had been considered for centuries as a sacred place by the Arapaho, Cheyenne, and Lakota Native peoples. The blasting and reforming of the site is still deemed desecration and there are calls for the much-visited national park site to be returned to Native peoples.

Most recently, there has been talk of adding another figure to the quartet, but that suggestion has been widely dismissed as both physically impossible and delusionally narcissistic.

There are two more sculptors with close ties to Lincoln that I should discuss before heading back to New York. I have noted both Augustus Saint-Gaudens and Daniel Chester French in passing before, and now it is time to check in with them in more detail.

Saint-Gaudens is best known for some of the most iconic Lincoln and Civil War related statues. Born in Dublin, Ireland (his mother was Irish, his father French), but raised in New York City from the age of six months, Saint-Gaudens studied art at Cooper Union while working as an apprentice cameo cutter. According to his later assistant, James Earle Fraser, whose own *Lincoln the Mystic* is now in Jersey City, Saint-Gaudens had told him he saw the president-elect pass through Manhattan on his way to the inauguration. "Lincoln stood tall in the carriage," he said, "his dark uncovered head bent in contemplative acknowledgement of the waiting people, and the broadcloth of his black coat shown rich and silken in the sunlight." The description could easily describe the Saint-Gaudens standing-Lincoln statue in Chicago. Four years later, he joined the "interminable" line of mourners to see Lincoln's body as it lay in state in Manhattan's city hall. The painful experience stuck with him; he would later create one of the most famous statues of Lincoln in existence, the imposing *Abraham Lincoln: The Man* in Lincoln Park, Chicago. Considered one of the best portrait statues ever made, a version of it stands in Parliament Square, London. Equally appealing is another statue created by Saint-Gaudens, this one the seated *Abraham Lincoln: The Head of State*, in Chicago's Grant Park.[8]

Lincoln was not Saint-Gaudens's only subject. His first major commission was the large bronze Admiral David Farragut Memorial in New York's Madison Square Park. Other Civil War statues include tributes to General John A. Logan in Chicago and General William Tecumseh Sherman just outside Central Park in New York. Closer to my own home is the hauntingly beautiful Adams Memorial in Washington, DC's Rock Creek Cemetery. There is also the massive bronze bas-relief known as the *Robert Gould Shaw and 54th Massachusetts Regiment Memorial* that I saw across from the Massachusetts State House on the edge of Boston Common. On one of my many side trips while touring New England, I stopped at what is now the Saint-Gaudens National Historical Park in Cornish, New Hampshire. Many of his most famous statues have been recast and placed around the property, his home and studio for many years, including the standing Lincoln, David Farragut, and Robert Gould Shaw memorials, as well as non–Civil War statues such as *The Puritan* and *Diana*, the latter of which stood on the tower of the old Madison Square Garden until it was demolished and the statue moved to the Philadelphia Museum of Art. It was at this park that I first learned of Saint-Gaudens's involvement in designing coinage, carving cameos, and the Cornish Art Colony. I also discovered here that Augustus Saint-Gaudens' brother, Louis, was the sculptor of the six massive sculptures representing deities and Ancient Greek thinkers related to rail transport in the United States, all of which stand guard over the main entrance of Washington, DC's Union Station.

A smaller version of two Saint-Gaudens statues—*Lincoln: The Man* and *Diana*—are in the Metropolitan Museum of Art in New York, which gives me an appropriate segue to revisiting with Harold Holzer. While Holzer was amassing a prodigious reputation and body of work in Lincoln scholarship, he was also serving for a quarter century as an executive at the Met. Many of his books relate to Lincoln's image, photographic and legacy, which led to a commission by Chesterwood to write the definitive biography of sculptor Daniel Chester French, the man who makes up the third, but certainly not least, member of the Lincoln sculptor triumvirate.[9]

I finally had a chance to visit Chesterwood in western Massachusetts. The person I had been in contact with previously, Donna Hassler, had retired so I reached out to Margaret Cherin, the interim executive director at the time of my visit. Lincoln passed through the area as he worked his way back to Illinois. My erratic GPS took me over unpaved back roads through the woods to get there, where I joined a tour just beginning through the visitor center museum and the studio. The museum was filled with examples of French's work and studies for larger statues.

There was the design of the Dupont Memorial, a three-sided base for a fountain whose allegorical figures of *Wind*, *Sky*, and *Sea* harmonize with the Washington, DC, neighborhood's elegant mansions. Studies and small models showed the *Minute Man* statue that stands by Old North Bridge in Concord, Massachusetts, the one in the shadow of the Ralph Waldo Emerson/Nathaniel Hawthorne house I saw overlooking the "shot heard round the world" starting the Revolutionary War. There were also depictions of some of French's other statues, like the one of John Harvard I saw in Harvard Yard, the statue of Lewis Cass I saw in the US Capitol's statuary hall, the one of abolitionist Wendell Phillips I saw in Boston's Public Garden, and of my hometown celebrity politician, Rufus Choate, now in the old courthouse in Boston. French did dozens of other large monuments including one of William Seward, the *Standing Lincoln* guarding the entrance to the Nebraska State House (in Lincoln, Nebraska), and the colossal statue of *The Republic* that was the centerpiece of the 1893 World's Columbian Exposition in Chicago. This latter event managed to create connections between Abraham and Robert Lincoln, Nikola Tesla, Thomas Edison, and the frequent tag team of Daniel Chester French and Henry Bacon. Meanwhile, as the tour guide Nancy took us through the studio, I could see both the miniature and the midsize models of what would become French's most spectacular and most well-known work of art—the magnificent, seated *Abraham Lincoln* that graces the inner chamber of the Lincoln Memorial in Washington, DC.[10]

I mentioned previously that I had the privilege of being the lead organizer and then master of ceremonies for the epic Lincoln Memorial Centennial event in 2022. I have a particular affinity for the Memorial and French's statue of Lincoln. Soon after I moved to the Washington, DC, area I began making regular pilgrimages to the Memorial, often standing at Lincoln's feet and imagining I could glean wisdom and insight from his downturned face. Or I would stand on the steps gazing along the reflecting pool at the great obelisk of the Washington Monument and the dome of the Capitol building in the distance. Each year for the last decade I would participate in the laying of a wreath in front of Lincoln as part of the annual Lincoln Birthday ceremony organized by the Military Order of the Loyal Legion of the United States and the National Park Service.

Model statues by Daniel Chester French as studies for the Lincoln Memorial. Note the mini-statue at Lincoln's feet. Chesterwood, Stockbridge, Massachusetts.

In 2024, I was the featured speaker for the event, introducing and reading the Gettysburg Address, perhaps Lincoln's greatest speech.

All of this continues the legacy of Abraham Lincoln, which Borglum, Saint-Gaudens, French, and others all helped define through their sculptures. Doing so was not always easy. Lincoln's son, Robert Todd Lincoln, assigned himself as the keeper and protector of his father's image and legacy, controlling who could see the official and private papers and offering his often harshly critical opinions on books and sculptures. I recently spoke with Jason Emerson, author of the definitive biography of Robert Lincoln, *Giant in the Shadows*, who told me that Robert was an unforgiving critic of the statuary. In a perhaps tone-deaf moment of frankness, he told Vinnie Ream, the young female sculptor, that he had "never seen any statue of my father which gave me a pleasant impression as a portrait." I can imagine how Ream took that criticism given that her impressive statue of Lincoln that she began in the White House when she was only seventeen currently stands in the Capitol's rotunda. (Spoiler: I like it; Robert and his mother did not.) Robert's attitude might at least in part be ego, complaining that of all the statues made of his father, only two sculptors had bothered to ask his opinion. "These were Mr. Saint-Gaudens, as to both his statues, and Mr. French, in regard to the statue he is now making for the Lincoln Memorial" in Washington. He noted that in both cases he "was able to make suggestions which they professed themselves glad to have." Not surprisingly, he liked those statues better.[11]

He stayed true to form as the long process of creating the Lincoln Memorial progressed at a snail's pace due to political infighting and the onset of World War I. He carried on a brisk correspondence with William Howard Taft, former president, future chief justice of the Supreme Court, and then-chair of the Lincoln Memorial Commission. A year after providing a written history of his father to be placed in a copper box laid in the cornerstone, Robert visited French's studio in Cornish, New Hampshire, and offered suggestions on its likeness that French, whether ingenuously or tactfully, professed to be most helpful. In 1922, the aging Robert attended the dedication ceremony that inspired the Centennial celebration I emceed a hundred years later.[12]

Before leaving Chesterwood, I decided to experience the walk through a dense forest that Daniel Chester French must have taken many times to clear his head (and his lungs of plaster dust). Somehow, I got lost from the path, only to find my way out to a large standing bronze, a recast of the statue that stands in front of the Nebraska State House. I would have missed it otherwise, so it felt like it was my destiny to find Abraham Lincoln everywhere I traveled.

While Lincoln traveled by train out of New England, never to return, I decided to check out the two New England states Lincoln never saw in his lifetime—Maine and Vermont. Although Lincoln missed them, both states played important roles in his presidency and the development of his legacy.

Chapter Fourteen

The Missing New England— Maine and Vermont

"You can't get there from here," I said in my best Down East accent. Growing up I had been a huge fan of *Bert and I*, the oddball Maine humor stories told in the 1950s and 1960s by Marshall Dodge and Robert Bryan. My father used to play their records (yes, 33 rpm LPs) when I was a kid. My mother cleaned the house of Robert Bryan, who lived in my hometown and established the Quebec-Labrador Foundation to provide support to remote communities in those two Canadian provinces. The story, "Which Way to Millinocket?" includes a long, confusing, attempt of a Mainer to give directions to an out-of-towner before realizing that the route was too difficult to communicate, hence, "You can't get there from here."[1]

While Lincoln was rushing from one New Hampshire town to the next, he received a request from the Republican City Committee of Portland, Maine, to "visit our city" at Lincoln's convenience "within a few weeks, and address our citizens on political questions."[2] Lincoln was already overbooked as it was, and a long side trip to Maine was impossible. He just could not get there from where he was. But Maine would play an important role in his presidency, not the least of which because it was the home of his first vice president, Hannibal Hamlin.

Growing up in northeastern Massachusetts put my family as close to Maine as we were to Boston. Like most Bay Staters, we always referred to Maine as "Down East." Our summer vacations usually consisted of us

The Missing New England—Maine and Vermont

kids piling into the back of the family station wagon for a drive "down" the Maine coast. That might seem nonsensical to some, but if you check the map of New England, you can see that virtually the entire state of Maine lies geographically east of Boston, the main hub of early Massachusetts history. The "down" part originates from nautical terminology and refers to prevailing wind direction rather than spatial direction. Ships from Boston had to sail downwind to go east, hence "Down East."

On these summer drives we might veer off for a stop at Indian Head in New Hampshire, a rock formation high on the cliffs overlooking the road and resembling the distinctive facial features of one of the many local Native peoples' tribes. Or we might go farther inland to Lake Winnipesaukee and along the Kancamagus Highway, the narrow, windy road with at least one treacherous hairpin turn that is a favorite of "Lookie loos," the tourists backing up the road for miles every fall foliage season. From there we inevitably went past Old Man of the Mountain, another cliff rock face that stood in the White Mountains until finally collapsing in 2003, and then on to Mount Washington, which at nearly 6,300 feet is the highest peak in the northeastern United States and the most topographically prominent mountain east of the Mississippi River. If you have heard anything about Mount Washington, it is probably that it is notorious for its erratic weather, bone-chilling winter temperatures, and incredibly high gusty winds.

But mostly these Down East trips took us weaving along the Maine coast, or as it used to be known, Upper Massachusetts. The land only became Maine in 1820 as part of a deal managed by Henry Clay known as the Missouri Compromise. The compromise became necessary because of a combination of technological advancement and geographical expansion. When the Constitutional Convention of 1787 managed to cobble enough support from the original thirteen states to create a replacement for the grossly inadequate Articles of Confederation, all states still had legal slavery. The invention of the cotton gin by Eli Whitney a few years later would soon improve the profitability of slavery. Then Thomas Jefferson stumbled into the Louisiana Purchase in 1803, essentially doubling the size of the United States. Jefferson had only planned to buy New Orleans from France, but the cash-poor Napoleon, deep into more wars than he could handle, decided to sell him the entire area France had been claiming. Not much changed until 1819 when the upper counties of Massachusetts petitioned for separate statehood, which the Southern slave states vociferously opposed because it would give the North an advantage of one extra free state. To maintain the balance of free and slave states, the Compromise created both Maine and Missouri. It also set aside all the land from the Louisiana Purchase north of the southern border of Missouri (except Missouri itself, obviously) as forever free from slavery. South of that line would be open to slavery if they so chose (which, to no one's surprise, they did).

Thinking the Northern territories would not be good land for growing cotton anyway, the South was relatively happy with this Missouri Compromise. So, in 1820 we gained two new states, and a lot of territory filed away as either free or slave based on latitude. That would be the case until 1854 when the Kansas-Nebraska Act would rouse Lincoln "as never before" back into politics.

I have talked about the Mexican War, the Compromise of 1850 (including the Fugitive Slave Act), and the Kansas-Nebraska Act before so I will not rehash it here, but these massive shifts toward the expansion of slavery aroused many more people than just Lincoln into action. Mainer William Pitt Fessenden, a senator and, briefly, Lincoln's secretary of the treasury, called the Kansas-Nebraska Act "a terrible outrage," arguing that "it needs but little to make me an out-and-out abolitionist."[3] Another Maine senator, Lot M. Morrill, was equally enraged.[4] And then there was yet another Maine senator (they traded seats a lot), Hannibal Hamlin.

Hamlin was born in Paris, Maine, a small town in what was then still Massachusetts. Six months younger than Lincoln, Hamlin became an attorney, served in the Maine legislature, and then two terms in the US House of Representatives, all as a member of the Democratic Party. He had antislavery sentiments from the beginning, but like Lincoln, became incensed by the Fugitive Slave Act and the Kansas-Nebraska Act. Not only did he leave the Democratic Party because of their ongoing support for the expansion of slavery, he helped co-found the Republican Party in Maine. Despite telling friends that he had no interest in the job,

Hannibal Hamlin, Lincoln's first vice president, on obverse of campaign medallion (Lincoln is on the other side) PUBLIC DOMAIN, LIBRARY OF CONGRESS

Hamlin was nominated for vice president at the Republican convention, beating Lincoln's early New England travel companion Cassius M. Clay on the second ballot.[5] Hamlin was a friend of William Seward but had his misgivings about whether Seward would be a good president at that moment. Still, like most other Republicans at the time, he expected Seward to win the nomination and in a letter to his wife said the party "must make the best of it, though I am sure a much wiser nomination could be made."[6] When Seward lost out to Lincoln, the strong Seward state of Maine suddenly became a viable source of vice presidents, and Hamlin as a former Democrat and an experienced Easterner balanced out the former Whig from the West, the outsider Lincoln.

Lincoln did not meet Hamlin until after their respective Republican nominations in 1860, but they were similar both in their opposition to slavery and their demeanor. We all know that Lincoln rarely made a good first impression due to his disheveled and poorly fitting suits and homely visage. Hamlin had also been described as a sloppy dresser, although he was reportedly more "good looking" than Lincoln, "with a complexion and hair and eyes as dark as those of Daniel Webster."[7]

According to Michael Burlingame, when they did first meet, Lincoln told Hamlin: "I have just been recalling the time when, in '48, I went to the Senate to hear you speak. Your subject was not new, but the ideas were sound. You were talking about slavery, and I now take occasion to thank you for so well expressing what were my own sentiments at the time." This was a memory that Hamlin told a C. J. Prescott long after Lincoln had been assassinated, so that might account for the rather stilted language supposedly quoting Lincoln, but it is certainly plausible given that Hamlin gave an antislavery speech on July 22, 1848, and Lincoln was in the Capitol that day voting on an appropriations bill.[8]

As was the norm in those days, the vice president had only two responsibilities: serve as "president of the Senate" (which was mostly banging the occasional gavel) and stand around in case something happened to the president (the only two Whig presidents died early in office, so Hamlin had a better chance than most vice presidents). Hamlin was largely left out of the loop on Lincoln's policy decisions and then was replaced by the party with the Democrat Andrew Johnson for Lincoln's second term. Given what we know now about Johnson's term in office, I have to believe the party would have been better off sticking with Hamlin.

Two quick thoughts before I leave Maine. Remember when Lincoln first went to Massachusetts in 1848 and dined with a former governor and distant relative, Levi Lincoln, in Worcester? Levi's brother Enoch was governor of Maine around the same time. And remember that the Emancipation Memorial by Thomas Ball had been targeted to the point of Boston removing it from its pedestal (the original in Washington, DC, was saved)? Well, there is a much smaller version of it with a somewhat tweaked design on display in the Colby College Museum of Art in Waterville, Maine. So even though Lincoln never visited the state, Lincoln is remembered in Maine.

The Missing New England—Maine and Vermont

While Bernie Sanders is the politician most people think of from Vermont (even though he was born in New York City), Stephen A. Douglas is usually remembered as "the other Illinoisan," even though he was born in Vermont. Other famous Green Mountain Staters include future presidents Chester A. Arthur and Calvin Coolidge, agricultural inventor John Deere, and Senator Justin Morrill, originator of the Morrill Land-Grant College Act strongly supported and signed into law by President Lincoln. While Lincoln himself never visited the state, his wife Mary went to Vermont during the Civil War. Mary's first visit was in 1863, where she had gone to avoid the heat and pestilence that permeated the Washington, DC, air every summer. Lincoln moved up to what is now known as President Lincoln's Cottage at the Soldiers' Home, about three miles north of the White House. Mary was accompanied by Tad and Mrs. General Abner Doubleday that first summer, checking into the Equinox House hotel in Manchester. The Equinox was opened in 1853 and owned by Franklin Henry Orvis, who also opened the Orvis fly-fishing and sporting goods company nearby. According to the hotel advertising, Manchester was "unsurpassed for beauty and scenery and picturesque views" and quickly became a celebrated summer resort for the connected and the wealthy with trains running from New York City, Boston, and elsewhere. Robert made his way up from Harvard to join his mother when Mary returned in 1864, after which she made reservations for herself and Abraham for the summer of 1865. Lincoln was assassinated in April, so that never happened.[9] It was time for me to visit Hildene.

It was a perfect day in April, sunny, high in the 70s, and on the cusp of Lincoln's assassination anniversary, so it felt like a good time to travel to Hildene. I had spent the night in Ipswich, so I left early in the morning to take the scenic route across the upper part of Massachusetts. I drove through Lawrence, another old mill town that nearly died once the mills shut down but has seen a resurgence as it converted some of the old mill buildings into offices and art working spaces. When Lincoln wrote Mary from Exeter in 1860, he said he changed trains in Lawrence, "the place of the Pemberton Mill tragedy," a five-story textile mill that collapsed and killed up to 145 people, including many Irish and Scottish immigrants, most of them young women.[10]

The last one hundred miles or so was beautifully scenic, driving across small creeks and then for the last fifty miles or so alongside a lazy river on what is called the Mohawk Trail. Passing through Williamstown (the first location outside Connecticut to start a Wide Awake club), I turned north a short distance across the border into Vermont. My first stop had a peripheral connection to Lincoln. Lincoln was an avid reader of poetry, especially that of Scottish poet Robert Burns. He could recite long passages from memory, as well as some of Shakespeare's soliloquies. He even wrote some poetry himself, including a long ditty that sounds silly on the surface but when digging deeper shows a sadness upon his return to Indiana long after he had moved to Illinois. Burns did not have a house in Vermont, but American poet Robert Frost did, in the town of Shaftsbury. Frost was not on my road trip plans, but the most famous line he ever wrote, and the one most misquoted, came to mind: "Two roads diverged in a wood, and I—/I took the one less traveled by, And that has made all the difference."[11] That seemed like a command, so I diverged from the highway to follow winding country lanes to a set of buildings called the Robert Frost Stone House Museum, now owned by Bennington College. The museum was closed for the season, but I did commune with a cool statue of Frost sitting on a bench among the trees, his pen poised to write the next line of a poem.

After more side trips I finally made it to Manchester, Vermont, not to be confused with the Manchester in New Hampshire, in Maine, in Connecticut, or in Massachusetts (apparently Rhode Island was too small for its own Manchester). I had booked a room at the Equinox Golf Resort and Spa mostly because Mary and Robert Lincoln had stayed there. It was that visit and subsequent visits to the home of a later colleague that led Robert to build a custom summer home, complete with an observatory to pursue his interest in astronomy.

Christine Furman met me at the door when I arrived at Hildene the next morning. Following the mile-long entrance road up to the visitor center, I was already enjoying the sunny and warm, even hot, day, an anomaly for this area. Christine welcomed me with a great deal of energy and spirit, both of which would rub off on me over the next several hours. Before we left the visitor center, three other people came down from the

The Robert Lincoln summer home at Hildene, Manchester, Vermont

upstairs offices to meet me. They included Stephanie Moffatt-Hynds, Hildene's program director, who I had traded emails with the previous year when I was planning the Lincoln Memorial Centennial program. Joining her were Brian Keefe, Hildene's president, and Ken Moriarty, chairman of Hildene's board of directors, both of whom treated me like a celebrity because of my involvement with the Centennial and my position as president of the Lincoln Group of DC. We stood for some time chatting, which attracted looks from incoming visitors wondering why I was getting so much attention. I would see most of the staff again when I returned to Hildene for the Lincoln Forum conference in April 2025. Ken had retired and Bob Hallenbeck had taken over as chairman. But now it was time for the house itself.

Christine started by explaining the origin of the name Hildene. I had always wondered how the wealthy came up with names for their estates (us normal people just call our houses, "my house"). The answer was both clever and unoriginal, if that is possible. The 412-acre estate spans two sections rather obviously defined by their geography: the hill on which the main house sits; and the valley which holds the farmland, goats, and other sections. Those features provide the name, which is derived from two old English words: *Hil* for the upper part, and *dene*, which means a valley with stream, for the lower half of the property. Christine also explained that Robert's granddaughter Peggy lived in the house from Robert's death in 1926 to her own in 1975, soon after which it came under the control of the nonprofit that currently runs it. That continuity explains why the property is still almost completely intact.[12]

Christine then walked me up to the main house, which was technically his summer home. For most of the year he lived in Washington, DC, during his time in government, then Chicago for his law practice and his duties with the Pullman company. Hildene was a place to relax and get away from the stresses of public and professional life. The house is reached by a curving walkway from the visitor center. Along the way we passed a construction zone. Christine explained that they were building Lincoln Hall, to be used for formal functions, lectures, and other events. Two years later, I attended a special spring Lincoln Forum conference in that same, now completed, Lincoln Hall. As we approached the home, my eyes strayed to the small domed structure at the edge of the woods. About twelve feet in diameter and maybe twenty feet tall, Robert's observatory was much smaller than I expected, but I was totally enchanted by the original telescope that had been returned after traveling about a bit. Lincoln had a fascination with astronomy from a young age, but Robert took it to a higher level. According to Robert's biographer, Jason Emerson, Robert became a voracious reader of books on astronomy, about thirty of which remain in his library at Hildene. "I belong to the class of old-young amateurs in astronomy, but I enjoy my study of it very much," he told a colleague. A former scientist myself, I would have loved to hang out with Robert gazing at the stars.

Christine and I were joined outside the house by Jesse Keel, the collections and exhibitions manager for Hildene at the time. Her enthusiasm for the place was electric, which led to at least a couple of surprises.

Before going inside, Jesse pointed out the bricked rectangular outline in the grass just outside the covered carport that serves as the entrance to the building. The bricks represent the foundation of the log cabin where Abraham Lincoln was born in Kentucky. The organization that owns Hildene put it in to demonstrate how in a single generation the Lincoln family had jumped from a one-room log cabin on the frontier to a twenty-four-room Georgian Revival mansion as a summer home (in addition to his main homes; the Chicago home is long gone but the Washington, DC, home still exists as the Laird-Dunlop House in Georgetown). Robert took a hands-on approach to designing the house, even surveying it himself.

Jesse took Christine and me on a tour of the entire house, including at least one area not usually open to visitors. While the house seems large from the outside, most of the twenty-four rooms are relatively small. Once inside I realized the house is much wider than it is deep. The family room next to the foyer has pictures of the Robert Lincoln family. He and Mary Harlan Lincoln had three children. The oldest, Abraham Lincoln II, but called Jack, was Robert's favorite and seemed destined to carry the family name into a prestigious future. Unfortunately, Jack died young, like Robert's three brothers. Virtually all the artifacts and furniture in the house are original because Robert and his descendants lived in it until 1975, then the Church of Christ, Scientist, kept it for a short time before it went to the Friends of Hildene nonprofit that has held it since 1978. Some of the house's features are unique. For example, a huge dumbwaiter the size of a small elevator dominated one hallway. Much bigger than the kind normally used to move food from the basement to the dining rooms of old houses, this one was primarily used for moving luggage up and down stairs during the family's annual transfers between Hildene and the main winter houses. These were impressive endeavors, especially as the family expanded to grandchildren. A typical move from Chicago to Vermont for the summer would include about nine servants, who joined the six that maintained Hildene all year long. The female servants all lived upstairs in rooms that seemed way too small, while male servants lived in a small outer building. The one exception was the main butler, who had his own room downstairs at the end of the hall, not far from the kitchen.

My favorite room on the first floor was Robert's office. Over the years I have become a rather obsessive bibliophile, collecting books about Abraham Lincoln totaling over 1,800 volumes. I did not count them, but Robert's office walls contained beautiful wooden bookcases filled with books that he and his family enjoyed when in residence. Virtually all are original books belonging to Robert. Passing through a door behind the office is a room that had once been an open porch for him to enjoy the pastoral view, but which later had been enclosed to provide a space for his ever-present assistant. Despite Hildene being a comfortable relaxation home, the assistant helped deal with correspondence related to Robert's continuing work as lawyer and then president of the Pullman car company. Jason Emerson recently told me about his time conducting research at Hildene, during which he was given permission to open the myriad drawers lining the assistant's office walls. In them he found many significant letters that had lain untouched for nearly one hundred years.

As we toured the second floor, Jessie showed us that one of the guest rooms had photos of William Howard Taft, a frequent visitor. Taft served as president for one term, but it was later as chief justice of the United States that he presided over the dedication of the Lincoln Memorial, at which the aging Robert Lincoln was present.

Jesse then brought us through the private living quarters. Originally, Robert and Mary Harlan had separate bedrooms on the second floor, each with its own bathroom. Their bedrooms conveniently had a large sitting room between them, where they relaxed, read, and entertained the children and grandchildren. In his old age, however, Robert moved his bedroom down to the first floor. Robert died at the ripe old age of eighty-two in 1926, while Mary carried on another eleven years until she passed away at age ninety.

Upstairs, in what was previously the female servants' quarters, was a small room displaying artifacts related to the last Lincoln who lived in the house. Mary Lincoln Beckwith hated being named after her famous great-grandmother. Robert started calling her Peggy to avoid confusion with his mother and his wife Mary Harlan Lincoln.[13] The name stuck. Her mother, Jessie Harlan Lincoln, was the youngest of Robert and Mary Harlan's three children. She eloped with Warren Wallace Beckwith because her parents did not approve of him being a college football and minor-league baseball player. Peggy was the oldest of two children—her younger brother was confusingly named Robert Todd Lincoln Beckwith—and neither one saw their father again after he divorced their mother when she was nine years old. She grew up at Hildene with her mother and grandparents.

I think Peggy was by far the most interesting Lincoln descendant. Born in 1898 as the Gilded Age drew to a close, Peggy defied the ladylike norms of the day by chain-smoking and filling positions usually held by men. Historian Michael Beschloss speculated that "Peggy was apparently a lesbian," although he offered no evidence of that.[14] She briefly served on a committee on public information in Cuba. During World War I she took to laboring on, and then managing, the family farm. Over the years she picked up her grandfather's favorite sport, golf, and learned how to fly a plane. She went so far as to build a private landing strip at Hildene and owned a variety of airplanes. When not flying, golfing, or operating the Hildene farm, Peggy would do a little oil painting and sculpture. She also became an accomplished photographer. When Peggy passed away, she honored her late mother's wishes and willed the house and all the Hildene property to the Church. According to Christine, the Church had no idea what to do with it and after three years sold it to the newly formed Friends of Hildene, which maintains it as a nonprofit to this day.

While Christine and I chatted about Peggy, Jesse asked us to wait in the narrow hallway while she went for a key. Returning a few minutes later, she unlocked the room directly across from the "Peggy" room. Normally this room is not open to the public. Like all the rooms in the mansion, this one was small, but it was jam-packed with Abraham Lincoln relics. There were books owned and inscribed by Lincoln, paintings, manuscripts, and other Lincoln artifacts that did not seem to fit the Robert Lincoln theme of the estate but were obviously far too valuable to ship elsewhere. One painting caught my eye immediately—a portrait of Tad Lincoln done by Francis Bicknell Carpenter. "Carpenter? Are you sure?" I asked Jesse. Carpenter indeed, she repeated. I don't recall specifically, but I am sure I said "Wow!"[15]

To understand my excitement, it helps to know that Carpenter famously talked Lincoln into letting him spend half a year living and painting at the Executive Mansion, which he reminisced about in a book called *Six Months at the White House with Abraham Lincoln*. Born in Upstate New York, Carpenter had been a young prodigy, opening his own studio in New York City by the time he was twenty-one. In 1852, the persuasive young painter managed to get commissioned to paint a portrait of President Millard Fillmore, another Upstate New Yorker. That portrait must have met with Fillmore's approval because commissions followed to paint Presidents Franklin Pierce and John Tyler, as well as the founder of Cornell University, Ezra Cornell, poet and antislavery activist James Russell Lowell, clergyman Henry Ward Beecher, and *New-York Tribune* editor Horace Greeley. Carpenter had also painted John C. Fremont, the first Republican candidate for president, who had ultimately lost to James Buchanan, the president Abraham Lincoln would succeed. With such a political pedigree, Lincoln likely felt obligated to be the next in line to sit for Carpenter's brush.

Lincoln was not an ideal model for a grand portrait. Throughout his political career he was called homely, even ugly. This was not something said only behind his back; people often offered to him directly, so much so that he turned it into self-deprecating advantage in his political career, once reportedly quipping when accused of being two-faced, "If I were two-faced, would I be wearing this one?" Lincoln also found it difficult to sit still long enough for adequate posing. Carpenter, like so many artists of the time, finally commissioned a photograph of Lincoln to use when making the final touches on his face. The same happened for the rest of Lincoln's Cabinet for what became Carpenter's most famous painting, *First Reading of the Emancipation Proclamation of Abraham Lincoln*, completed in 1864. The painting received an enthusiastic public reception when Lincoln had it displayed in the East Room of the White House, after which an engraving was widely sold in the United States. After Lincoln's assassination, Carpenter tried to get Congress to purchase the painting. Already deeply in debt because of the war, Congress refused the opportunity. Carpenter finally charmed a wealthy woman by the name of Elizabeth Thompson into buying the painting for $25,000 and donating it to Congress. Carpenter attended the joint session of Congress held on

Lincoln's birthday in 1878 that accepted the painting. It now hangs on the Senate side of the US Capitol building in Washington, DC.[16]

At the other end of the second floor was another slightly larger display room dedicated to Abraham Lincoln, this one open to the public. Words from Lincoln's second inaugural speech were parsed out around the wall. Among the artifacts was one of Lincoln's famous stovepipe hats, which added another ten inches to Lincoln's already towering height. Hildene's hat has perfect provenance, having been kept in the family since Lincoln had it in his possession. It is unequivocally Lincoln's hat, Jesse guaranteed.

After thanking Jesse for the insiders' tour, Christine and I ventured downhill to another big draw for tourists at Hildene, the Pullman car, fully restored and moved to the estate only in 2011. When we reached the Pullman car we were joined by Tom Taylor, the official Pullman docent for the day. Tom gave us a tour both outside (a series of information boards explained the history of the car) and inside (including the pull-down beds neatly tucked in their overhead compartments above the opulent seating). The wooden car—its name is *Sunbeam*—was built in 1903 when Robert was president of the Pullman Company.

The *Sunbeam* Pullman car at Hildene, Manchester, Vermont

As Tom explained, this car was only for the very wealthy, that is, those with substantial amounts of money that allowed them to travel in style. Each car held eighteen passengers and would have two porters to wait on their every need. The seats are converted into beds for the long trips.

Pullman porters, who were all African-American, worked up to hundred-hour weeks with lousy pay but could make some additional money with tips from the wealthy travelers. While it was not company founder George Pullman's, or Robert's, intent, Pullman porters jumpstarted the Civil Rights Movement, in part because they could see the vast amounts of wealth held by passengers that they were kept from attaining themselves.

Abraham Lincoln is often referred to as the "Great Emancipator" because of his Emancipation Proclamation ("thenceforward and forever free") and strong support for the Thirteenth Amendment that constitutionally abolished slavery. A fuller picture of emancipation requires acknowledgment of the steps African Americans, both Freemen and Freedmen, took to accomplish their own freedom in consort with policy changes. While the three Reconstruction Amendments supposedly guaranteed freedom, citizenship, and voting rights for African Americans, the reality is that conservative forces denied those rights through restrictive black codes, violence, and murder throughout decades of Jim Crow segregation. African Americans routinely fought for their rights, and one of the groups that did so was made up of Pullman porters.

Among Robert Lincoln's many accomplishments was becoming president of the Pullman Palace Car Company following the death of its founder, George Pullman. Robert had been the company's general counsel when workers went on strike in 1894, and while both he and Pullman were generally caring of their employees, they also were businessmen who wanted to keep costs low and profits high. In 1906, the Pullman Company paid out $45 million in stock dividends to its shareholders.

The 1894 strike involved over four thousand white workers teaming up with the American Railway Union led by Eugene Debs but led to little change in working conditions. The all-Black porters were excluded from the initial union and the strike. However, a 1904 pamphlet entitled *Freemen Yet Slaves under 'Abe' Lincoln's Son, or Service and Wages of Pullman*

The Missing New England—Maine and Vermont

Porters, published by a former Pullman porter, accused Robert of "industrial slavery" conditions "even worse in some respects" than was the chattel slavery Lincoln had ended. In 1925, after many more years of unbearable workloads and continued low wages, the African-American porters formed their own union, the Brotherhood of Sleeping Car Porters (BSCP), led by A. Philip Randolph. The BSCP went on to play a key role in the Civil Rights Movement and helped organize the 1963 march on Washington that featured Martin Luther King's "I Have a Dream" speech.[17]

Back on the *Sunbeam*, I could envision the porters working their expected four hundred hours a month—sometimes twenty hours at a stretch—for their incredibly low wages supplemented by tips that required significant forbearance of the constant debasement and abuse by white patrons. Porters were expected to pay for their own meals and supply their own uniforms and shoe polish. Hildene does a great job of presenting the full picture of Robert's relationship with the Pullman Company and its porters, but it is easy to see why the porters formed their own union to fight for their rights.[18]

After Hildene I headed for Peekskill to begin my journey to New York and home. Abraham Lincoln also made two stops in Peekskill, one on the way to his inaugural, the other on the way to his burial. After his New England tour of 1860, he made one more stop in New York City before heading home.

Chapter Fifteen

The End and the Beginning— Heading Home

Abraham Lincoln had intended only to make a quick stop— "I may be delayed in New York City an hour or two," he had written Mary from Exeter—but his late arrival on Saturday night meant he was stuck in the city until Monday. He decided to use his Sunday to go to church. Twice.

The fact that Lincoln went to church so often on this trip is surprising. He was not a regular churchgoer at home, and his religiosity continues to be debated to this day. Yet he had gone to church in Exeter, telling his wife that "according to Bob's orders, I am to go to church once today."[1] He had already been to Reverend Beecher's Plymouth Church the day before his Cooper Union speech and was about to go there again on his return to New York. Quite a difference from his early days where he had to defend himself against charges he was an "infidel," that is, a mocker of religion.

Henry Ward Beecher was as famous an abolitionist as William Lloyd Garrison. His sermons were regularly printed in the *New York Independent*, ensuring that the 2,800-person capacity of Plymouth Church was regularly overflowing. "Travelers visited it, just as they went to Washington or Niagara," one parishioner reminisced, adding that "it was 'the thing'" to do. His wife had told him he must do it, so Lincoln did it. Rising early that Sunday morning, he took the ferry from Fulton Street to Atlantic Avenue on the Brooklyn side of the icy East River. Henry C. Bowen, publisher of the *Independent*, met Lincoln in his pew

Reverend Henry Ward Beecher's Plymouth Church in Brooklyn, New York PUBLIC DOMAIN, LIBRARY OF CONGRESS

near the front of the church, his presence quickly being noticed by other parishioners. Beecher gave an inspirational speech on what makes a man a gentleman. After the service, Lincoln spoke with Beecher, which again attracted the interest of everyone else wanting a view until Lincoln finally begged off to travel back to New York to fine-tune his speech.[2]

Stuck in New York on this return trip, Lincoln again took the ferry across the river to Beecher's church in Brooklyn. This time he was accompanied by James A. Briggs. He was late arriving, which disrupted the service already underway as people turned to see him lingering near the back, at least until someone stood up to give him a seat in the packed church. By this time, Beecher had heard reports of Lincoln's Cooper Union speech and his tour through New England, which had all but "settled" in his mind that Lincoln, and not Seward, should be the Republican nominee.[3] Again, Lincoln was besieged by parishioners wanting to get a closer look and shake his hand.

Returning to Manhattan, Lincoln met up with Hiram Barney, a member of the host committee for the Cooper Union address, and the two visited Five Points, a poverty-stricken slum neighborhood known for its vice, crime, overcrowding, and unsanitary conditions. The area inspired the 2002 film *Gangs of New York*, the gritty, violent look at gang feuds erupting during Irish immigrant protests against conscription (i.e., being drafted) in the Civil War. Incidentally, the film stars Daniel Day-Lewis, who later played Lincoln in the 2012 film *Lincoln*. A mix of Irish, German, and Italian immigrants, along with free African Americans, Five Points had become a cause célèbre attracting politicians, celebrities, and anti-poverty reformers, including Charles Dickens, and now, Abraham Lincoln. Lincoln and Barney visited the Five Points House of Industry, a charity mission, which housed around 150 abandoned children. According to reminiscences years later, Lincoln listened to the stories of the children and told of his own meager upbringing, inspiring hope for all.[4] Before leaving, he was handed a copy of *The Lost and Found; or Life among the Poor*, which Mary Lincoln read "with much interest" and shared with her friends in Springfield.

Lincoln was not quite finished. After stopping for tea at Barney's home, he joined James Briggs for an evening service at the Church of Divine Unity on Broadway, led by the Universalist preacher Edwin Hubbell Chapin.[5]

While Lincoln was visiting churches and orphanages in New York City, I was leaving the Equinox Hotel near Hildene and back on the road toward two other places in New York that Lincoln visited later in his presidency. My first stop was West Point, home of the US Military Academy. Overlooking the Hudson River, West Point is the oldest of the five service academies and educates cadets for commissioning in the US Army. It originally was a Revolutionary-era fort, but I stopped because

The End and the Beginning—Heading Home

Abraham Lincoln had made a clandestine visit here in June 1862 to confer with General Winfield Scott.

After a breezy three-hour drive from Vermont, I pulled into the West Point parking lot and immediately spied one of the two people I had come to meet. Tony Czarnecki is a past president and board member of the Lincoln Society in Peekskill and had invited me to speak at their annual dinner. He has published articles on Lincoln's visit to West Point and his stops in the Peekskill train depot. Within minutes after meeting at the entrance to the West Point Museum, we were joined by the main host of our visit, Emily Lapisardi. Emily was the sitting vice president of the society the day we met; the next day she was formally installed as the group's president. More importantly for our purposes that day, she was the music director of the Catholic Chapel at West Point and therefore had special access onto the otherwise restricted military academy grounds.

Hopping into Emily's SUV, the three of us stopped briefly at the security gate, where Emily flashed her pass, and we were in. Since we were meeting at noon, our first stop was at a dining facility, which used to be an officers-only club but is now open to all West Pointers and their families. We grabbed our lunch from the à la carte line and ate at a table next to huge windows overlooking the incredible vista of the Hudson River from the Highland Heights.

After lunch we drove a bit farther into the academy and parked in one of the lots surrounding the parade grounds, where they were practicing landings and takeoffs of military helicopters. From there we walked up to the "million-dollar view" overlooking the river. Here we could see the location of the tremendous chain American revolutionaries had pulled across the narrow strait at a sharp curve in the river to block British ships from moving up the Hudson. It was clear this was no easy task—a short length of the chain had been preserved as part of a memorial on the bluff, and each link was about two feet long. The chain and gun batteries on cliffs overlooking the river successfully kept the British navy from destroying George Washington's army.

Lincoln had a much easier time during his visit. Winfield Scott was a hero of the Mexican War and had been general-in-chief early in the

Civil War before age and infirmities retired him. Lincoln was here to discuss war strategies, including any tips that might get the new general in charge, George B. McClellan, to start putting his troops into battle, something he seemed hesitant to do. Scott was confident there was enough troop strength to win the war handily if they attacked the Confederate armies. On the other hand, Scott thought the force at Fredericksburg seemed "entirely out of position" and not particularly useful for McClellan. Lincoln left satisfied with Scott's advice, although the Second Battle of Bull Run two months later proved disastrous and Lincoln soon after that sent McClellan packing.[6]

Our next stop was the Catholic Chapel itself, where Emily showed us walls covered in plaques honoring important Civil War military leaders who received their training at West Point. Union generals represented included Ulysses S. Grant, McClellan, George Meade, Phillip Sheridan, William Tecumseh Sherman, and George Armstrong Custer (who finished last in his class in 1861). But West Point also trained soldiers who would turn their backs on the United States and join the Confederacy, such as Robert E. Lee, Stonewall Jackson, James Longstreet, and J. E. B. Stuart.

A velvet rope blocking the steps to the choir loft in the rear of the chapel was no barrier to Emily, who deftly unhooked it to let us pass. Snaking our way up the narrow stairs, we skittered through the surprisingly small area mostly taken up by the organ pipes until we reached the far wall. There, tucked about as far away from the other plaques as possible, was a small tablet that at first looked blank. A closer look, and insider information from Emily, revealed it to be the plaque for Benedict Arnold. Because of Arnold's treason, visitors and cadets have taken to rubbing Arnold's name and credentials from the plaque. The original name of the fort was Fort Arnold, named after its commander during the Revolutionary War. Then in an act of unmitigated treason, Commander Arnold tried to turn the fort over to the British. Foiled from doing so, Arnold took tail to England and the fort was renamed Fort Clinton after the more patriotic General James Clinton, whose brother George and son DeWitt would later serve as governors of New York.

Behind the chapel is the main cemetery of West Point. A dress-uniform burial was happening as we approached, so we respectfully

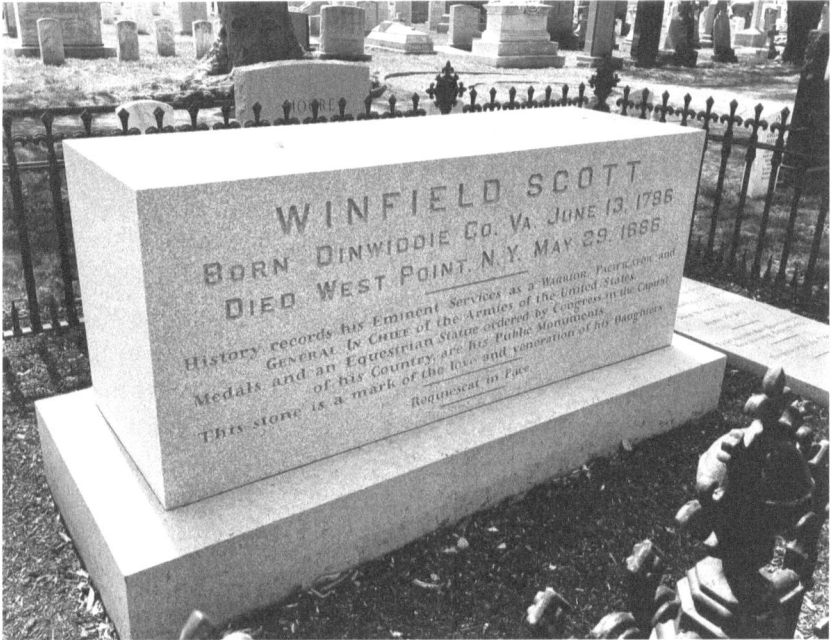

Gravestone of General Winfield Scott, Lincoln's Civil War general, West Point, New York

circled around to another side of the cemetery in search of General Winfield Scott's grave. We also saw the graves of other Civil War veterans, all academy graduates.

Having seen the Catholic Chapel, we then drove up to the main West Point Cadet Chapel. This huge monolith of native granite looks like a cross between Gothic cathedrals and a medieval fortress. Having lived in Europe for three years, I recognized the traditional interior, which was big enough to fit several Catholic Chapels with room to spare. The tremendous stained-glass windows included a large sanctuary window inscribed with the motto of the Academy: "Duty, Honor, Country."

But what really caught my eye was the massive organ designed by M. P. Moeller. Begun in 1911 and enlarged by memorial gifts over the years, the organ is now the largest church organ in the world. Emily excused herself for a moment while Tony and I chatted about Lincoln's 1862 visit, and when she returned, she was carrying the key to the organ.

"Let me see if I can get this thing running," she said. "It's been a few months since I last had a chance to play this one." She usually had to limit herself to the smaller Catholic Chapel organ, but like any good musician, she could not pass up an opportunity to play the "big one." After a minute or so of pushing buttons, pulling knobs, and pumping foot pedals, she went into full Phantom of the Opera mode and started playing. While Tony and I marveled at the immensity of the sound roaring out of the 23,511 pipes (the largest in any religious edifice in the world), we were joined by a small tour group that I had noticed creeping up the aisle. A family with three young children sidled up to the organ, so I stepped back to let them get closer. We were a few feet from Emily as she played, the impromptu mini concert a major treat for all of us. The kids were absolutely entranced by the music, and Emily clearly enjoyed having an audience. I felt privileged and inspired to be there.

That privilege extended to a private tour that Emily had arranged at the West Point Museum just outside the main gate, in particular the academy history and the Civil War sections. These were interesting in themselves, but the docent took us through an unmarked door into the back hallways of the museum and upstairs using one of those open grillwork elevators you see in old black-and-white movies. Opening a locked door even in this exclusive place, the docent brought us into a room reminiscent of my grandmother's attic. Laid out on a small table was a small "VIP display" of Civil War–era artifacts that were not in the public exhibits because of their rarity. For example, there were General Ulysses S. Grant's field glasses and two-star shoulder strap, one of his canes, and a Civil War Medal of Honor. Again, an extraordinary special adventure that most visitors do not have the privilege of seeing.

It was after 5 p.m. and it was time to call it a day. Back at the car, Emily gave me a signed copy of her book on Rose Greenhow called *My Imprisonment*. Greenhow was a widowed Washington, DC, socialite who became an enemy spy during the early part of the Civil War, including passing key information to Confederate general P. G. T. Beauregard that led to Union defeat at the First Battle of Bull Run. Arrested, she was held under house arrest in her own 16th Street home for about six months before being moved to Old Capitol Prison for another four months, then expelled to the Confederacy. Greenhow wrote a diary of sorts during her imprisonment, which Emily had annotated. Emily also gives first-person reenactments of Rose Greenhow for a variety of Civil War Round Tables, schools, and community centers.

I said goodbye to Emily and Tony, both of whom I would see the next day, then drove half an hour or so to Peekskill and checked in at my hotel. Famished, I ventured out to a restaurant overlooking the river, dowsing a hefty portion of pork Bolognese with a small local beer.

I woke up the next morning to a partly cloudy day in the low 70s. There was a chance of rain later in the day, but I had hopes it would hold off because I was meeting Tony again for a visit of the Lincoln Depot Museum. After eating breakfast at the hotel, I followed my GPS until I saw the museum sign with Tony already waiting for me in the small parking lot. On the way in we met Michael Macedonia, the outgoing president of the Lincoln Society of Peekskill, who was carting away materials in preparation for their annual dinner dance that night, which I would be keynoting. Once inside the visitor center, Tony introduced me to Paul Martin, chair of the Lincoln Depot Foundation and primary curator and docent of the Lincoln Depot Museum. After fielding phone calls, Paul gave me the grand tour and explained the museum's origins.

Lincoln had passed through the depot on two occasions. The first was in February 1861, as he wended his way around the Northern states to his inauguration. His train made a short side trip into Peekskill so that Lincoln could honor his former congressional colleague, William Nelson, representing Westchester County. According to Paul, the train was at the Peekskill Freight Depot for only about seven minutes, just long enough to refill the water tanks and take on wood fuel for the steam boilers. Ever the politician, Lincoln used the time to give a brief speech to the thousand or so people swarming the town once they heard he would stop there.[7] The next time Lincoln passed through the depot was after the assassination as his body largely retraced the inaugural path in reverse back to Springfield, Illinois.

As with many other places with a Lincoln connection, the small city of Peekskill made the most out of their little piece of Lincoln lore. The depot remained under corporate control for more than a century after

Lincoln's visit and thus was unavailable for use as a museum. As a consolation prize of sorts, in 1925 the city placed a memorial called the *Lincoln Exedra* on the South Street bluff overlooking the depot. The land was donated by John Smith Jr., who had held the rank of captain in the Civil War and had served as president of the Lincoln Society in Peekskill in 1917. It seemed altogether fitting and proper that it should become a site honoring Lincoln. As the exedra aged, the Lincoln Society in Peekskill raised money and had it fully restored.[8]

But what about the depot itself? After the train station fell into disrepair, the century-old vision of preserving the facility finally got its chance in 2005 thanks to the former mayor of Peekskill, who just happened to be the governor of New York State at that point, George Pataki. Ever proud of his hometown, Pataki secured the initial funding to acquire the building and renovate it into a museum. It opened to the public in 2014 in the direct sightline of the Exedra. More recently, the foundation and society had built a second building on the grounds to serve as a visitor center and speaker venue.

At this point we finally left the visitor center to cross the short distance to the depot. Before going inside, we stopped for photos in front of the Richard Masloski sculpture *Lincoln in Peekskill*, which graces the entrance. A Cornwall, New York, native, Masloski has sculpted magnificent memorials to subjects ranging from Mark Twain and Edgar Allan Poe to Rip Van Winkle to John F. Kennedy, and, of course, to Abraham Lincoln. The seven-foot-tall Peekskill statue depicts Lincoln standing at the back railing of the train, eagerly braving the wind as he offers a few words to the crowd.[9]

Inside the museum, Paul showed us the displays documenting Lincoln's visit to the depot. One exhibit, *New York and Abraham Lincoln: The Indispensable Relationship*, shows not only the impact of Lincoln to Peekskill and the Hudson Valley region but also to New York as a whole. There were maps, sculpture models, artwork, signed documents, pamphlets, and an original signed letter from New York City mayor Fernando Wood to Lincoln voicing his Confederate sympathies. Since the depot also hosted a stop of the funeral car after the assassination, there were artifacts and photographs related to that event, including a timetable of

Statue of Lincoln at Lincoln Depot Museum, Peekskill, New York

the funeral train and other items. Before I left, Paul presented me with a framed, limited edition and signed print of a pencil sketch he had drawn depicting Lincoln giving his inauguration train speech, the same view that the Masloski sculpture depicts.

The Lincoln Society dinner dance that night was a happy affair. I signed copies of my book, *Lincoln: The Fire of Genius*, for about an hour, then joined Tony and others for dinner. There I met Rob Kaplan, the current vice president and future president of the Lincoln Group of New York, based in New York City. Rob and I chatted as best as we could while the spirited, and booming, headliner band called Vinyl Siding kept the eighty members in attendance up and dancing away the evening. Between songs, Rob and I tried to one-up each other on the number of Lincoln books we own. He was impressed with my collection of about 1,800 Lincoln books, and I was impressed with his nearly 5,000 books total, the result of a career in the publishing business. I felt better when I realized only about 800 of those books were about Lincoln. Around 9 p.m. the band took a break, and I stood up to give my keynote address about how Lincoln's commitment to science and technology helped modernize the country. My speech went well enough based on the response, and the society gave me their Lincoln Legacy Award, then officially promoted Emily to president. Everyone applauded and then Vinyl Siding came back to lead us past midnight. Lincoln may have only been in Peekskill for seven minutes, but my time there was both much longer and more exhilarating.

Lincoln was desperate to get home to Springfield. Leaving early the morning of Monday, March 12 on the Erie Railroad, it took him two days and multiple train lines before he arrived in the wee hours of the 14th at the Great Western Depot in Springfield "in excellent health and his usual spirits." The *New-York Tribune* notes the success of Lincoln's New York and New England tour, opining that "Mr. Lincoln has done a good work and made many warm friends."

That same day, Lincoln began writing responses to letters he either did not have time to answer while traveling or that had arrived in Springfield while he was away. The first was to William A. Beers and Sereno

The End and the Beginning—Heading Home

Mansfield, photographers in New Haven, apologizing for missing the opportunity to sit for them while he was in their city. The next went to an A. Chester, again apologizing for not being able to accept an invitation to speak in Chicago. Yet another apology that day went to attorney Alexander W. Harvey, who had wanted Lincoln to speak as he passed through Buffalo on his way home, which Lincoln declined because his other commitments had "carried me so far beyond my allotted time" that he could not add another. By the next day he was starting to deal with requests to assist various political candidates with their forthcoming elections.[10] Meanwhile, he was finalizing the production of the Lincoln-Douglas Debates book to be published in the spring.[11]

He was also beginning to get prods from friends suggesting that he, Lincoln, could potentially be "available" (i.e., electable) for the Republican nomination. One of the great debates among Lincoln scholars is when he started thinking of himself as a viable candidate for president. Back in those days it was considered unseemly to actively campaign for such high elective office. Even the series of Lincoln-Douglas debates was ostensibly to make the case for the party such that enough local representatives could be elected to provide a sufficient majority in the state legislature, since it was the legislature who chose the US senators, the case until the Seventeenth Amendment in 1913 changed it to the direct vote we have today. Lincoln was invited along with other likely presidential contenders to attend an April 1859 dinner in Boston celebrating Thomas Jefferson's birthday.[12] That may have been a recognition of his minor celebrity status following the 1858 debates, but later that year, business magnate and influencer Jesse Fell coaxed Lincoln into providing an autobiographical sketch that was expanded and widely distributed across the country. This growing publicity gave Lincoln enough viability to garner an invitation to give the Cooper Union speech, following which several of his New England hosts introduced him as presidential or vice presidential material. On his return trip to New York, James Briggs told Lincoln that "I think your chance of being the next President is equal to that of any man in our country."[13] Not long after he returned to Springfield, he replied to an Ohio businessman who had suggested that the

Ohio legislature supported Lincoln as the Republican nominee. It is in this letter where Lincoln first voices the idea that he is likely not the first choice of a very great many (those going to Seward, Chase, Bates, or a given state's native son) and thus "our policy, then, is to give no offence to others—leave them in a mood to come to us, if they shall be compelled to give up their first love."[14]

Lincoln's long New England trip had finally ended, but his path to the presidency was just beginning.

Epilogue

Abraham Lincoln became the Republican nominee for president two months after he returned from his second New England trip. Less than six months later he was elected president of the United States. How much did Lincoln's two tours through New England matter, if at all? As with most things, the answer depends on perspective.

From a long-term perspective, you could argue that his 1848 speeches in Massachusetts were unimportant. While he received local attention at the time, not one newspaper remembered his earlier trip when he returned in 1860. Whether Lincoln even influenced the 1848 elections themselves is unclear. Sure, Zachary Taylor did carry Massachusetts and the election that fall, but the Free Soil candidate, Martin Van Buren, received 10 percent of the national vote. Van Buren did even better in Massachusetts, totaling over 28 percent of the vote, more than the Democrat, Lewis Cass, meaning that the Free Soil Party had siphoned off enough Whig votes to make the election much closer than it should have been. Not only did Lincoln fail to keep the Massachusetts Free Soilers in the Whig fold, but just two years later that splinter party also went on to form a coalition with Democrats to oust the Whigs from the major state offices.

Evaluating from a different perspective, however, the 1848 trip proved to be critically important to Lincoln's personal and political growth. He gained considerable insights into several factors that informed his later runs for the Senate and the presidency.

First, he learned that the candidate matters. Zachary Taylor was nominated by the Whigs because the country wanted him, rather than his strong Whig credentials. While Lincoln argued that Taylor's apolitical background was a strength—he would defer to congressional Whigs as representatives of the people to guide his time in office—he carried significant baggage that exacerbated the already delicate balance within the Whig Party itself. Whigs had argued the Mexican War was unconstitutional, a "Manifest Destiny" power grab not only to gain more land but to enable the spread of slavery. And yet here they were nominating a hero of that war, made worse by the fact that he was a Southern plantation owner actively enslaving hundreds of Black Americans. Many in the Whig Party felt these factors disqualified their own candidate.

Second, party divisions matter. The Whigs had always been a blended party, progressive in many ways but also a mix of national factions running the ideological span from liberal to conservative. This was especially evident in Massachusetts, where Cotton Whigs relying on slave-grown cotton to feed their profitable textile mills sometimes clashed with the growing number of Conscience Whigs who found any association with the slave-labor camps of the South objectionable. This ideological split, combined with the incomprehensible choice of Taylor as the nominee, led to a number of its most active leaders spurring the Whigs to form the Free Soil Party. Lincoln had argued that a vote for Free Soilers was handing the election to the Democrats and worked against the common antislavery expansion beliefs of the Whigs. Unity around a single common central goal is better than quibbling on differences around the edges.

Third, abolitionist fever was growing. As a young Illinois legislator in 1837, Lincoln had opined on how slavery was founded on both injustice and bad policy, but also that abolitionist doctrines increased rather than abated slavery's evils (by hardening proslavery defensiveness).[1] But times had changed. The immorality of slavery had grown to the point where abolitionism was becoming more mainstream in the North. New England abolitionists like William Lloyd Garrison, Theodore Parker, and Frederick Douglass, along with influential writers such as Ralph Waldo Emerson, Henry David Thoreau, Louisa May Alcott, and Nathaniel Hawthorne helped shift public sentiment from more conservative antislavery (sometimes with colonization) to more radical abolitionism (sometimes with calls for full equality). Lincoln always understood that "public sentiment is everything," and that a shift in the public's attitude about slavery was not something that could be ignored.

Epilogue

Fourth, while Northern states had effectively abolished slavery, they were not free from complicity in the "peculiar institution." Much of the wealth acquired by the North early in the nation's history had come from some connection to slavery, be it shipbuilding, slave trading, or acceptance of financial contributions and students from the South to its finest colleges. As the Northern economy shifted away from direct slavery, the growth of textile industry and the sale of materials and food crops to the South continued to bind together the two sections. That interdependence meant that eliminating slavery would be even more difficult than the task that overwhelmed the Framers of the Constitution.

Fifth, humor only goes so far. Lincoln was best known for his humorous stories, and all too often, his biting sarcasm. His 1848 speeches drew substantial crowds more for their entertainment value, the "hayseed in my hair" from the West who could rally the populace without being taken too seriously as a policymaker. While he had made a few forays into denouncing slavery before, it would only be after this Massachusetts tour that he would start to see it as the driving force in national politics. Meeting William Seward, already a national and Whig leader, at his last speech in Boston must have given him something to think about.

And then he was out of politics for a dozen years. Well, not completely out of politics. It is true that he did not hold elective office from the time he left Congress in early 1849 until the time he was elected president in late 1860. During that time, he built a substantial law practice and continued riding the circuit courts in central Illinois. But he remained active in politics, regularly giving speeches to support other candidates for office. His longtime foil in Illinois, Senator Stephen A. Douglas, had taken over the responsibility of pushing through the Compromise of 1850 with its formidable new Fugitive Slave Act. Four years later, Douglas advanced the Kansas-Nebraska Act, which repealed the Missouri Compromise and opened all the western territories to the potential of slavery, including the previously protected Northern areas remaining from the Louisiana Purchase. Lincoln was incensed.

Meanwhile, the 1850s saw the slave- versus free-labor conflict grow exponentially as both sides raced to populate the territory of Kansas, leading to "Bleeding Kansas," a half decade of violent power struggle

Stephen A. Douglas by Mathew Brady, 1859 PUBLIC DOMAIN, LIBRARY OF CONGRESS

over slavery. A day after the sacking of Lawrence, Kansas, by proslavery forces, Massachusetts senator Charles Sumner was beaten nearly to death by a cane wielded by South Carolina representative Preston Brooks. In 1857, the US Supreme Court issued its Dred Scott decision, which not only denied Scott his freedom but also made sweeping pronouncements that no Black man had any rights that white men were bound to respect and that the federal government had no authority to bar slavery from the territories. Lincoln spoke out against all these attacks on democracy and freedom. And then John Brown staged a failed insurrection at Harpers Ferry, Virginia, intending to set off a slave rebellion. Instead, it further entrenched the slave states, exacerbating their fear that they were losing control of the federal government and must take steps to form their own country based on what they say is the falsehood of Jefferson's ideal of "all men are created equal."

Realizing he needed to be in office to play a larger role in fighting the expansion of slavery, Lincoln turned down an election to return to the state legislature so he could run for Senate. He lost, but only because the conservative forces in Illinois still controlled the legislature that selected the senators. When the new Republican Party ran its first presidential candidate, John C. Fremont, Lincoln traveled through Illinois, Indiana, Ohio, and Wisconsin to give speeches supporting that candidacy. After Fremont came close but lost, Lincoln ran again for Senate as a Republican against Stephen A. Douglas. Again, he lost, even though he helped Republicans gain more seats in the legislature, but not enough to appoint Lincoln. His seven joint debates with Douglas got him national attention and effectively set the party platforms for the next several years. Lincoln was still out of political office but now had gained more national recognition. This sudden celebrity status brought him requests to join other political leaders at a birthday dinner in Boston for Thomas Jefferson, author of the Declaration of Independence. It also got him an invitation to give the speech that became known as the Cooper Union address.

In contrast to his first trip to New England, his 1860 tour was vital to his nomination and election. In 1848 Massachusetts he had been there specifically to campaign for the Whig nominee, Zachary Taylor, but the nomination convention was still three months away at the time of Cooper Union. That meant Lincoln was arguing for the Republican Party as a whole and not a specific candidate, which opened the possibility that Lincoln himself could be that candidate. Learning from his previous New England tour and integrating that knowledge with the fundamental shift in political and social society during the turbulent 1850s, Lincoln went to Rhode Island, New Hampshire, and Connecticut with a more focused set of key guiding principles and came away with updated insights that informed his political strategy.

First, that the candidate still matters. Fremont had won New England and the northernmost states in the 1856 election, but not Pennsylvania, Indiana, Illinois, or California, all states crucial to a Republican win in 1860. Counting votes and evaluating public sentiment, Lincoln assessed that the presumptive Republican nominee, William H. Seward, was unlikely to win all those states. Perhaps Lincoln, as a lesser-known westerner who had fewer influential friends, but also fewer enemies, could capture them.

Second, party divisions again still mattered (Part I). As the Whigs splintered, new alliances were born. No longer Conscience versus Cotton, the new Republican Party captured the main northern Whig factions as well as the antislavery portions of the Free Soilers, Democrats, and Know-Nothings, shedding former Whigs in the South to the Democrats. This reflected the greater ideological split between anti- and proslavery sentiments in North versus South, but also between pro-Union versus pro-Secession motivations.

Third, party unity was critical. The new Republican Party was sectional, essentially limited to Northern states, in large part because the South would not allow antislavery or Republican organizers to exist in their section. Understanding that the Republican candidate would have to win based solely on Northern votes, Lincoln worked hard to dispel internal splitting along regional priorities. Rather than damage the party by arguing over disagreements with Massachusetts's anti-immigration bill or Pennsylvania's issues with tariffs, the entire Republican Party needed to focus on the one big thing they could all agree on—opposition to the expansion of slavery into the western territories. Abolitionists would have to put aside their attempts to end slavery where it still existed in the slave states long enough to get a Republican into the executive mansion.

Epilogue

Fourth, party divisions still mattered (Part II). While working to keep Republican Party unity, Lincoln exploited the rift between Northern and Southern Democrats. Stephen A. Douglas had been the presumptive Democratic nominee but had fallen out of favor with President Buchanan and the Southern Democrats over his insistence that popular sovereignty allowed territories to exclude slavery if they preferred to be a free state. The South was adamant that the Dred Scott decision authorized them to bring their enslaved "property" wherever they wanted, including the territories and even into free states. The South did not trust Douglas to protect their ability to enslave people. Lincoln had helped expand this rift by committing Douglas to the "Freeport Doctrine" during the 1858 debates, then he used his Cooper Union address to widen the chasm by employing Douglas's own words against him. After Douglas noted that "Our fathers, when they framed the Government under which we live, understood this question just as well, and even better, than we do now," and contrary to Douglas's false characterization of what the framers intended, Lincoln demonstrated that the founders had known that slavery was morally wrong and took steps to put it on a path to its ultimate extinction. The rhetorical "thin edge of the wedge" helped split the Democratic Party further into a proslavery but pro-Union North and a proslavery and pro-secession South. That split cost the Democrats the election.

The fact that slavery had now become a moral cause—"I am naturally anti-slavery. If slavery is not wrong, nothing is wrong. I cannot remember when I did not so think and feel"—became the main theme of his post–Cooper Union tour of New England. From city to city, he repeated and reinforced his Cooper Union message. He added insights relevant to local political races (like his support of the Lynn shoemakers' strike) and used subtle anecdotes rather than the sarcasm of his previous trip. Rather than touring to help keep the fracturing Whigs together as he did in 1848, his goal in 1860 was to demonstrate that the choice was between the Republican Party of freedom and union versus a Democratic Party of enslavement and disunion.

Did Lincoln's New England trips make any difference at the Republican National Convention held in May in Chicago? It seemed so. Voting at the convention went from East to West, which meant New England got the first votes. Going into the convention the assumption was that these states would favor Seward, the former governor and current senator from neighboring New York, and the Republican Party's best-known leader. On the first ballot, Maine began by giving Seward ten of its sixteen votes but surprised everyone by giving the rest to Lincoln instead of someone like Salmon P. Chase. Then New Hampshire gave seven of its ten votes to Lincoln and only one to Seward. Vermont, Connecticut, and Rhode Island ignored Seward (and Lincoln) altogether, going for native sons. Things got worse for Seward on the second ballot when Vermont switched all its votes from its native son to Lincoln. By the third ballot Lincoln had passed Seward, and a final shift put him over the top for the nomination.

The fact that New England went first and shunned Seward certainly affected the votes of other states as the balloting proceeded west. Most of the New England delegates were convinced that Seward could not be elected in November and therefore were looking for an alternative. Whereas Seward had a long track record of public service, and thus had established a somewhat radical reputation, Lincoln seemed more moderate and measured in his actions. Just as Lincoln had anticipated, many in the Republican Party were looking for an alternative to Seward that could win over the states Fremont had lost, and the entertaining "sucker" from the West turned into national leader and "Little Giant" killer might be that man. Lincoln's opportunely timed venture into New England reinforced his plausibility as a viable alternative to Seward.

*　*　*

Any series of long road trips like this offer considerable time to contemplate. I thought about what lessons we could learn from Lincoln for today's world. This trip was focused on New England, but in the past, I had also traveled throughout the South and Midwest, spending many hours visiting rural areas that are not much different than the small town I grew up in. Today, New England (other than the most rural northern section of Maine) routinely votes for Democrats, its current iteration the most like Lincoln's progressive Republican Party. Today's South and rural

Midwest generally vote for Republicans, akin to the conservative, and especially the Southern/Confederate Democrats of Lincoln's time. And yet everywhere I went I found people who want the best for their families. Unfortunately, that desire does not always translate well in a nation where all but a small percentage of people vote according to the "D" or "R" attached to the candidate rather than the integrity of the candidate him- or herself. So, what would Lincoln teach us?

First, we are all Americans. While Lincoln despised slavery and thought it must be constrained such that it could in due course cease existence, he never believed Southerners themselves were evil. In his 1854 Peoria speech, Lincoln argued that "if slavery did not now exist amongst them, they would not introduce it. If it did now exist amongst us, we should not instantly give it up."[2] He understood that the North had benefited from the existence of slavery, and in his second inaugural address acknowledged that "both North and South" were given "this terrible war."[3] We must work together to find paths forward, not turn on each other.

Second, the wealthy have undue influence over what issues we argue. Prior to and during the Civil War, most of the wealth in the Southern states was held by a small number of plantation-owning slaveholders. Only about 20 percent of white Southerners enslaved Black Americans, although the percentage was higher in some states like South Carolina, and virtually everyone white benefited from the white supremacist social structure. More importantly, wealth brings political, social, and economic influence. Many white Southerners went to war believing they were being attacked by the North, when in fact the South seceded and began the war to protect slavery. Poor and working-class whites in the South went along, in part out of ideology but mostly out of necessity. Similarly, while there was a greater emphasis on small business in the North, there were wealthy mill owners who tempered the fight against injustice, thus perpetuating a system reliant on slavery. We, the working and middle classes, must be driven by solution-oriented reality, not misdirection based on falsehoods designed to distract us from the real sources of conflict.

Third, social equality and education are good for the nation. Lincoln believed that the Declaration of Independence's credo of "all men are created equal" applied to all men (and women), not just white men. "In giving freedom to the slave, we assure freedom to the free," he wrote in his annual message to Congress in 1862. None of us loses rights when those rights are enjoyed by all Americans.[4] He also believed that education "is the most important subject which we as a people can be engaged in."[5] We should be embracing knowledge, not disdaining it.

In our current age, too many of us choose to believe things that are objectively false while dismissing those things that are objectively true. In both my former scientific and current historian careers, I have learned that giving more information does not necessarily lead to more wisdom. We are all so overwhelmed by information that we select which to absorb, often based on whether it reinforces our preformed attitudes. Lincoln understood the approaching danger even in his time. "If destruction be our lot," he noted in his Lyceum Address, "we must ourselves be its author and finisher."[6] He could see that arguments among ourselves open us to manipulation by the unscrupulous. Deceit and protection of the wealth for a small number of influential people dragged masses of Americans from North and South into a war against ourselves. The same is true today.

To finish Lincoln's quote above from the Lyceum address, "As a nation of freemen, we must live through all time, or die by suicide."

After finishing my tour of New England, I revisited three places that played important roles in the story. First was the mural on the side of the old textile mill in my hometown of Ipswich, Massachusetts. Lincoln's presence there reminds us of his two tours of New England and how much had changed in the interregnum. Lincoln became more mature, and the nation became unstable over the continued presence of slavery.

Second was the Lincoln Memorial. I have often climbed the steps and stood in the main hall communing with Daniel Chester French's grand statue of Lincoln surveying the populace and the District of Columbia, gazing down the reflecting pool to the Washington Monument, and beyond to the US Capitol with its gleaming dome. This is the same dome Lincoln had insisted must be completed even as the Civil War raged.

And finally, I am drawn back to Statuary Hall in that Capitol. It was Abraham Lincoln who signed the law creating Statuary Hall in

Epilogue

The author in front of the Daniel Chester French statue of Lincoln in the Lincoln Memorial, Washington, DC

1864. Vermont-born Justin Morrill, whom Lincoln had worked closely with on several projects including the creation of land-grant colleges, had proposed that the old House of Representatives be turned into a place where each state could display memorials to their most respected representatives. While some changes have been made over the years, two of the more controversial statues remain: Mississippi's statue of Confederate president Jefferson Davis and Georgia's statue of Confederate vice president Alexander Stephens. Recently, however, an informal proposal was made to replace the Stephens statue—all white marble installed during the Jim Crow era—with a more modern statue of former Georgia governor and US president Jimmy Carter, who died in late 2024 at the age of one hundred.

Placing Carter in Statuary Hall seems like the perfect way for the nation to shift its focus from a Union versus Confederacy mindset to one of what Lincoln called "our one common country." In the words of Lincoln: "The dogmas of the quiet past are inadequate to the stormy present. The occasion is piled high with difficulty, and we must rise—with the occasion. As our case is new, so we must think anew, and act anew. We must disenthrall ourselves, and then we shall save our country."

Adding,

Fellow citizens, we cannot escape history . . . we will be remembered in spite of ourselves.

That seems like a good place to start.

Notes

Introduction
1. Alan Pearsall, *American Town: The History of Ipswich, Massachusetts* (EBSCO Publishing, 2009).

Chapter 1: Zachary Taylor, the Whig?—New England Beckons
1. Installation was delayed during the governorship of Republican Glenn Youngkin. As of this writing, no date has been set for Johns to appear in Statuary Hall.
2. Roy P. Basler, *The Collected Works of Abraham Lincoln*, Vol. 1 (Rutgers University Press, 1953), 431–42.
3. Basler, *Collected Works*, Vol. 1, 468.
4. Robert W. Merry, *Decade of Disunion: How Massachusetts and South Carolina Led the Way to Civil War, 1849–1861* (Simon & Schuster, 2024), 32.
5. Merry, *Decade of Disunion*, 33.
6. Basler, *Collected Works*, Vol. 1, 514.
7. Wayne C. Temple, *Lincoln's Connections with the Illinois Michigan Canal, His Return from Congress in '48, and His Invention* (Illinois Bell, 1986), citing *Illinois Journal*, August 23, 1848, 1.
8. Basler, *Collected Works*, Vol. 2, 1.
9. Wayne C. Temple passed away on March 31, 2025, while I was editing the manuscript for this book.
10. Historian William F. Hanna received his bachelor's degree at Southeastern Massachusetts University (SMU), where I later did a year of graduate school before transferring to Rutgers University. SMU has since been absorbed into the University of Massachusetts system as UMass-Dartmouth.
11. Basler, *Collected Works*, Vol. 1, 516.
12. Burlingame has led the way investigating this issue and has published evidence that it was John Hay's workmanship, but a debate still rages among Lincoln scholars.
13. Temple, *Connections*; William F. Hanna, *Abraham Among the Yankees: Abraham Lincoln's 1848 Visit to Massachusetts* (Old Colony Historical Society, 1983), 17–26.
14. Basler, *Collected Works*, Vol. 10, 11–12.

NOTES

Chapter 2: The Party Divided—Worcester Free Soilers Rebel
1. *Boston Advertiser*, September 14, 1848.
2. Bruce Chadwick, *Lincoln for President: An Unlikely Candidate, An Audacious Strategy, and the Victory No One Saw Coming* (Sourcebooks, 2009), 21; David H. Donald, *Lincoln* (Simon & Schuster, 1995), 131.
3. This is Samuel Adams Sr., whose son Samuel Adams Jr. had been a leader in the Revolutionary War era.
4. Ivan Sandrof, *Your Worcester Streets*, n.d., 5, https://mywpl.org/sites/default/files/pdf/Your-worcester-street.pdf.
5. John W. Starr Jr., *Lincoln and the Railroads* (Dodd, Mead & Company, 1927), 49–50.
6. Hanna, *Abraham Among the Yankees*, 15.
7. Basler, *Collected Works*, Vol. 2, 1–5.
8. David Demaree, "A Stumping Sucker: Reception of Abraham Lincoln in Massachusetts, September 11–23,1848," *Civil War History*, vol. 68, no. 1 (2022), 100; Kenneth Cmiel, *Democratic Eloquence: The Fight over Popular Speech in Nineteenth-Century America* (Morrow, 1990), 61; Douglas L. Wilson and Rodney O. Davis, *Herndon's Informants: Letters, Interviews, and Statements about Abraham Lincoln* (University of Illinois Press, 1998), 699.
9. https://mhc-macris.net/details?mhcid=wor.688; Hanna, *Abraham Among the Yankees*; Arthur P. Rugg, *Abraham Lincoln in Worcester* (Belisle Printing and Publishing Co., 1909).
10. Not to be confused with his father, Levi Lincoln Sr., who had also been Massachusetts governor and moved to Worcester.
11. John Hancock, Caleb Strong, and Michael Dukakis each served more total years, but not consecutively.
12. Also sometimes known as Constitution Highway, it is the longest road in the United States, running for 3,365 miles from Boston, Massachusetts, to Newport, Oregon.
13. David J. Kent, *Lincoln: The Fire of Genius: How Abraham Lincoln's Commitment to Science and Technology Helped Modernize America* (Lyons Press, 2022).

Chapter 3: The Abolitionists—New Bedford Whaling and Wailing
1. Signage outside these landmarks.
2. Jonathan W. White, *Shipwrecked: A True Civil War Story of Mutinies, Jailbreaks, Blockade-Running, and the Slave Trade* (Rowman & Littlefield, 2023), 146–47; Herman Melville, *Moby-Dick; or, The Whale* (Harper & Brothers, 1851).
3. Signage outside these landmarks.
4. Michael Burlingame, *Abraham Lincoln: A Life* (Johns Hopkins University Press, 2008), 823, citing Zephaniah W. Pease, ed., *The Diary of Samuel Rodman: A New Bedford Chronicle of Thirty-Seven Years, 1821–1859* (Reynolds, 287, entry for September 15, 1848).
5. See Grinnell Mansion website, https://www.grinnellmansion.com/.
6. Interestingly, Stephen A. Douglas originally was spelled with a second "s" but he dropped it the year after Frederick Douglass published his first autobiography; see Martin H. Quitt, *Stephen A. Douglas and Antebellum Democracy* (Cambridge University Press, 2012). Also see National Park Service site, https://www.nps.gov/places/nathan-and-polly-johnson-house.htm.

7. Frederick Douglass, *Frederick Douglass: My Bondage and My Freedom* (Miller, Orton & Mulligan,1855); Matthew Stewart, *An Emancipation of the Mind: Radical Philosophy, the War Over Slavery, and the Refounding of America* (W.W. Norton, 2024), 7.

8. Douglass, *My Bondage and My Freedom*, 90; Stewart, *Emancipation of the Mind*, 7.

9. See Massachusetts Historical Society Collections Online, https://www.masshist.org/database/1698.

10. Herndon gave Lincoln Theodore Parker's lecture on "The Effect of Slavery on the American People," delivered in the Music Hall in Boston. Lincoln read it and marked a passage that will sound familiar to us today: "Democracy is direct self-government, over all the people, for all the people, by all the people."

Chapter 4: The Textile Mills—Lowell and the Power of Cotton

1. Hanna, *Abraham Among the Yankees*, 52; https://www.lowellma.gov/City-Hall-Historic-District; National Park Service, Lowell National Historical Park, https://www.nps.gov/places/old-city-hall.htm.

2. Basler, *Collected Works*, Vol. 2, 6; Hanna, *Abraham Among the Yankees*, 38–41; Samuel P. Hadley, "Recollections of Lincoln in Lowell in 1848 and Reading of Concluding Portion of the Emancipation Proclamation," in *The Abraham Lincoln Centennial* (Lowell Historical Society, 1909), 370–72; *Lowell Courier*, September 18, 1848, 2; Boston *Atlas*, September 19, 1848, 2; Lincoln quote, Library of Congress Abraham Lincoln Papers, Series 3, Abraham Lincoln to Jesse Fell, autobiographical statement, December 20, 1859.

3. Hanna, *Abraham Among the Yankees*, 52.

4. The presidency in 2000 was decided by a 5–4 Supreme Court decision stopping the ballot recount in Florida, giving the presidency to Bush by a single electoral vote.

5. James Oakes, *The Crooked Path to Abolition: Abraham Lincoln and the Antislavery Constitution* (W.W. Norton, 2021), xxvi, 56.

6. Anne Farrow, Joel Lang, and Jenifer Frank, *Complicity: How the North Promoted, Prolonged, and Profited From Slavery* (Ballantine Books, 2005).

7. Farrow, Lang, and Frank, *Complicity*, 9. The unsatiable need for more cotton production acreage was one impetus behind the 1830 Indian Removal Act that forced Native peoples known as the Five Civilized Tribes out of the mid-south into the barren land now largely the state of Oklahoma, then called "Indian Territory."

8. Craig Steven Wilder, *Ebony & Ivy: Race, Slavery, and the Troubled History of America's Universities* (Bloomsbury Press, 2013), 285; Jeffrey Boutwell, *Boutwell: Radical Republican and Champion of Democracy* (W.W. Norton, 2025), 13; Farrow, Lang, and Frank, *Complicity*, 6, 25.

9. Farrow, Lang, and Frank, *Complicity*, 26, 49.

10. https://teachingamericanhistory.org/document/rough-draft-of-the-declaration-of-independence/.

11. Ira Berlin, *Many Thousands Gone: The First Two Centuries of Slavery in North America* (Belknap Press, 1998), 8.

12. Berlin, *Many Thousands Gone*, 6–10; Nancy Bradeen Spannaus, *Defeating Slavery: Hamilton's American System Showed the Way* (iUniverse, 2023), 18; Joanne B. Freeman, *The Field of Blood: Violence in Congress and the Road to Civil War* (Farrar, Straus and Giroux, 2018).

13. Burlingame, *Abraham Lincoln: A Life*, 818.

14. Later, the Republican Party in 1856 modified this into "Free Soil, Free Labor, Free Speech, Free Men, Frémont!"

15. See transcript, National Archives, https://www.archives.gov/founding-docs/declaration-transcript.

16. Farrow, Lang, and Frank, *Complicity*; Burlingame, *Abraham Lincoln: A Life*; Kinley Brauer, *Cotton Versus Conscience: Massachusetts Whig Politics and Southwestern Expansion, 1843–1848* (Ross & Haines, 1967).

17. Farrow, Lang, and Frank, *Complicity*, xxvi.

18. Thomas H. O'Connor, *Lords of the Loom: The Cotton Whigs and the Coming of the Civil War* (Charles Scribner's Sons, 1968), 80; Glenna Lang, "The Political Career of U.S. Senator Charles Sumner: Abolitionist, Radical Reformer, and Civil Rights Activist," *Longfellow House Bulletin*, 2020, 4–5.

19. O'Connor, *Lords of the Loom*, 58–59; quote from Samuel G. Brown, ed., *The Works of Rufus Choate, with a Memoir of his Life* (Little, Brown and Company, 1826), Vol. II, 274.

20. Stephen Puleo, *The Caning: The Assault That Drove America to Civil War* (Westholme Publishing, 2012), 38–39; James M. McPherson, *Battle Cry of Freedom: The Civil War Era* (Oxford University Press, 1988), 120.

21. Puleo, *Caning*, 6.

Chapter 5: The Ancestors—Boston Burbs and the New England Lincolns

1. Boston *Courier*, September 20, 1848, 2; Boston *Atlas*, September 20, 1848, 2; Hanna, *Abraham Among the Yankees*, 58.

2. Hanna, *Abraham Among the Yankees*, https://www.dorchesteratheneum.org/project/abrajam-lincolns-visit-to-dorchester/.

3. https://www.chelseaprospers.org/post/parks-and-open-space.

4. George Monroe, "Lincoln's Visit to Dedham," printed manuscript in the collection of the Dedham Historical Society, cited in Hanna, *Abraham Among the Yankees*, 60.

5. James L. Parr, *Dedham: Historic and Heroic Tales from Shiretown* (History Press, 2009).

6. Hanna, *Abraham Among the Yankees*, 42; See also University of Massachusetts Lowell Library, https://libguides.uml.edu/early_lowell/Frederick_Douglass_in_Lowell_1844.

7. Kent, *Fire of Genius*, 238; Anonymous, "DNA Tests: Nancy Hanks Is Daughter of Lucey Hanks," *For the People*, vol. 17, no. 4 (2015), 3; Edward Steers Jr., *The Lincoln Tree: 300 Years of Lincoln Ancestry, 1500 to 1837*, independently published, 2023, 11–15.

8. Burlingame, *Abraham Lincoln: A Life*, 820, citing Solomon Lincoln to Artemas Hale, Hingham, March 2, 1848, photostatic copy, Lincoln Miscellaneous Collection, University of Chicago.

9. Basler, *Collected Works*, Vol. 1, 455–56; Basler, *Collected Works*, Vol. 1, 459–60.

10. Basler, *Collected Works*, Vol. 1, 459; Basler, *Collected Works*, Vol. 1, 461–62.

11. Basler, *Collected Works*, Vol. 2, 217–18.

12. Basler, *Collected Works*, Vol. 4, 37.

13. Burlingame, *Abraham Lincoln: A Life*, 1195; Jon Meacham, *And There Was Light: Abraham Lincoln and the American Struggle* (Random House, 2022), 153; Wilson and

Davis, *Herndon's Informants*, 406, statement from Henry C. Whitney to Herndon, November 1866.

14. Steers, *Lincoln Tree*; Steers and I each had long careers as scientists before turning full-time to our lifelong studies of Abraham Lincoln.

15. He may have been only fifteen years old at the time and some historians think he misrepresented his age to make the voyage, although it was common for the very young to travel to the colonies.

16. Steers, *Lincoln Tree*, 31.

17. Katie Brace, "Driver Said She Swerved to Avoid Squirrel Before Crashing into Historic House," NBCBoston.com, July 15, 2021.

18. The Lincoln Sculpture Project map can be found at https://dbwiegers.zenfolio.com/lincoln-sculpture-map.

19. "The British Surrender at Yorktown, 1781," Eyewitness to History, www.eyewitnesstohistory.com, 2002.

20. Steers, *Lincoln Tree*, 33.

21. Taunton *Daily Gazette*, September 23, 1848, 2, cited in Hanna, *Abraham Among the Yankees*, 70.

22. Basler, *Collected Works*, Vol. 1, 6–9; Hanna, *Abraham Among the Yankees*, 72–73.

Chapter 6: The Writers—Concord in the Shadow of the Revolution

1. The C-SPAN video for the event can be watched here: https://www.c-span.org/program/american-history-tv/lincoln-memorial-centennial-ceremony/612712.

2. Concord Museum, https://concordmuseum.org/.

3. Basler, *Collected Works*, Vol. 2, 220–21.

4. Basler, *Collected Works*, Vol. 1, 115.

5. Paul Brooks, *The People of Concord: American Intellectuals and Their Timeless Ideas* (Fulcrum Publishing, 1990), 207; Ralph Waldo Emerson, *Journals*, Vol. 7, 100.

6. Douglas L. Wilson and Rodney O. Davis, *Herndon on Lincoln: Letters* (University of Illinois Press, 2016), 209–10.

7. Wilson and Davis, *Herndon on Lincoln: Letters*, 238.

8. Brooks, *People of Concord*, 141.

9. Kent, *Fire of Genius*, 154–63.

10. Brooks, *People of Concord*, 82

11. Brooks, *People of Concord*, 34–35, 37ff.

12. For full poem, see https://www.poetryfoundation.org/poems/45870/concord-hymn.

13. "The Old Manse," National Park Service, https://www.nps.gov/places/the-old-manse.htm.

14. Harold Holzer, ed., *The Lincoln Anthology: Great Writers on His Life and Legacy from 1860 to Now* (Library of America, 2009), 32.

15. Basler, *Collected Works*, Vol. 5, 158; *New York Times*, March 22, 1862, 4:6.

16. Holzer, *Anthology*, 32–37, with the restored prose.

17. David J. Kent, *Abraham Lincoln and Nikola Tesla: Connected by Fate* (Science Traveler Books, 2015).

Notes

18. Stephen Cushman, *Belligerent Muse: Five Northern Writers and How They Shaped Our Understanding of the Civil War* (University of North Carolina Press, 2014), 11.

19. Stanley Harrold, *Lincoln and the Abolitionists* (Southern Illinois University Press, 2018), 81–82; Cushman, *Belligerent Muse*, 9–10; Stewart, *Emancipation of the Mind*, 167; *Complete Works of Emerson*, Vol. 11, 296 (https://quod.lib.umich.edu/e/emerson/4957107.0011.001/1:18?rgn=div1;view=fulltext); For an excellent discussion of Nathaniel Gordon, see Ron Soodalter, *Hanging Captain Gordon: The Life and Trial of an American Slave Trader* (Washington Square Press, 2006).

20. Meacham, *And There Was Light*, 132.

21. Signage at Concord Museum.

22. Gordon Harris, "Abolition and the Underground Railroad in Essex County," Historic Ipswich, see https://historicipswich.net/2023/09/19/the-underground-railroad-in-ipswich/.

23. Two months prior to Lincoln's 1848 tour, Gerrit Smith's cousin, Elizabeth Cady Stanton, led the convention in Seneca Falls, New York, fighting for women's suffrage, so Lincoln may have been aware of this reform effort as well.

Chapter 7: The Hub of the Universe—Boston and Cambridge

1. See https://www.thefreedomtrail.org/trail-sites/kings-chapel-kings-chapel-burying-ground; https://www.thefreedomtrail.org/trail-sites/granary-burying-ground.

2. Pronounced in Boston as Treh-mont, not Tree-mont.

3. See https://www.mygenealogyhound.com/vintage-photographs/massachusetts-photographs/MA-Boston-Massachusetts-Joseph-Tapping-Tombstone-Kings-Chapel-Burying-Ground-2009-photo.html.

4. Justin G. Turner and Linda Levitt Turner, *Mary Todd Lincoln: Her Life and Letters* (Fromm International Publishing, 1987), 463.

5. If that is not complicated enough, there is some evidence that she and the children were with Lincoln when he got to Niagara Falls during the trip home to Illinois. The author has a manuscript in preparation for the *Journal of the Abraham Lincoln Association* on this topic.

6. Basler, *Collected Works*, Vol. 2, 5; Hanna, *Abraham Among the Yankees*, 50. Locofoco is a derogatory name used by the Whigs for the Democratic Party.

7. See http://www.celebrateboston.com/culture/the-hub-origin.htm.

8. Lincoln Sculptures Project map, https://dbwiegers.zenfolio.com/lincoln-sculpture-map.

9. Hanna, *Abraham Among the Yankees*, 78, citing Boston *Daily Bee*, September 22, 1848, 2.

10. Kent, *Lincoln: The Fire of Genius*, 204–6.

11. Personal correspondence, November 22, 2024.

12. Kent, *Fire of Genius*, 186.

13. For the Tremont Temple story, see https://tremonttemple.com/our-story.

14. Hanna, *Abraham Among the Yankees*, 75; *Boston Post*, June 10, 1848, 2; James Schouler, "Abraham Lincoln at Tremont Temple in 1848," *Proceedings of the Massachusetts Historical Society*, 1909, 76 (James Schouler is *Atlas* editor William Schouler's son).

15. Boston *Atlas*, September 23, 1848, 2; Hanna, *Abraham Among the Yankees*, 79.

16. Burlingame, *Abraham Lincoln: A Life*, 826, citing *Boston Journal*, n.d., copied in *New-York Tribune*, September 25, 1848.

17. Meacham, *And There Was Light*, 106, citing *Buffalo Commercial Advertiser*, September 26, 1848.

18. Boston *Atlas*, September 23, 1848.

19. Hanna, *Abraham Among the Yankees*, 80; Boston *Atlas*, September 23, 1848.

20. Kevin Peraino, *Lincoln in the World: The Making of a Statesman and the Dawn of American Power* (Crown Publishers, 2013), 78, citing Seward's autobiography edited by his son (see next).

21. Frederick W. Seward, *Seward at Washington as Senator and Secretary of State: A Memoir of His Life, with Selections from His Letters, 1846–1872*, 2 vols. (Derby and Miller, 1891), 79–80.

22. Cushman, *Belligerent Muse*, 167.

23. Basler, *Collected Works*, Vol. 1, 451–52.

Interregnum: 1848–1860

1. Boutwell, *Boutwell*, 42–43, personal communications.

2. Merry, *Decade of Disunion*.

3. For more details, see https://millercenter.org/us-presidents-and-slavery.

4. See especially, Freeman, *Field of Blood*.

5. Basler, *Collected Works*, Vol. 3, 511–12.

6. Basler, *Collected Works*, Vol. 3, 511–12.

7. Basler, *Collected Works*, Vol. 2, 247–83.

8. Basler, *Collected Works*, Vol. 3, 511–12; Basler, *Collected Works*, Vol. 2, 320–23.

9. Doughface refers to Northern politicians who favored Southern proslavery positions.

10. *Dred Scott v. Sandford* (1857), https://www.archives.gov/milestone-documents/dred-scott-v-sandford.

Chapter 8: The Speech of a Lifetime—Cooper Union

1. Library of Congress Abraham Lincoln Papers, Series 1, James A. Briggs to Abraham Lincoln, telegram, October 12, 1859.

2. Harold Holzer, *Lincoln at Cooper Union: The Speech That Made Abraham Lincoln President* (Simon & Schuster, 2004), 106; Andrew A. Freeman, *Abraham Lincoln Goes to New York* (Coward-McCann, Inc., 1960), 80; https://web.archive.org/web/20141129153953/http://www.trademarkproperties.com/elevator.

3. Holzer, *Cooper Union*, 5.

4. Stephen A. Douglas, "The Dividing Line Between Federal and Local Authority: Popular Sovereignty and the Territories," *Harper's New Monthly Magazine*, vol. 19 (September 1859), 519.

5. Tom Link, personal communication, November 18, 2024; Harold Holzer, *Brought Forth on This Continent: Abraham Lincoln and American Immigration* (Dutton, 2024), 118.

6. For an analysis, see https://teachingamericanhistory.org/document/an-irrepressible-conflict/.

7. Basler, *Collected Works*, Vol. 3, 522–50; Holzer in his *Cooper Union* book has an excellent analysis.
8. See https://www.battlefields.org/learn/primary-sources/cornerstone-speech.
9. *New-York Tribune*, February 29, March 6, 1860.

Chapter 9: *The Seward Rivalry Begins—Providence*

1. Basler, *Collected Works*, Vol. 3, 550–51; *Illinois State Journal*, March 7, 1860, copied from the Providence *Journal*.
2. His collection is now the Frank and Virginia Williams Collection of Lincolniana at Mississippi State University.
3. Frank J. Williams, "A Candidate Speaks in Rhode Island: Abraham Lincoln Visits Providence and Woonsocket, 1860," *Rhode Island History*, vol. 51, no. 4 (1993), 107–19; William F. Hanna, "Abraham Lincoln's 1860 Visit to Rhode Island," *Lincoln Herald*, Fall 1979, 198; *Providence Daily Post*, February 28, 1860, 2.
4. Hanna, "1860 Visit to Rhode Island," 199, citing *Daily Post*, March 3, 1860, 2 and *Daily Journal*, February 29, 1860, 2.
5. Wilder, *Ebony & Ivy*, 73–74; Nathaniel Philbrick, *Travels with George: In Search of Washington and His Legacy* (Penguin Books, 2022), 164.
6. Wilder, *Ebony & Ivy*, 98, 109, 278.
7. Wilder, *Ebony & Ivy*, 285.
8. Wilder, *Ebony & Ivy*, 286; Kent, *Fire of Genius*, 186–87; James T. Campbell et al., *Slavery and Justice: Report of the Brown University Steering Committee on Slavery and Justice*, Brown University, October 2006, 12–25.
9. Philbrick, *Travels with George*, 165–66.
10. Hanna, "1860 Visit to Rhode Island," 200–201; *Woonsocket Patriot*, *Providence Daily Journal*, March 9, 1860, 2.
11. Percy Coe Eggleston, *Lincoln in New England* (Tudor Press, 1922), 7.
12. https://tile.loc.gov/storage-services/public/gdcmassbookdig/stateofcountrysp01lcsewa/stateofcountrysp01lcsewa.pdf.

Chapter 10: *The Robert Visit—New Hampshire*

1. Basler, *Collected Works*, Vol. 3, 511–12.
2. Jason Emerson, *Giant in the Shadows: The Life of Robert T. Lincoln* (Southern Illinois University Press, 2012), 39, FN 439.
3. Emerson, *Giant in the Shadows*, 47, FN97, 98, 443; "Reminiscences of Robert Lincoln and Abraham Lincoln," Phillips Exeter Academy, 7.
4. Emerson, *Giant in the Shadows*, 40–41; Elwin L. Page and Mike Pride, *Abraham Lincoln in New Hampshire* (Monitor Publishing Co., 2009), 23.
5. Emerson, *Giant in the Shadows*, 42–43; Robert T. Lincoln to Reverend J. B. L. Soule, April 11, 1881, Robert Todd Lincoln Letterpress Books, Abraham Lincoln Presidential Library, Springfield, IL, 4 (microfilm reel 6), 112.
6. Page and Pride, *Lincoln in New Hampshire*, 37.
7. Basler, *Collected Works*, Vol. 10, 48–49.
8. Basler, *Collected Works*, Vol. 4, 87.
9. Emerson, *Giant in the Shadows*, 10.

10. Emerson, *Giant in the Shadows*, 44.
11. Basler, *Collected Works*, Vol. 3, 547–48, italics in original.
12. Basler, *Collected Works*, Vol. 3, 550.
13. Page and Pride, *Lincoln in New Hampshire*, 69; Basler, *Collected Works*, Vol. 10, 49.
14. Basler, *Collected Works*, Vol. 3, 552; *Inquirer* (Dover, NH), March 8, 1860.
15. Page and Pride, *Lincoln in New Hampshire*, 73.
16. Kent, *Fire of Genius*.
17. Ron Soodalter, "Lincoln Campaigns in New Hampshire," *America's Civil War*, September 3, 2010; personal communication; Walter B. Stevens, *A Reporter's Lincoln* (Missouri Historical Society, 1916), 44.
18. Emerson, *Giant in the Shadows*, 378.
19. Earlier reports suggested that he stayed with old friend and congressional colleague Amos Tuck, but a later letter from Tuck shows that he was out of town at the time and apologized for missing him.
20. Basler, *Collected Works*, Vol. 10, 49.
21. Basler, *Collected Works*, Vol. 3, 554 (letters to Pomeroy and Briggs); Vol. 10, 50 (follow-up letter to Briggs).

Chapter 11: The Bedful of Snakes—Central Connecticut

1. Eggleston, *Lincoln in New England*, 14.
2. For a brief biography of Buckingham, see https://www.nga.org/governor/william-alfred-buckingham.
3. On June 16, 1862, Lincoln borrowed from the Library of Congress "Stowe's Key to Uncle Tom," formally: Harriet Beecher Stowe, *A Key to Uncle Tom's Cabin; Presenting the Original Facts and Documents Upon Which the Story Is Founded. Together with Corroborative Statements Verifying the Work* (John P. Jewett & Co., 1853).
4. Details of sculptures from Riverfront brochure, https://riverfront.org/wp-content/uploads/2021/02/LSWMap.pdf.
5. Richard Carwardine, *Lincoln's Sense of Humor* (Southern Illinois University Press, 2017), 26, 30, 99.
6. Basler, *Collected Works*, Vol. 4, 1–30.
7. All quotes in this section from Basler, *Collected Works*, Vol. 4, 1–30.
8. Carwardine, *Lincoln's Sense of Humor*, 26.
9. Jon Grinspan, *Wide Awake: The Forgotten Force that Elected Lincoln and Spurred the Civil War* (Bloomsbury Publishing, 2024); Jon Grinspan, "Taking Up the Torch," *Smithsonian Magazine*, May 2024; personal communication.
10. Julius G. Rathbun, "The Wide Awakes: The Great Political Organization of 1860," *Connecticut Quarterly*, vol. 1 (October 1895), 335.
11. Justin Kaplan, *Mr. Clemens and Mark Twain* (Simon & Schuster, 1966), 187.
12. Kent, *Fire of Genius*, 187.
13. Kent, *Fire of Genius*; Find-a-Grave.
14. Basler, *Collected Works*, Vol. 3, 471–82.
15. Basler, *Collected Works*, Vol. 4, 24.
16. Hartford *Evening Press*, March 6, 1860.
17. Holzer, *Lincoln at Cooper Union*, 197.

NOTES

Chapter 12: The Vice Presidential Abyss—Eastern Connecticut and Rhode Island

1. Eggleston, *Lincoln in New England*, 17–20.
2. Eggleston, *Lincoln in New England*, 21.
3. Dale Plummer, "Saving the Wauregan: Historic Downtown Hotel Came Close to Demolition," Norwich *Bulletin*, October 27, 2019; "Norwich Reclaims a Piece of History," *Hartford Courant*, August 26, 2021.
4. Meacham, *And There Was Light*, 152.
5. Holzer, *Lincoln at Cooper Union*, 162.
6. Eggleston, *Lincoln in New England*, 13.
7. Basler, *Collected Works*, Vol. 4, 38; Holzer, *Lincoln at Cooper Union*, 191, 214–15.
8. Holzer, *Lincoln at Cooper Union*, 169.
9. Basler, *Collected Works*, Vol. 4, 45–46.

Chapter 13: The Sculptors and the Showman—Southwestern Connecticut

1. Wilson and Davis, *Herndon's Informants*, 261; Holzer, *Lincoln at Cooper Union*, 198–201.Ho
2. Holzer, *Lincoln at Cooper Union*, 198–201.
3. Andrew Fowler, "Abraham Lincoln in Connecticut," *Yankee Institute*, 2025, https://yankeeinstitute.org/2025/01/17/abraham-lincoln-in-connecticut/.
4. David B. Parker, "A New Look at 'You Can Fool All the People,'" *For the People*, vol. 7, no. 3 (2005), 1–2.
5. Peter Manseau, *The Apparitionists: A Tale of Phantoms, Fraud, Photography, and the Man Who Captured Lincoln's Ghost* (Mariner Books, Houghton Mifflin Company, 2017), 102, 185; Holzer, *Lincoln at Cooper Union*, 69.
6. *Lincoln Lore*, no. 1467 (May 1960); James B. Conroy, *Lincoln's White House: The People's House in Wartime* (Rowman & Littlefield Publishers, 2017), 181–82.
7. Kent, *Fire of Genius*, 138.
8. James A. Percoco, *Summers with Lincoln: Looking for the Man in the Monuments* (Fordham University Press, 2008), 111, citing Fraser, "Essay on Saint-Gaudens"; Holzer, *Brought Forth on This Continent*, 334; Francis S. Barry, *Back Roads and Better Angels* (Steerforth, 2024), 177.
9. Harold Holzer, *Monument Man: The Life & Art of Daniel Chester French* (Princeton Architectural Press, 2019); https://www.metmuseum.org/press-releases/lincoln-2012-news.
10. Holzer, *Monument Man*.
11. Emerson, *Giant in the Shadows*, 280; personal communication.
12. Emerson, *Giant in the Shadows*, 406; Jason Emerson, "The Son of the Great Emancipator: Robert Todd Lincoln and African Americans," *Lincoln Lore*, no. 1945 (Spring 2025), 17–24.

Chapter 14: The Missing New England—Maine and Vermont

1. Marshall Dodge and Robert Bryan, *Bert and I and Other Stories from Down East* (Bert and I Books, 1981).
2. Holzer, *Lincoln at Cooper Union*, 188.

3. Joshua Zeitz, *Lincoln's God: How Faith Transformed a President and a Nation* (Viking Press, 2023), 108.

4. Meacham, *And There Was Light*, 317.

5. Charles Eugene Hamlin, *The Life and Times of Hannibal Hamlin* (Riverside Press, 1899), 194, 367; Edward Achorn, *The Lincoln Miracle: Inside the Republican Convention That Changed History* (Atlantic Monthly Press, 2023), 367. Lincoln appointed Clay to be ambassador to Russia in 1861.

6. Achorn, *Lincoln Miracle*, 314.

7. Achorn, *Lincoln Miracle*, 362, citing *New York Daily Herald*.

8. Burlingame, *Abraham Lincoln: A Life*, 827; Hamlin, *Life and Times of Hannibal Hamlin*, 194, 367; TheLincolnLog.com.

9. C. J. King, *Four Marys and a Jessie* (Friends of Hildene, Inc., 2005), 54–62; Emerson, *Giant in the Shadows*, 81.

10. Basler, *Collected Works*, Vol. 10, 49; http://www.celebrateboston.com/disasters/pemberton-mill-collapse.htm.

11. Robert Frost, *The Road Not Taken*, public domain, https://www.poetryfoundation.org/poems/44272/the-road-not-taken.

12. More history of Hildene at https://hildene.org/about/history.

13. See King, *Four Marys and a Jessie* for more details.

14. Michael Beschloss, "Last of the Lincolns," *New Yorker*, February 20, 1994.

15. When I returned to Hildene in April 2025, Jesse had moved on and Gary Parzych, the new exhibits manager, confirmed the painting was indeed of Tad and painted by Carpenter. It is on loan from a private collector.

16. *A Genealogical History of the Rehoboth Branch of the Carpenter Family in America*, also known as the *Carpenter Memorial*.

17. Emerson, "The Son of the Great Emancipator," *Lincoln Lore*, no. 1945 (Spring 2025), 17–24.

18. Emerson, *Giant in the Shadows*, 365–68; Barry, *Back Roads and Better Angels*, 177; https://digital.lib.niu.edu/illinois/gildedage/pullman; Parzych, The History We See, from Hildene website; also https://www.wttw.com/a/chicago-stories-pullman-porters.

Chapter 15: The End and the Beginning—Heading Home

1. Basler, *Collected Works*, Vol. 10, 49.

2. Holzer, *Lincoln at Cooper Union*, 74, 78, citing Stephen M. Griswold, *Sixty Years with Plymouth Church* (Fleming H. Revell Publishers, 1907), 28, 35; Tom Link, personal communication.

3. Holzer, *Lincoln at Cooper Union*, 202.

4. Holzer, *Lincoln at Cooper Union*, 202–5.

5. *Evening Post* (New York), August 16, 1867, 2–4.

6. Anthony J. Czarnecki, "Mr. Lincoln's Visit to Peekskill," *Westchester Historian*, vol. 87, no. 1 (2011), 4–33; https://www.mrlincolnandnewyork.org/mr-lincolns-visits/visit-to-west-point/index.html.

7. "Mr. Lincoln at Peekskill," *Highland Democrat* (Peekskill, NY), February 23, 1861.

8. https://www.lincolnsocietyinpeekskill.org/about.html.

9. See https://www.johngtesta.com/lincolnstatue.html.
10. Basler, *Collected Works*, Vol. 4, 30–33.
11. David H. Leroy, *Mr. Lincoln's Book: Publishing the Lincoln-Douglas Debates* (Oak Knoll Press, 2009); Harold Holzer, ed., *The Lincoln-Douglas Debates: The First Complete, Unexpurgated Text* (HarperCollins Publishers, 1993).
12. Jeffrey Boutwell, "The Most Important Dinner That Abraham Lincoln Never Attended," *Lincoln Forum Bulletin*, vol. 55 (2024), 18–19.
13. Holzer, *Lincoln at Cooper Union*, 205.
14. Basler, *Collected Works*, Vol. 4, 33.

Epilogue

1. David J. Kent, "Abraham Lincoln's Long Road to Emancipation." *Lincolnian*, vol. 37, no. 2 (2020), 7–10.
2. Basler, *Collected Works*, Vol. 2, 255.
3. Basler, *Collected Works*, Vol. 8, 332–33.
4. Basler, *Collected Works*, Vol. 5, 537.
5. Basler, *Collected Works*, Vol. 1, 5–9.
6. Basler, *Collected Works*, Vol. 1, 108–15.

Acknowledgments

Every book takes a village, and I will start by thanking all of you who have taken this journey with me. That begins with all the readers of my previous books who decided that going for another ride was a worthwhile endeavor. While I traveled alone for most of the thousands of miles I drove researching this book, I always felt that I had you all with me.

Many renowned Lincoln scholars have generously shared their wisdom over the years that I have had the privilege of knowing them. I have tried to pass along that wisdom to readers. My thanks go out to such gracious luminaries (in alphabetical order) as Sidney Blumenthal, Jeffrey Boutwell, Michael Burlingame, Jason Emerson, David Gerleman, Jon Grinspan, Bill Hanna, Harold Holzer, Tom Horrocks, Steve Inskeep, Carolyn Ivanoff, Michelle Krowl, Tom Link, Erin Carlson Mast, Edna Greene Medford, Lucas Morel, Nathan Richardson, John Rodrigue, Rod Ross, Scott Schroeder, Ron Soodalter, Nancy Spannaus, Ed Steers, James Swanson, Wayne Temple, Jonathan White, Dan Weinberg, David Wiegers, Bob Willard, Frank Williams, Melissa Winn, and many others I apologize in advance for unintentionally omitting.

The idea for this book began with the wonderful mural painted by artist Alan Pearsall on the outside wall of the former textile mill, now EBSCO Publishing, along the Ipswich Riverwalk. Thanks, Alan, for including Lincoln in the history of the town and inspiring this journey, and thanks to Gordon Harris for helping me understand the history. I met many people on the road during my travels and spoke with many more before and after the trips. I want to offer my appreciation to Tony Czarnecki, Christine Furman, Gordon Harris, Brian Keefe, Jesse Keel, Emily Lapisardi, Paul Martin, Stephanie Moffett-Hynds, Gary Parzych, Judy Roderiques, Tom Taylor, and the docents not otherwise named at

Acknowledgments

Hildene, Chesterwood, Saint-Gaudens National Historical Park, the Norman Rockwell Museum, the William H. Seward House Museum, and numerous state and National Park Service sites.

I have been associated with several organizations whose members provide me with constant opportunity to learn about our sixteenth president, including the Lincoln Group of the District of Columbia, Abraham Lincoln Institute, Abraham Lincoln Association, Lincoln Forum, President Lincoln's Cottage, Lincoln Presidential Foundation, Ford's Theatre, White House Historical Association, Civil War Round Table of the District of Columbia, and others. Thank you for demonstrating Lincoln's relevance to the modern world.

Many thanks to my literary agent, Marilyn Allen, for finding a stellar publisher for this volume and continuing to have faith in my efforts over many years and many books. Thank you to my editors, Kate Ayers and Greta Schmitz, and their team at Globe Pequot for guiding this project into life.

Special thanks to my family, who keep me grounded in the New England values of hard work and integrity. No matter where I am, you always make a welcome home. Extra special thanks to Ru Sun for her encouragement, constructive criticism, and exceptional attention to detail. This book and I are much better because of you.

Index

1857 Dred Scott Decision, xv, 114

Abolition Row Park, 39
Abraham Among the Yankees, 14
Allen, Charles, 20, 25

Barney, Hiram, 222
Barnum, P. T., 194
Beecher, Henry Ward, 119, 220
Benjamin Lincoln House, 74
Booth, John Wilkes, 156
Boott Cotton Mills Museum, 54
Boott, Kirk, 54
Borglum, Gutzon, 197
Boston Common, 95
Boston, Massachusetts, 63, 91, 149
Boston Whig Club, 95
Brady, Matthew, 123
Bridgeport, Connecticut, 190
Briggs, James, 124
Brooklyn, New York, 221
Brown brothers, 140
Brown, John, 114, 129
Brown University, 139
Bryant, William Cullen, 126
Buchanan, James, 113
Buckingham, Governor William A., 161
Bullock, Alexander, 23, 31
Burlingame, Michael, 176
Burnside, General Ambrose, 139
Burnside Park, 139

Burns, Robert, 210
Bushnell Park, 163

Cadet Chapel (West Point), 225
Cambridge Common, 99
Cambridge, Massachusetts, 98
Carpenter, Francis Bicknell, 215
Carwardine, Richard, 166
Cass, Senator Lewis, 9
Chapel of the Most Holy Trinity (West Point), 224
Chelsea, Massachusetts, 64
Choate, Rufus, 23, 29
Clay, Cassius Marcellus, 167
Clay, Henry, 12, 108, 205
Compromise of 1850, 108
Concord Female Antislavery Society, 87
Concord, Massachusetts, 77
Concord Museum, 78
Concord, New Hampshire, 150
Conscience Whigs, 58
Cooper Union, 119
Cornish, New Hampshire, 202
Cotton Whigs, 58
Custom House Square, 46

Dawes Island, 99
Dedham Community House, 64
Dedham, Massachusetts, 64
Douglas, Stephen, 114, 122, 239
Douglass, Frederick, 41

INDEX

Dover City Hall, 155
Dover, New Hampshire, 154

Eddy, John, 133, 145
Eggleston, Julius W., 175
Eggleston, Percy Coe, 175
Emerson, Ralph Waldo, 79, 85
Equinox House, 209
Exeter, New Hampshire, 148, 156
Exeter Town Hall, 156

Federal Building, 135
Fillmore, Millard, 107
Free Soil Party, 24, 31
French, Daniel Chester, 198
Frost, Robert, 210
Fugitive Slave Act, 109
Furman, Christine, 210

Gardner, Henry J., 28
Garrison, William Lloyd, 43, 59, 82, 88
Granary Burying Ground, 91
Greene, Nathaniel, 3
Grinnell, Congressman Joseph, 38
Grinspan, Jon, 166
Grove Street Cemetery, 171
Gulliver, John, 189

Hadley, Samuel, 50
Hale, Artemas, 67
Hale, John Parker, 155
Hale, Lucy Lambert, 156
Hall, Junius, 14
Hamlin, Hannibal, 206
Hanks, Stedman Wright, 66
Hanna, Bill, 135
Hanna, William F., 14
Harris, Edward, 180
Harris, Gordon, 29
Hartford City Hall, 160
Hartford, Connecticut, 160
Harvard University, 98
Harvard Yard, 99

Hawthorne, Nathaniel, 82
Helper, Hinton Rowan, 136
Herndon, William, 66, 80, 189
Hildene, 209
Hingham, Massachusetts, 67, 70
Holzer, Harold, 121, 165
Hopper College, 170

Ipswich, Massachusetts, 43
Island Cemetery, 144
Ivanoff, Carolyn, 192

Johnson, President Andrew, 69

Keel, Jason, 212
Kennedy Plaza, 138
Krishnamoorthi, Raja, 17

LaHood, Darin, 17
Lapisardi, Emily, 223
Latham, George, 149, 153
Lawrence, Kansas, 112
Levi Lincoln Jr. House, 27
Liberator, The, 43
Liberty Hall, 37
Lincoln Beckwith, Mary, 214
Lincoln, Benjamin, 74
Lincoln Depot Museum, 227
Lincoln Financial Sculpture Walk at Riverfront, Hartford, 161
Lincoln, Levi Jr., 27, 29
Lincoln, Mary, 93, 107, 209
Lincoln, Mary Harlan, 213
Lincoln, Mordecai, 72, 75
Lincoln Oak Memorial, 170
Lincoln, Rhode Island, 177
Lincoln, Robert, 146, 149, 153, 156, 202, 212
Lincoln, Samuel, 70
Lincoln sculpture (Hingham), 73
Lincoln, Solomon, 67
Link, Tom, 123
Lovejoy, Elijah, 32

INDEX

Lowell City Hall, 48
Lowell, Francis Cabot, 55
Lowell, Massachusetts, 48
Lowell National Historical Park, 54

Manchester, Vermont, 209, 210
Manhattan, New York, 119, 222
Mark Twain House, 169
Martin, Paul, 227
Massachusetts Institute of Technology (MIT), 99
Massachusetts State House, 95
McClellan, George B., 224
McLevy Hall (Bridgeport), 191
Merchants National Bank, 37
Mexican-American War, 24
Missouri Compromise, 205
Moby-Dick, 36
Monroe, George, 64
Mystic, Connecticut, 176

Nature, 79
New Bedford Historical Society, 41
New Bedford, Massachusetts, 33
New Bedford Whaling National Historical Park, 33
New Hampshire Capitol building, 151
New Haven City Hall, 173
New Haven, Connecticut, 170
New Haven Green, 170
New London, Connecticut, 175
Newport, Rhode Island, 142
New York City, New York, 220
New-York Tribune, 131
Norwich City Hall, 180
Norwich, Connecticut, 180, 189
Norwich Town Hall, 182

Old Manse, 82

Padelford, Seth, 136
Page, Elwin L., 146
Parker, Theodore, 46

Pawtuxet, Rhode Island, 177
Peekskill, New York, 227
Phenix Hall, 153
Phillips Exeter Academy, 148, 158
Phillips, Wendell, 45, 82
Plymouth Church, 220
Polk, President James K., 6
President Lincoln Memorial (Lowell), 48
Providence, Rhode Island, 133, 149
Pullman Company, 217
Pullman porters, 218

Railroad Hall, 135
Revolutionary War, 83
Roderiques, Judy, 33, 37
Rotch-Jones-Duff House and Museum, 36
Rotch, William Jr., 36

Saint-Gaudens, Augustus, 198
Samuel Lincoln House, 70
Schouler, William, 15
Scituate, Massachusetts, 75
Scott, Winfield, 223
Seaside Park, 193
Seward, William, 101, 145, 183
Seward, William Henry, 124
Slave society, 57
Sleepy Hollow Cemetery, 88
Smyth, Frederick, 186
Societies with slaves, 57
Soodalter, Ron, 156
South Shore (Massachusetts), 69
Sprague, William, IV, 136
Springfield, Illinois, 230
Stamford, Connecticut, 196
Statuary Hall (United States Capitol), 3
Steers, Edward, Jr., 69
Stevens, General Isaac, 142
Stevens, Major Hazard, 144
Stowe, Harriet Beecher, 161
St. Paul's Chapel, 123

261

INDEX

Stratton, Charles S., 196
Sunbeam car, 217

Taft, William Howard, 214
Taunton, Massachusetts, 76
Taylor, General Zachary, 3, 7
Taylor, Zachary, 25, 107, 233
Temple, Wayne, 14
Thoreau, Henry David, 81, 86
Tremont House, 63, 92
Tremont Temple, 101
Tuck, Amos, 148
Twain, Mark, 169

Union Hall (New Haven), 172
University of Bridgeport, 192
USS *Merrimack*, 150

Van Buren, President Martin, 51

Waterville, Maine, 208
Webster, Daniel, 12, 20, 29, 151
Weed, Thurlow, 187
West Point, 222
West Point Museum, 223, 226
Whitney, Eli, 171
Wide Awakes, 166
Wilson, Henry, 25, 58
Winthrop, Senator Robert C., 23
Woonsocket, Rhode Island, 175, 180
Worcester, Massachusetts, 19

Yale College, 170

About the Author

David J. Kent is an award-winning Abraham Lincoln scholar and avid traveler. He is a native New Englander whose upbringing, recurring presence, and thousands of miles of travel in New England provided significant insights and a "travel-along" atmosphere to this book. In addition to traveling to nearly ninety countries, David has driven 20,000 miles exploring Abraham Lincoln sites across the United States. He is immediate past president of the Lincoln Group of DC with a decade of ongoing group leadership, as well as on the boards of the Abraham Lincoln Institute and the Lincoln Forum. This is his seventh book, including *Lincoln: The Fire of Genius*. When he is not on the road, he lives in northern Virginia outside Washington, DC.

    Website: http://www.davidjkent-writer.com/.
    Facebook: @DavidJKentWriter
    Twitter: @DavidJKentWrite
    Bluesky: @djkblue.bsky.social
    Instagram: @DavidJKentWrite

www.ingramcontent.com/pod-product-compliance
Lightning Source LLC
LaVergne TN
LVHW041623060526
838200LV00040B/1410